The Equality of the Sexes

The Equality of the Sexes

Three Feminist Texts of the Seventeenth Century

TRANSLATED WITH AN INTRODUCTION
AND NOTES BY
Desmond M. Clarke

OXFORD
UNIVERSITY PRESS

OXFORD
UNIVERSITY PRESS

Great Clarendon Street, Oxford, OX2 6DP,
United Kingdom

Oxford University Press is a department of the University of Oxford.
It furthers the University's objective of excellence in research, scholarship,
and education by publishing worldwide. Oxford is a registered trade mark of
Oxford University Press in the UK and in certain other countries

Published in the United States of America by Oxford University Press
198 Madison Avenue, New York, NY 10016, United States of America

British Library Cataloguing in Publication Data
Data available

Library of Congress Control Number: 2013942044

ISBN 978-0-19-967351-3

For the next generation: Aida, Isabella,
Emily, and Eric Desmond

Acknowledgements

It is a pleasure to acknowledge the spontaneous generosity with which colleagues and correspondents replied to requests for assistance in the course of preparing these translations. Foremost among them was Oliver Ranner, who kindly translated the phrases in ancient Greek that van Schurman scattered liberally throughout her Latin dissertation, and identified her quotation from Pseudo-Plutarch's *Placita philosophorum*. Theo Verbeek identified some obscure and incomplete references in one of van Schurman's footnotes. Mark Chu advised about Torquato Tasso's *Discorso*, while Andrew Mayes confirmed the citation from Psalm 92 that van Schurman quoted in Hebrew. Theresa Urbainczyk found the source of Gournay's reference to Theodoret in *Graecarum affectionum curatio* and provided a photocopy of the original text, while Doug Hutchinson clarified the possible influence of Aristotle's *Protrepticus* on a commonplace about the irrelevance of physical strength when assessing human accomplishments.

Marie-Frédérique Pellegrin organized a conference in Lyon on the work of Poulain de la Barre in October 2012, and also edited a selection of essays on women philosophers in the *Revue philosophique de la France et de l'Étranger* (July/September, 2013). I used my contributions to both initiatives to draft the commentaries on Poulain and van Schurman in the Introduction. Finally, Eileen O'Neill extended my interest in this literature when she invited participants to a conference on Seventeenth-Century Women Philosophers at the University of Massachusetts, Amherst, in 1997, and assigned me responsibility for Anna Maria van Schurman. The librarians at Marsh's Library, Dublin (which includes Stillingfleet's book library), provided access to van Schurman's works and to many of the more recondite sources to which all three authors in this edition referred. The British Library compensated for inevitable limitations in the personal libraries of Marsh and Stillingfleet, and did so with a degree of friendly and efficient service unrivalled among other national libraries.

The challenge of identifying undocumented citations and references in these texts has been facilitated by the work of previous editors, from whose results I have borrowed and to which I have added some corrections or further relevant sources. Two anonymous readers on behalf of Oxford University Press also made helpful suggestions, though in the interests of brevity I have left some loose ends for future development by others.

Contents

Note on the Texts and Translations   xi

Introduction   1

Marie le Jars de Gournay
  The Equality of Men and Women   54
  The Ladies' Complaint   74

Anna Maria van Schurman
  A Dissertation on the Natural Capacity of Women for
    Study and Learning   79
  Excerpts from the Correspondence   94
  Excerpts from *Eukleria*   112

François Poulain de la Barre
  A Physical and Moral Discourse concerning the
    Equality of Both Sexes   119
  Conversations concerning the Education of
    Ladies [Excerpt]   201

Further Reading   213
Index   217

Note on the Texts and Translations

A la Reyne, l'Égalité des hommes et des femmes was first published privately in 1622, while *Grief des dames* appeared initially as a chapter in *L'Ombre de la Damoiselle De Gournay* (Paris: Jean Libert, 1626). Gournay revised both texts a number of times in subsequent collections of her complete works. I have translated the final versions that appeared in *Les Advis, Ou, Les Presens de la Demoiselle de Gournay* (1641) and, for that purpose, have used the critical edition of the *Oeuvres complètes*, ed. Jean-Claude Arnould *et al.* (Paris: Champion, 2002). Van Schurman's *Dissertatio* was written in Latin, and is translated from the first edition published as *Dissertatio de Ingenii muliebris ad Doctrinam, & meliores Litteras aptitudine* (Leiden: Elsevier, 1641). I have used italics to identify words or phrases that van Schurman used or quoted in ancient Greek, and have identified her infrequent use of other languages in notes. The selections from her correspondence are translated from *Opuscula Hebraea, Graeca, Gallica, Prosaica & Metrica* (Leiden: Elzevier, 1648), and those from her autobiography, which was also written in Latin, are translated from *Eukleria seu Melioris Partis Electio* (Altona: C. van der Meulen, 1673). Finally, the Poulain texts are translated from Poulain de la Barre, *De l'égalité des deux sexes. De l'éducation des dames. De l'excellence des hommes*, ed. Marie-Frédérique Pellegrin (Paris: Vrin, 2011). I have also consulted the first edition of *Discours physique et moral de l'égalité des deux sexes, où l'on voit l'importance de se défaire des préjugez* (Paris: Jean Du Puis, 1673), and have adopted that version of the title in the translation below.

There were no footnotes in Gournay's texts. Van Schurman's relatively few footnotes are identified in the text with superscript letters; however, her references are usually incomplete by today's standards, and I have expanded them when necessary and cited accessible modern editions of the sources to which she refers. Editorial notes and explanations are marked by Arabic numerals. I have adopted the same pattern to distinguish Poulain's infrequent footnotes from editorial notes.

The citation of book titles in English in the text of the Introduction may be misleading, and therefore requires a brief comment. Many of the books mentioned were published in Latin, French, Italian, or other languages, and it seemed useful for readers to have their titles translated into English.

Accordingly, I have adopted the practice of translating into English the titles of all works that are cited in the body of the Introduction. However, some of these books were also translated and published in English—some anonymously, some more than once—and I have attempted, by adding footnotes, to avoid confusion between citing published English translations and merely translating the titles of books that appeared in foreign languages.

Quotations from the Bible present special challenges, since no single English translation is likely to reflect the theological preferences of all three authors translated in this volume. I have used the Douay-Rheims version for quotations in Gournay's work (since she quotes the Latin Vulgate), and the King James version for biblical quotations that occur in van Schurman and Poulain, although evidently, none of the authors consulted or quoted an English Bible.

The translation of two synonymous words, in French and Latin, require a brief comment because, in one case, the original terms were ambiguous, and in the other we lack an equivalent simple term in contemporary English. The word *homo* in Latin and *l'homme* in French were often used by these authors to refer indiscriminately to human beings of both genders. The inclusive use of the term *homo* was already evident in the Latin edition of the Bible known as the Vulgate, which was used by Gournay when she quoted Genesis 1:27 ('God created man to his own image…male and female he created them'). Unless the context implied that an author meant males, I have generally translated *homines* and *hommes* in the plural as 'people' or 'human beings', and have adopted similar solutions for uses in the singular. In some contexts, however, these French and Latin terms are used to designate men only (though Latin also has the term *vir* to identify males). To avoid repeating this ambiguity in English, I have used the terms 'man' or 'men' in the translated texts only in cases where the corresponding French or Latin terms were applied exclusively to males.

The other words that gave some pause were *scientia* in Latin and *science* in French, though their original usage was not ambiguous. Both words were used in their scholastic sense by all three authors to refer to any systematic body of knowledge that was constructed according to the prevailing norms for the discipline in question. Accordingly, philosophy and theology both satisfied the relevant criteria and were called *scientiae* in Latin or *sciences* in French. In contrast, the word 'science' in English has been used since the nineteenth century to mean only certain kinds of empirical knowledge such as physics or chemistry, or, in a wider sense, mathematical or logical disciplines that are closely associated with empirical studies. Nonetheless, despite the obvious difference in meaning and extension, I have reluctantly adopted the English term 'science' as a translation of *scientia* and *science*, especially when the latter terms are used in the plural, to avoid cumbersome phrases such as 'systematic bodies of knowledge'. This was also the solution adopted in English translations of Poulain in the eighteenth and nineteenth centuries. Readers might bear in mind, therefore, that a science in the early modern period was not the same as a science in the twenty-first century, and that the English word 'science' in these translations applies equally to physics, legal studies, or theology.

Finally, the word 'feminist' in the title of this volume is not self-explanatory. The *Oxford English Dictionary* is surprisingly brief and uninformative about how this term is used today to describe a very wide range of ideological or political perspectives. It offers a definition of the adjective 'feminist' as 'of or pertaining to feminism, or to women'; 'feminism' is defined as 'advocacy of the rights of women (based on the theory of the equality of the sexes)'. The texts translated here are feminist in the sense that they reject the misogynistic traditions that esteemed women (as such) less than men: they offer arguments to challenge the inferior status of women that prevailed in civil and ecclesiastical societies in the seventeenth century; they argue for women's right of equal access to educational opportunities; and, fundamentally, they claim that women in general are equal to men. In a word, these authors were feminists because they rejected what today is called 'gender' as a valid criterion for discriminating between human beings.

The following abbreviations and short titles are used for works cited frequently:

ANF   *Anti-Nicene Fathers*, ed. A. Roberts and J. Donaldson. Peabody, MA: Hendrickson, 1999.

AR   *The Complete Works of Aristotle*, ed. Jonathan Barnes. 2 vols. Princeton, NJ: Princeton University Press, 1984.

AT   *Oeuvres de Descartes*, ed. C. Adam and P. Tannery. 8 vols. Rev. edn. Paris: Vrin, 1964–76.

CCSL   *Corpus Christianorum, Series Latina.* Turnhout, Belgium: Brepols.

Decrees Norman P. Tanner, ed., *Decrees of the Ecumenical Councils.* 2 vols. London: Sheed and Ward, 1990.

Essais   Michel de Montaigne, *Les essais: édition conforme au texte de l'exemplaire de Bordeaux*, ed. Pierre Villey; new edn. with a preface by V.-L. Saulnier. 3 vols. Paris: Presses universitaires de France, 1965.

Essays   Michel de Montaigne, *The Complete Essays*, trans. M. A. Screech. London: Penguin, 1991.

GO   Marie le Jars de Gournay, *Oeuvres complètes*, ed. Jean-Claude Arnould *et al.* 2 vols. Paris: Champion, 2002.

LCL   Loeb Classical Library, Harvard University Press, followed by the volume number.

NE   Aristotle, *The Nicomachean Ethics*, trans. Roger Crisp. Cambridge: Cambridge University Press, 2000.

NPNF   *Nicene and Post-Nicene Fathers of the Christian Church*. 2nd series. Peabody, MA: Hendrickson, 1999.

PG   *Patrologia cursus completus ... Series Graeca*, ed. J.-P. Migne. 161 vols. Paris, 1857–64.

PL   *Patrologia cursus completus ... Series Latina*, ed. J.-P Migne. 221 vols. Paris, 1844–64.

PO   *De l'égalité des deux sexes. De l'éducation des dames. De l'excellence des hommes*, ed. Marie-Frédérique Pellegrin. Paris: Vrin, 2011.

S   *Seneca: Dialogues and Essays*, trans. John Davie, with an Introduction by T. Reinhardt. Oxford: Oxford University Press (World's Classics), 2007.

ST   Nicolas Malebranche, *The Search after Truth, and Elucidations of the Search after Truth*, trans. T. M. Lennon and P. J. Olscamp. 2nd edn. Cambridge; Cambridge University Press, 1997.

Introduction

Alexis Trousset (alias Jacques Olivier) emerged briefly from obscurity in 1617, when he published a misogynistic tract entitled *Alphabet of the Imperfection and Malice of Women*. Trousset composed his diatribe as alphabetically ordered descriptions of female vices, beginning with the letter 'A' ('a very avaricious animal') and dedicated it to 'the worst creature in the world.' The following extract from the preface exemplifies the style and content of the whole book:

Woman! If your arrogant and fickle mind could know the fate of your misery and the vanity of your condition, you would flee from the light of day and seek out the shadows; you would hide in caverns and caves; you would curse your misfortune, regret your birth and hate yourself. Nonetheless, the extreme blindness that deprives you of this knowledge makes you live in society as the most imperfect creature in the universe, the scum of nature, the breeding ground of evils, the source of controversy, the laughing stock of the insane, the scourge of wisdom, the firebrand of hell, the instigator of vice, the cesspool of filth, a monster in nature, a necessary evil, a multiform chimera, a harmful pleasure, the bait of the devil, the enemy of the angels, the mask of God, deforming and undermining the wisdom of the very God who created you.[1]

When an equally undistinguished M. Vigoureux argued that the faults attributed to women occurred just as frequently among men,[2] Trousset replied (within months of publishing the original *Alphabet*) by contrasting the alleged ignorance of his critic with the unimpeachable authorities on which he relied:

It is said, and it is true, that it is not the business of a blind man to judge colours. I say that it is not the business of an ignorant soldier like you to criticize and reproach those who prove their claims with good arguments and by reference to authorities drawn from holy Scripture and reliable authors, both philosophers and theologians.[3]

---

[1] *Alphabet de l'imperfection et malice des femmes* (Paris: Jean Petit-Pas, 1617), 3–4.

[2] Le Sieur Vigoureux, *La Défense des femmes, contre l'alphabet de leur pretendue malice & imperfection* (Paris: Pierre Chevalier, 1617).

[3] *Response aux impertinences de l'aposté capitaine Vigoureux: sur la defence des femmes* (Paris: Jean Petit-Pas, 1617), 29. Trousset had similarly claimed, in the *Alphabet*, that he relied on 'the reading of the Holy Scriptures and the most serious and profound authors of past and present centuries' (p. 332).

The French edition of Trousset's virulent alphabet was reprinted frequently throughout the seventeenth century and was 'newly translated out of the *French* into *English*' as *A Discourse of Women, Shewing their Imperfections Alphabetically*.[4] Its subsequent republication in English testifies to the enduring popularity of misogyny among readers in both languages.

This brief interlude in the *querelle des femmes*, though it may appear atypical, illustrates many features of the ongoing controversy about the status of women and their alleged natural incapacities. In particular, it identifies the two authorities—namely, the Bible and the writings of ancient 'reliable authors'—to which most participants appealed to support disparate conclusions, and it highlights the challenges faced by those who wished to escape from traditional rhetoric and add a new dimension to the debate.

The dispute about women's natural talents and roles in society had oscillated in the sixteenth century between two diametrically opposite views—those that claimed that women were inferior to men, and those that argued that they were superior. Erasmus (1467–1536) reported a standard version of the inferiority thesis in 1514, allegedly on the authority of Plato, in his widely read and quoted *Praise of Folly*:

When Plato shows himself in doubt whether to place woman in the class of rational creatures or in that of brutes, he only wishes to point out how flagrant is the folly of the sex. For if by chance some woman wishes to be thought of as wise, she does nothing but show herself twice a fool. It is as if one took a bull to the masseuse, a thing quite 'against the grain', as the phrase is. It is doubly a fault, you know, when against nature one assumes the color of a virtue, warping one's character in a direction not its own. Just as according to the proverb of the Greeks, 'an ape is always an ape, though dressed in scarlet', so a woman is always a woman—that is, a fool—whatever part she may have chosen to play.[5]

Although the original text of the *Timaeus* does not support this interpretation, Erasmus' comment became a commonplace Platonic source to 'prove' that women are less rational than men. The opposite thesis—that women are superior to men—was defended by Erasmus' contemporary, Cornelius

---

[4] There were later French editions in 1619, 1626, 1628, 1634, 1640, 1646, 1658, and 1683. The English edition omitted the author's name and the prefatory material quoted in the text above. It was presented as 'The Anatomy of Women; Described in Two and Twenty several *Vices* Alphabetically' (although there were twenty-three chapters), and was published in London by Henry Brome in 1662 (reprinted, 1673).

[5] Erasmus, *Opera Omnia* (Leiden, 1706), IV, 418; *The Praise of Folly*, trans. H. H. Hudson (Princeton, NJ: Princeton University Press, 1941/1970), 23–4. Erasmus relies on *Timaeus* 91A–D.

Agrippa (1486–1535), in the *Declamation on the Nobility and Pre-eminence of the Female Sex* (1529). Agrippa conceded that, while 'one sex is not pre-eminent over the other because of the nature of the soul...in everything else apart from the divine essence of the soul, women...are almost infinitely superior to the uncouth male gender.'[6]

Similar contradictory claims about women continued to appear in the seventeenth century. Rolet's *Historical Account of the Wiles and Craftiness of Women* (1623) suggested that women were the exclusive source of all the evils in the world. According to Rolet, 'there is no animal in the world more dangerous than woman' and, since their malice is almost infinite, he would have exhausted his supply of paper had he attempted to provide a comprehensive account of female malice from the beginning of time.[7] In contrast, Jacquette Guillaume's book announces its thesis in the title: *Illustrious Women: or it is proved by sound and convincing reasons that the female sex surpasses the male sex in all kinds of ways*.[8] Gabriel Gilbert and François Du Soucy likewise argued for the superiority of women.[9] In addition to these tracts about the inferiority or superiority of women, there was also a distinct genre that avoided direct comparison of the sexes by simply reporting famous women who became eminent because of their virtues and achievements. Boccaccio had provided an exemplar of this in *Concerning Famous Women*, which was mined by many subsequent writers for historical examples of illustrious women.[10] Those who adopted Boccaccio's approach in the seventeenth century included Louis Machon, *Discourse or Apologetic Lecture in Support of Women* (1641), Madeleine de Scudéry, *Illustrious Women* (1642), and Pierre Le Moyne, *The Gallery of Great Women* (1647).[11]

[6] *De Nobilitate & Praecellentia Foeminei sexus* (1529), 4A.

[7] L.S.R., *Tableau historique des ruses et subtilitez des femmes* (Paris: Rolet Boutonne, 1623), 3–4, 86.

[8] *Les dames illustres ou par bonnes et fortes raisons, il se prouve, que le Sexe feminin surpasse en toutes sortes de genres le Sexe masculin* (Paris: Thomas Jolly, 1665).

[9] Gilbert, *Panegyrique des Dames* (Paris: Augustin Courbé, 1650): 'I planned to show that women are more perfect than men' (p. 4); Du Soucy, *Le Triomphe des Dames* (Paris: chez l'autheur, 1646), 199–201, 214.

[10] *De mulieribus claris*, which was written in Italian in 1361/62, and first published in Latin in 1463.

[11] Machon, *Discours ou Sermon apologetique, en faveur des femmes. Question nouvelle, curieuse, & non jamais sostenue* (Paris: T. Blaise, 1641); George de Scudéry, *Les femmes illustres, ou les harangues heroiques de Monsieur de Scudery, avec les veritables portraits de ces Heroines, tirez des Medailles Antiques* (Paris: Antoine de Sommaville & A. Courbé, 1642) which was published by Madeleine de Scudéry under her brother's name; Le Moyne, *La Gallerie des femmes fortes* (Paris: Antoine de Sommaville, 1647).

In this turmoil of conflicting ideas and polarized claims, the three authors translated in this edition made a novel contribution by arguing for the *equality* of men and women. Despite significant differences in their educational experiences and religious affiliations, they also shared a measure of intellectual independence that made it possible for them to defend feminist egalitarianism against prevailing orthodoxies in the civil and ecclesiastical consensus of the early modern period. Their biographies testify to their relative autonomy, natural resilience, and the extent to which they challenged received wisdom.

Marie le Jars de Gournay (1568–1645), the eldest of six children, was born in Paris but spent a significant period of her youth at the family estate at Gournay-sur-Aronde, in Picardie, after her father's death in 1577.[12] She had no formal education, though she taught herself Latin and some Greek before the intellectual awakening that she experienced on reading Montaigne's *Essays* in 1584. When Montaigne came to Paris four years later, Gournay asked to meet him and, following their conversations, she described herself as his *fille d'alliance* or adoptive daughter. Montaigne subsequently visited Gournay for a few months at Gournay-sur-Aronde; despite the significant age gap between them, these brief encounters resulted in correspondence between Montaigne and his enthusiastic disciple until Montaigne's death (in 1592) at his chateau in the south of France. The death of Gournay's mother the previous year left her doubly bereaved; she effectively assumed full responsibility for care of the family and for stabilizing its parlous financial situation. When the family estate in Picardie was inherited by her younger brother, Marie le Jars returned to Paris, where she spent the rest of her life.

Gournay was then twenty-four years old. The relatively limited range of lifestyle options available to young women in France at that time included marriage, life in a convent, or employment as a servant. Marie le Jars declined to marry, despite her mother's insistent encouragement, and she rejected the convent life that her younger sister Léonore followed. Nor was Gournay a noble lady with financial resources to provide the free time required to engage in serious studies. Instead she set about constructing a novel and distinctive social status for herself as a professional writer of very

---

[12] For this biographical sketch I have borrowed from Gournay's *Apologie pour celle qui écrit* (1634) and from Marjorie J. Ilsley, *A Daughter of the Renaissance: Marie le Jars de Gournay. Her Life and Works* (The Hague: Mouton, 1963).

modest means. This choice was anomalous; in fact, Gournay was at odds with the spirit of the times in many features of her life. She assumed the role of editor of posthumous editions of Montaigne's *Essays* despite her lack of a formal education, and thereby incurred the scorn of some contemporary scholars.[13] She was at odds with public opinion when, in an open letter to the Queen that she subsequently came to regret, she defended the Jesuits following the regicide of Henry IV.[14] Gournay was also a Catholic moralist in an age when the market was already replete with pamphlets by Huguenots, Jesuits, Oratorians, Jansenists, sceptics, and others who provided readers with a surfeit of advice about how to live their lives. She published poems that were generally not highly rated by readers or critics, and expressed tolerant views about alternative Christian churches when religious toleration was hardly popular in France. This profile of an independent unmarried woman as a professional writer, living in very modest means in an attic apartment in central Paris, accompanied only by her maid, was further complicated by her public expressions of feminism.

Gournay's first publication—a short novel entitled *The Promenade of Monsieur de Montaigne* (1594)—revealed her feminist sympathies in frequent rhetorical digressions, such as: 'It is commonly believed that, in order to be chaste, a woman should not be educated; truly, one fails to honour chastity if one believes that it can be found attractive only by those who are blind.'[15] Some of these narratively misplaced defences of women's virtue and natural ability were deleted from later editions of the *Promenade* and were integrated into *The Equality of Men and Women*, which was published in 1622. Likewise, her Preface for Montaigne's *Essays* in 1595 included the ironic sentiments about the 'blessed' condition of women that reappeared, in 1626, in the opening sentences of *The Ladies' Complaint*.[16] This brief tract revealed more clearly than *Equality* how strongly Gournay felt about the inferior condition of women. When it first appeared, its author was

---

[13] There were notable exceptions, such as the Dutch humanist, Justus Lipsius (1547–1606).

[14] *Adieu, de l'ame du roy de France et de Navarre Henry le Grand à la Royne. Avec, La defence des Peres Jesuites (1610)*, GO I, 191–235.

[15] GO, II, 1355, note 9 (1594 edn.).

[16] 'Blessed are you, reader, if you are not a member of the sex that has been excluded from all goods, forbidden to be free, and also forbidden from all the virtues because it has been excluded from the power and moderation by the use of which the virtues are acquired.' GO, I, 283–4, note A. This was deleted from later editions of the Preface but then re-used in *The Ladies' Complaint*. The original titles of these texts were *l'Égalité des hommes et des femmes* (Paris: 1622) and *Grief des dames* (Paris: 1626).

already fifty-eight years old. Gournay, however, survived into her eight-ieth year, and during the following two decades she continued to edit Montaigne, to contribute to the literary, religious, and political discussions of polite society in Paris, and to publish revised editions of her own work. When she died in Paris on 13 July 1645, her life's work seemed to have died with her. None of her writings was republished until the twentieth century, and most critical commentary about her during the intervening centuries was negative.[17] In this respect at least, she had much in common with one of her correspondents, Anna Maria van Schurman.

Van Schurman (1607–1678) was born, four decades after Gournay, into a strict Calvinist family in Germany, to where her grandparents had moved from Antwerp during the Spanish occupation.[18] In 1615 she returned to The Netherlands and settled in Utrecht, where she spent most of her adult life and where she was educated at home until her father's death in 1623. Her decision to remain unmarried, like that of Gournay, seems to have been motivated partly by her religious beliefs, and partly by the obligation of taking care of her widowed mother and maiden aunts. In contrast with Gournay, however, van Schurman became an internationally renowned scholar. She displayed an amazing ability to learn languages from a very young age, and she mastered (among other languages) ancient Greek, Latin, and Hebrew. When the University of Utrecht was founded in 1636, Gisbertus Voetius (1589–1676) was appointed the first professor of theol-ogy, and he allowed van Schurman to hear his lectures unofficially if she sat behind a curtain to conceal her attendance.

It was during this period that she composed her *Dissertation* in Latin, as a young scholarly lady who was unequivocally committed to the strict Calvinism that Voetius defended against the liberal wing of the Reformed Church in the United Provinces. The *Dissertation* was published in a French translation in 1646, with the amended title: *A Famous Question: Is it neces-sary, or not, that girls be learned? Debated on each side by Miss Ann Marie van Schurman, a Dutch woman, and M. Andrew Rivet from Poitou.* It was also trans-lated into English in 1659 as *The Learned Maid; or, Whether a Maid may be a*

---

[17] The first republication of Gournay's writings, after 1641, was Mario Schiff, *La fille d'alliance de Montaigne, Marie de Gournay* (Paris: Champion, 1910).

[18] See van Schurman's autobiography, *Eukleria seu melioris partis electio. Tractatus brevem vitae eius delineationem exhibens* (Altona: C. van der Meulem, 1673), and M. de Baar *et al.* eds., *Choosing the Better Part: Anna Maria van Schurman (1607–1678)* (Dordrecht: Kluwer, 1996).

Scholar? A Logick Exercise Written in Latine by that Incomparable Virgin Anna Maria à Schurman of Utrecht.[19] Although van Schurman remained a devout Christian for the rest of her life, she eventually abandoned both the strict theology of Voetius and the educational philosophy that she had defended in the *Dissertation*. This change of mind occurred due to the influence of a French preacher, Jean de Labadie (1610–1674). He was born into a Catholic family in France, was ordained as a Jesuit priest in 1638, and almost immediately left the Jesuits to become a secular priest in Amiens.[20] He seems to have been attracted to a mystical or evangelical style of Christianity that he failed to find in any of the church structures that were then available. Consequently, he moved frequently from one form of religious life to another, from sympathy towards Jansenism to becoming briefly a Carmelite, until he read Calvin's *Institutes* and adopted the congenial spirit of reform that he found there. Labadie settled in Geneva, where he remained for seven years, during which he was visited in 1662 by Van Schurman's brother, Johannes Godschalk van Schurman. He was subsequently invited by the Walloon church in Middelburg (The Netherlands) to assume leadership of their congregation. In 1666 that invitation brought him to Utrecht, where he met Van Schurman for the first time.

Van Schurman and Labadie met infrequently during the following three years, when Labadie was invariably in conflict with various synods of the Reformed Church about the orthodoxy of his preaching. He was eventually forced by the local magistrates to surrender his official ministry in the province of Zeeland in 1669; he then settled in Amsterdam, where he established a community of like-minded Christians. Van Schurman and a small number of women companions joined him there, though they were forced to move again the following year. This led to a series of frequent relocations, as this unorthodox community of Calvinist men and women sought asylum in some hospitable jurisdiction. They initially sailed to Bremen, and spent two years at Herford. They then moved north to Altona,

[19] *Question celebre. S'il est necessaire, ou non, que les Filles soient sçavantes. Agitée de part & d'autre, par Mademoiselle Anne Marie de Schurman Holandoise, & le Sr. André Rivet Poitevin* (Paris: Rolet le Duc, 1646). The English edition was published in London by Redmayne.

[20] For biographical information, see *Declaration de Jean de Labadie...contenant les raisons qui l'ont obligé à quitter la Communion de l'Eglise Romaine pour ranger à celle de l'Eglise Reformée* (Montauban: P. Braconier, 1650); F. Sambuc, *Jean de Labadie; sa vie et ses écrits* (Strasbourg: Heitz, 1869); T. J. Saxby, *The Quest for the New Jerusalem: Jean de Labadie and the Labadists, 1610–1744* (Dordrecht: Nijhoff, 1987).

near Hamburg, where van Schurman composed her autobiography, until they finally returned to Friesland, in the United Provinces, in 1675.

Throughout his career as an independent wandering preacher, Labadie preached a style of Christianity that was modelled on the early Christians who lived a simple life in relatively unstructured communities. It was characterized by respect for the Bible as the word of God, by belief in predestination and the powerlessness of human beings to realize their own salvation, and by the ideal of a mystical union with God. The 'illumination or irradiation' by grace that was believed to effect such a union did not result from study or human intelligence; it was independent of the education, sex, age, or social status of those to whom God granted his gifts freely and, according to Labadie, there were many people in history, including 'many children, young people, including even girls and village folk' who realized the highest aspirations of a Christian life.[21]

This ideal of simple religious faith was radically different from the presbyterian and highly scholastic theology of Voetius. At the age of sixty-two, however, van Schurman relinquished nearly all the religious and academic friendships of her previous life to embrace this communitarian ideal and to follow Labadie, both spiritually and geographically, in pursuit of an authentic Christian life. Following this religious conversion, she reviewed and rejected the reasons that she had offered in the *Dissertation* in favour of women's education; she no longer believed that knowledge of biblical languages and theology were conducive to being a good Christian. Van Schurman was now satisfied to adopt as her motto the words attributed to Christ, when he praised the contemplative attitude of Mary rather than the active assiduousness of her sister, Martha: 'one thing is needful; and Mary hath chosen that good part, which shall not be taken away from her' (Luke 10: 42). However, this re-evaluation of the importance of academic studies did not invalidate van Schurman's previous argument about the insignificance of gender for religious faith. As discussed below, it was consistent even with her revised religious faith to reject the suggestion that men, as such, have a unique role in the interpretation or transmission of a distinctly Christian way of life.

---

[21] Labadie, *Manuel de Pieté contenant quelques devoirs & actes religieux & Chrétiens* (Middelbourg: H. Smidt, 1668), 124; Labadie, *L'Empire du S. Esprit sur les Ames* (Amsterdam: L. Autein, 1671), p. 7 of unpaginated preface.

As in the case of Poulain (discussed below), the English translation of van
Schurman's work extended its readership briefly, and she is cited intermittently by various authors writing in English in the early eighteenth century. For example, the translator's Preface to *An English-Saxon Homily on the
Birthday of St. Gregory* mentions van Schurman's 'Scholastick' writing, and
the anonymous 'Sophia', in *Woman Not Inferior to Man*, refers to the learned
Dutch woman 'with a thesis in her hand, displaying nature in it's [*sic*] most
innocent useful lights'.[22] Nonetheless, a cursory review of the subsequent
literature suggests that van Schurman's *Dissertation* faded from view until
the revival, in the twentieth century, of academic interest in women authors.

Finally, François Poulain de la Barre (1647–1723) contrasts with the
other two authors translated here both in his formal education and his decision to change membership from one church to another. He was born into
a bourgeois Catholic family in Paris, and began the standard education at
the age of nine that was provided at that time for men in French colleges.[23]
Following completion of the college curriculum in 1663, when he was
awarded the degree of Master of Arts, he continued his studies in theology
until 1666. Poulain spent some years as a language teacher, in the course
of which he published a short comparative study of Latin and French.[24]
During the period between the conclusion of his studies (in 1666) and
his eventual departure to Geneva (in 1688), Poulain became increasingly
critical of the scholastic philosophy that provided the framework within
which Catholic theology was presented as a systematic and coherent unit.

[22] 'The useful Objections that are made by Gentlemen to Womens [*sic*] learning, are fully
answer'd in a Scholastick way, and in very elegant Latin, by the Glory of her Sex, Mrs [*sic*] *Anna
Maria a Schurman*': *An English-Saxon Homily on the Birthday of St. Gregory*, by Aelfric, Abbot of
Eynsham, trans. Elizabeth Elstob (London: W. Bowyer, 1709), p. iii; Sophia, *Woman not Inferior
to Man* (London: John Hawkins, 1739), 37.

[23] For biographical information, I am indebted to Maleleine Alcover, *Poullain de la Barre: une
aventure philosophique* (Seattle: Biblio 17, 1981) and Siep Stuurman, *François Poulain de la
Barre and the Invention of Modern Equality* (Cambridge, MA: Harvard University Press, 2004).
College education in seventeenth-century France is documented in L.W. D. Brockliss, *French
Higher Education in the Seventeenth and Eighteenth Centuries* (Oxford: Clarendon Press, 1987),
and Henry Phillips, *Church and Culture in Seventeenth-Century France* (Cambridge: Cambridge
University Press, 1997), Ch. 3. The Jesuit curriculum of college education was based on
the *Ratio studiorum*. See E. A. Fitzpatrick, *St. Ignatius and the Ratio Studiorum* (New York
and London: McGraw-Hill, 1933); F. de Dainville, *L'Education des jésuites (xvie–xviiie siècles)*
(Paris: Editions de Minuit, 1978), and Camille de Rochemonteix, *Un collège des jésuites au xvi-
i^ème et au xviiième siècles*, 4 vols. (Le Mans, 1889).

[24] *Les rapports de la langue Latine avec la Françoise, pour traduire elegamment et sans peine*
(Paris: 1673).

He had similar reservations about the claimed authority of the Church to provide a definitive interpretation of biblical passages, such as Matt. 26: 26–28. These first steps towards theological independence were confirmed by his acquaintance with Cartesian philosophy. Cartesianism had been banned in French universities and colleges, and was widely suspected of being conducive to religious heresy, even by Calvinist theologians such as Voetius. Some of Descartes' philosophical works had also been listed by the Catholic Church in its *Index of Forbidden Books* in 1663; members of the Church were forbidden to print, read, or even possess copies 'until such time as they were corrected'—an unlikely possibility, since the author had died thirteen years earlier.[25] Despite the almost universal condemnation, however, many supporters of Descartes' philosophy published new editions of his works in France during the 1660s and 1670s; they also held public conferences, and contributed to the dissemination of Cartesian ideas by writing new philosophical work that was inspired by Cartesian ideas.[26]

The primary conclusion that Poulain borrowed from Descartes was that one should not adopt philosophical opinions on the authority of any author, even of philosophers as famous as Plato or Aristotle. The only authorities that merit recognition are reason and experience; in philosophical matters, one should follow the evidence and adjust one's beliefs to the relative strength of supporting reasons. This critique of authority applied equally to Descartes as to anyone else:

> But please take care that I do not claim here that Descartes is infallible, that everything that he proposes is true or unobjectionable, that one should follow him blindly and that others cannot discover anything as good as, or even better than, what he gave us. I only say that I believe he is one of the most reasonable philosophers that we have, whose

[25] See D. M. Clarke, *Descartes: A Biography* (Cambridge: Cambridge University Press, 2006), 413–16. The controversies surrounding Cartesianism are summarized in D. M. Clarke, *Occult Powers & Hypotheses: Cartesian Natural Philosophy under Louis xiv* (Oxford: Clarendon Press, 1989), and Phillips, *Church & Culture*, Chap. 6.

[26] For example, Claude Clerselier edited a three-volume edition of Descartes' correspondence, which appeared in Paris in 1657, 1659 and 1667; Louis de la Forge edited *L'Homme de René Descartes* (Paris, 1664) and published his own Cartesian account of the union of mind and body in *Traitté de l'esprit de l'homme et de ses facultez et fonctions, et de son union avec le corps* (Paris: 1666). Jacques Rohault wrote a very successful summary of Cartesian natural philosophy, *Traité de physique* (Paris: 1671); Nicolas-Joseph Poisson issued his *Commentaire ou remarques sur le methode de M' Descartes* (Paris: 1671), and the most famous exponent of Cartesianism, Nicolas Malebranche, completed *De la recherche de la vérité* in two parts in 1674–75.

method is ...most appropriate for distinguishing between truth and falsehood, even in the works of the author of that method.[27]

Relatively little is known about this period of Poulain's life except that, following his exposure to Cartesianism, he published three books on the equality of the sexes in quick succession: *A Physical and Moral Discourse on the Equality of Both Sexes, which Shows that it is Important to Rid Oneself of Prejudices* (1673), in which the author is identified only as 'Sieur P.'; *The Education of Ladies to Guide the Mind in the Sciences and in Morals* (1674), in which Poulain's full name appears and in the course of which he also identifies himself as the author of the previous book. Finally, Poulain published an ironic defence of men's claims to superiority in *The Excellence of Men, against the Equality of the Sexes* (1675).[28] It also seems inexplicable, in retrospect, that despite the radical nature of his contributions to this debate and the unorthodox views about biblical interpretation that they included, Poulain was ordained a priest in 1679. He subsequently served as a curate in two village parishes in northern France, in La Flamengrie and then in Saint-Jean Baptiste de Versigny, before abandoning his priestly career. Poulain lived briefly in Paris, in 1688, and seems to have gradually adopted Calvinist sympathies during this transitional period.

The religious and philosophical conversions that Poulain underwent made his position as a former Catholic priest untenable in France. He moved to Geneva in 1688, where he married Marie Ravier and spent the remainder of his life. He earned a living initially by reverting to his earlier career; he taught French to the citizens of his newly adopted city and published a small monograph on the French language to assist his pupils.[29] In 1720 he published a critical examination of Catholic doctrine on the Eucharist and a defence of the capacity of individuals to read and interpret the Bible: *The Doctrine of Protestants about the freedom to read the Holy Scripture, church services in the vernacular, the invocation of saints, and the sacrament of the Eucharist; Confirmed by the Roman Missal and by Reflections on each of these issues, with a philosophical commentary on the following words of Jesus Christ: This*

---

[27] *De l'éducation des dames*, PO, 278. Malebranche recommends the same critical attitude towards Descartes (ST, 215).

[28] The original titles were: *Discours physique et moral de l'égalité des deux sexes, où l'on voit l'importance de se défaire des préjugez* (Paris: 1673); *De l'éducation des dames pour la conduite de l'esprit dans les sciences et dans les moeurs* (Paris: 1674); *De l'excellence des hommes contre l'égalité des sexes* (Paris: 1675).

[29] *Essai des remarques particulieres sur la langue françoise, pour la ville de Geneve* (Geneva: 1691).

is my body, This is my blood, Mt. XXVI, v. 26.[30] Poulain remained in Geneva until his death, at the age of seventy-six, in 1723.

Poulain's primary text on the equality of the sexes was reprinted in Paris in 1676, and a third edition appeared three years later. However, there were no published replies to this revolutionary thesis, which was almost completely ignored in the seventeenth century. It seems as if Poulain's thesis was simply too radical to merit even the objections of critics; he was proposing that women could exercise all the same offices and functions as men in civil and religious society in a country where misogyny, at its extreme, had been expressed in the torture and public burning of women as witches, especially in the first half of the seventeenth century.[31] As a result, except for a brief notoriety in the eighteenth century, Poulain's work faded into obscurity in France after his death. When Henri Piéron stumbled on a copy in the French national library at the beginning of the twentieth century, the pages were still uncut; no-one had ever read that copy of the book before.[32]

In contrast with its fortunes in France, however, Poulain's *Discours physique et moral* became a significant source text for feminist writing in English. It was translated into English as *The Woman as Good as the Man; or, The Equallity of Both Sexes* in 1677. This was subsequently plagiarized by an anonymous 'Sophia' in *Woman Not Inferior to Man: or, A Short and Modest Vindication of the Natural Rights of the FAIR-SEX to a Perfect Equality of Power, Dignity, and Esteem, with the Men* (London, 1739), of which a second, expanded edition appeared in *Beauty's Triumph: or, The Superiority of the Fair Sex Invincibly Proved* (London, 1751). Poulain's text was retranslated into English and edited in an anonymous pirated edition 'by a Lady' as *Female Rights Vindicated; or, The Equality of the Sexes Morally and Physically Proved* (London, 1758). The same translation appeared in two later editions as *Female Restoration, by a Moral and Physical Vindication of Female Talents* (London, 1780) and as *Female Rights Vindicated; or, the Equality of*

---

[30]   *La doctrine des protestans sur la liberté de lire l'Ecriture Sainte, le service divin en langue entendue, l'invocation des saints, le sacrement de l'eucharistie. Justifiée par le Missel Romain & par des Réfléxions sur chaque point. Avec un commentaire philosophique sur ces paroles de Jesus-Christ, Ceci est mon Corps; Ceci est mon Sang, Matth. Chap. XXVI, v. 26* (Geneva: Fabri & Barrillot, 1720).

[31]   See E. W. Monter, *Witchcraft in France and Switzerland: The Borderlands during the Reformation* (Ithaca and London: Cornell University Press, 1976). There is an earlier book by H. R. Trevor-Roper, *The European Witch-Craze of the 16th and 17th Centuries*, republished by Penguin, 1990.

[32]   H. Grappin, 'Notes sur un féministe oublié; le cartésien Poulain de la Barre,' *Revue d'histoire littéraire de la France* (1913), 852. This is merely a symptom of the lack of interest in Poulain that is documented in Alcover, *Poullain* and Stuurman, *François Poulain* (note 23).

the Sexes Proved (South Shields, 1833).[33] Thus the anonymous exploitation and English translations of Poulain's *Discours physique et moral* influenced feminist publications in English from Judith Drake to Mary Wollstonecraft, and inspired many eighteenth-century contributors on both sides of the debate about women's equality.[34] The reciprocal influence between French and English feminists came full circle when the publisher of *Female Rights Vindicated* (1833) inserted an acknowledgement in Poulain's text of the significance of Mary Wollstonecraft.[35]

Poulain's radical critique of tradition added a new dimension to the debate about women. He thereby made explicit the fundamental challenge faced by all three authors, if they were to avoid being mired in a contest of quoting biblical texts or ancient books which clearly favoured their opponents. They had to provide new reasons for the equality thesis that were sufficiently objective and persuasive to change the terms in which the debate had previously been conducted and, in doing so, to help define the meaning of equality as it applied to men and women. This can best be seen by reviewing some of the ways in which they each argued for the equality of men and women.

Marie de Gournay and Equality

Marie le Jars was among the first to argue for the equality of men and women, and thereby helped set the agenda for its discussion for the remainder of the seventeenth century.[36] This distinctive thesis is stated in the opening sentences of *Equality*:

> Most of those who defend the cause of women…adopt the completely opposite view by claiming superiority for women…I am content to make women equal to men, for nature is also as opposed to superiority as to inferiority in this respect.

---

[33] The history of pirated versions of Poulain's book in England was noted by Stuurman, *François Poulain de la Barre and the Invention of Modern Equality*, 282, and has been documented in detail by Guyonne Leduc, *Réécrites anglaises au XVIIIe siècle de l'ÉGALITÉ DES DEUX SEXES (1673) de François Poulain de la Barre* (Paris: l'Harmattan, 2010). I am indebted to Guyonne Leduc for bringing these anonymous texts to my attention.

[34] Drake, *An Essay in Defence of the Female Sex in a Letter to a Lady, Written by a Lady* (London: 1691); Wollsonecraft, *A Vindication of the Rights of Woman* (London: 1792).

[35] 'Nor ought I to omit mentioning the name of *Mary Wollstonecraft*, a writer of extraordinary talent, nor that of *Harriet Martineau*, who is yet living, and the very clever authoress of a series of Tales, illustrative of Political Economy.' *Female Rights Vindicated* (1833), 68.

[36] For previous proponents of equality, see Eileen O'Neill, 'The Equality of Men and Women,' in D. Clarke and C. Wilson, eds. *The Oxford Handbook of Philosophy in Early Modern Europe* (Oxford: Oxford University Press, 2011), 445–74.

The meaning of 'equality' emerges in the course of the arguments offered in its defence, and I return to that issue at the conclusion of this introduction.

The most obvious feature of Gournay's *Equality* that initially strikes a reader today is that it is replete with references to ancient and contemporary authors, in the style of Montaigne's *Essays*, and that it cites numerous examples of women who realized the virtues or achievements that she claimed were distributed equally among men and women. Despite that, Gournay denies that her aim is to prove her thesis with reasons or examples.

If I offer a favourable opinion about the dignity or ability of ladies, I do not claim to be able to prove it at this juncture with reasons (because those who are tenacious will be able to dispute them) or by examples (because they are too familiar), but only by the authority of God himself and of the Fathers who were buttresses of his Church, and of those great philosophers who have enlightened the universe. (p. 55)

One part of this statement of method is relatively clear: the ultimate authority for Gournay's equality thesis is divine revelation and its interpretation by theologians of the early Church who enjoyed the honorific title of 'Fathers'. But that leaves unresolved an apparent inconsistency between, on the one hand, the style and content of *Equality* and, on the other, the explicit rejection of examples or reasoning as evidence for its thesis. In fact, Gournay did introduce many counter-examples to combat opponents of equality and she also deployed some compelling arguments that are worth making explicit.

One of these arguments occurs towards the conclusion of *The Ladies' Complaint*, which criticizes the so-called 'learned' who claim to have established a general conclusion about the inferiority of women's abilities. Gournay dismisses their logic as follows: 'they are adequately conquered and penalized for displaying their stupidity when they refute the particular by the general—if one could assume that, in general, the ability of women is inferior' (p. 78). She had named many well-known examples of women who were as learned, virtuous, and competent as some men—these were uncontested facts—while her opponents defended a general proposition to the effect that women are inferior to men. It is a matter of logic that every universal claim is subject to falsification by even one counter-example. The observation of one non-black crow falsifies the general proposition that all crows are black and, in the general thesis at issue here, the counter-examples were very numerous. The specific examples of women who were notable for their outstanding virtues logically imply that any universal thesis about the inferiority of women is false. Rather than attempt fallaciously to refute 'the particular by the general', any valid argument based on historical data must proceed in the opposite direction, from particular cases (by induction) to a general claim.

The Equality of Men and Women also appealed to reason to show that those who proposed a general thesis about women's alleged inferiority were inconsistent with their own stated principles. Although that would not prove the equality of the sexes, it would at least help undermine opponents' arguments. Scholastic philosophers had, over many centuries, developed and defended a thesis that was attributed to Aristotle, according to which each naturally occurring type of reality has a unique 'form'. They understood a form as the specific property or cluster of properties that makes something the kind of thing that it is. This philosophical theory applied to every type of entity—animal, vegetable, or otherwise. In the case of human beings, it was almost universally taught that the defining feature of a human being was the possession of a rational soul or mind; accordingly, having a rational soul or mind was a necessary and sufficient condition for being human. It was also widely taught among Christian philosophers that the human soul could exist independently of the human body; otherwise it would be impossible (they thought) to provide an intelligible account of the personal immortality that was allegedly revealed in the New Testament.

This anthropology had been endorsed by centuries of dogmatic teaching within western Christianity. It became especially explicit in the fourteenth and fifteenth centuries, in response to neo-Aristotelians such as Pietro Pomponazzi (1462–1525), who was sympathetic to the Averroist theory that all human beings share in a single spiritual soul. The Fifth Lateran Council (1512–17) condemned that view and declared its official teaching as follows:

...we condemn and reject all those who insist that the intellectual soul is mortal, or that it is only one among all human beings, and those who suggest doubts on this topic. For the soul not only truly exists of itself and essentially as the form of the human body... but it is also immortal; and further, for the enormous number of bodies into which it is infused individually, it can and ought to be and is multiplied... And since truth cannot contradict truth, we define that every statement contrary to the enlightened truth of the faith is totally false and we strictly forbid teaching otherwise to be permitted.[37]

On this account, the defining feature of human beings is that each individual has their own immortal, spiritual soul, and it is impossible for anyone to be partly ensouled or less ensouled than someone else; either one has a spiritual soul or not. That provided an incontrovertible basis for arguing that men and women are essentially equal. Evidently, they may still differ in respect of inessential features—such as their size, shape, skin colour, linguistic facility, and so on—but they are essentially either human or not human. Gournay exploits that scholastic doctrine to argue that those who deny women's essential equality with men are inconsistent:

…the human animal, if understood correctly, is neither a man nor a woman because the sexes were not created unconditionally or in such a way that they constitute different species, but exclusively for the purpose of propagation.[38] The unique form and specific characteristic of this animal consists only in the rational soul; and if we are allowed to laugh in the course of this argument, it would not be inappropriate to jest that there is nothing more like the male cat on the windowsill than a female cat. Man and woman are so much one that, if man is more than woman, then woman is more than man.[39] (p. 65)

It is therefore inconsistent to endorse the scholastic teaching of Church councils and still deny the essential equality of the sexes.

Since the Lateran Council also rejected the suggestion that truths from different sources (that is, revelation and reason) may conflict, Pomponazzi had offered an alternative, consistent position for philosophers who were not subject to its jurisdiction. He proposed that, on purely philosophical grounds, one cannot prove the individuality and immortality of the human soul, but it could be accepted as a matter of religious faith. Gournay comes close to adopting that strategy. As is well known, she was an autodidact and did not have an opportunity to acquire a traditional scholastic education. She was therefore reluctant to become involved in the kind of philosophical and theological disputations that were popular in universities at

---

[37] *Decrees*, I, 605.

[38] The 1622 edition had the following alternative: 'the sexes were not made unconditionally [*simplement*], but *secundum quid*, as they say in the Schools; that is to say, exclusively for the purpose of propagation' (GO, I, 978, note 12). The French term '*simplement*' corresponds to the Latin term '*simpliciter*', with which '*secundum quid*' is usually contrasted by scholastics.

[39] Gournay returns to this theme in *The Ladies' Complaint*, when she refers to 'the eternal decree of God Himself, who produced no more than a single creation of two sexes' (p. 78).

that time.[40] In addition to this reservation about philosophical disputations, Gournay's extensive work on Montaigne's *Essays* may have inclined her towards Pyrrhonism. She may therefore have concluded, for sceptical reasons, that there were persuasive philosophical arguments to support both sides of the thesis about the human soul. For whatever reason, she seems to have concluded that biblical revelation—as understood in the Catholic Church to which she belonged—provided the most reliable guide to the truth in this matter and that she should rely primarily 'on authority of God himself' and the Fathers of the Church. That would limit the effectiveness of her argument to those who shared her faith; but even such a limited result in an almost universally Christian Europe would convict many opponents of inconsistency.

Gournay accordingly borrows what she accepted as God's revelation about the equality of the sexes from the Genesis account of creation and from other texts in the New Testament: 'mankind was created male and female, according to Scripture, while counting these two as only one creation' (p. 65). She relies in this context on Gen. 1:27: 'And God created man in his own image: to the image of God he created him: male and female he created them.' The gendered connotations of 'man' in English do not reflect the Latin text of the Bible that Gournay used, in which the term '*homo*' is applied inclusively to both men and women. This point was supported by her comment that, despite being called the 'Son of Man', Christ was evidently the son of a woman. She also appeals to Saint Basil to confirm her interpretation, even quoting the final phrase in Latin from the Vulgate version of Saint Mark's gospel: 'The virtues of man and of woman are the same because God bestowed on them the same creation and the same honour; *masculum et feminam fecit eos Deus*' (pp. 65–6). Other Church Fathers, including Gregory of Nyssa and Theodoret of Cyrrus, adopted similar interpretations of 'man' in their commentaries on Genesis. In the passage to which Gournay refers, Theodoret wrote:

It would have been very easy for God to command and to populate the whole world with inhabitants...by a single act; but to prevent people from believing that there is some difference in nature between people, he decided that all the innumerable human nations would be born from a single couple...It was for the same reason that he did not make the woman from a different material but he took the materials

---

[40] Poulain and other Cartesians subsequently interpreted such a lack of formal schooling as an advantage rather than the opposite, as will be seen below.

to form woman from man ...that is also why God prescribed to men and women the same laws, because the differences between them occur precisely in the structure of their bodies rather than their souls. Woman is endowed with reason, just like man; she is capable of understanding and being aware of her obligations; she knows what she should do and what she should not do, just like man ...Not only men but women also should have access to the divine temples; and the law that allows men to participate in the divine mysteries does not exclude women but commands them, in the same capacity as men, to be initiated and to participate in those mysteries. In addition, that law offers men and women the same rewards for virtue because they strive together to realize the virtues.[41]

When the Genesis account of creation was filtered through the categories of Greek philosophy by the Church Fathers, it was translated into the claim that men and women have the same nature. Gournay also adopts this terminology and concludes that, in respect of 'those whose nature is one and the same, one must conclude that their actions are also the same, and that their esteem and praise are therefore equal when their works are equal' (p. 66). The correspondence between actions and natures was borrowed from a scholastic principle that made it possible to argue in either direction—from knowledge of a given nature to the kind of actions that it can perform or, retroductively, from knowledge of certain actions to the underlying nature from which they result. The latter option is illustrated by the first syllogism of van Schurman's *Dissertation*:

The assumption [about women's ability] may be proved both by what is characteristic of the form of this subject—i.e. human reason—and also by its acts or effects, since it is obvious that women in fact learn various arts and sciences, and acts cannot occur without the corresponding principles. (p. 82)

Thus, while her Dutch counterpart subsequently inferred from the observable actions of some women (in learning, virtuous behaviour, and so on) that they must share the same nature as men, Gournay argued from the Genesis account of a common nature to the conclusion that women's actions are comparable to those of men.

Still borrowing from Genesis, Gournay's concluding remarks in *Equality* highlight the implausible implications of suggesting that women are images of God but not images of men.

---

[41] *Graecarum affectionum curatio seu Evangelicae veritatis ex gentilium philosophica cognitio* (*The Cure of Hellenic Maladies*), PG 83, 943; there is a French translation in Théodoret de Cyr, *Thérapeutique des Maladies Helléniques*, trans. P. Canivet, 2 vols. (Paris: Editions du Cerf, 1958), 244–5.

If one believed that Scripture commanded women to yield to men, as if it were unworthy on their part to oppose them, look at the absurdity of what that would imply: woman would find herself worthy of being made in the image of the Creator, of benefiting from the most holy Eucharist and the mysteries of redemption and of paradise, and of the vision—indeed, the possession—of God, but not of possessing the advantages or privileges of man. Would that not be equivalent to declaring that man is more precious and more exalted than all these things and, therefore, to committing the most serious blasphemy? (p. 730)

Nonetheless, Gournay's central claim—that women and men have exactly the same nature, or what she calls 'the unity of the sexes' (p. 73)—was compatible with assigning different roles to women in civil society or the Church. Since she relied on Scripture to support her main thesis, she could not deny the relevance of biblical passages that were frequently quoted by opponents who denied equality in the Church to women. Gournay could, however, interpret these biblical passages as merely local arrangements in the early Church or as unique decisions by God about specific issues, rather than as general statements of women's inferiority.

For example, Gen. 3:16 presents God as punishing Eve for her transgression in the Garden of Eden: 'To the woman also he said: I will multiply thy sorrows and thy conceptions: in sorrow shalt thou bring forth children, and thou shalt be under thy husband's power, and he shall have dominion over thee.' Gournay comments: 'However true it may be, as some maintain, that this submission was imposed on women as punishment for the sin of eating the apple, that is still a long way from showing the claimed superior dignity of men' (p. 73). In other words, to punish one person and not another does not imply that one is less human or worthy than the other; in fact, the very concept of punishment presupposes that those being punished are fully responsible for their actions as human beings. In a similar way Gournay understood the instruction of Saint Paul to one of the early churches—that 'the head of the woman is the man' (I Cor. 11:13)—as merely a practical arrangement to guarantee peace within marriages, because experience shows that many conjugal partners fail to live in peace and if one partner acceded to the other it would provide a way of avoiding controversy within marriage. Paul's other injunction against women preaching in church is understood similarly as nothing more than an attempt to avoid temptation to other churchgoers.

Finally, the Incarnation was understood traditionally as God appearing in the world as a human being. That necessitated adopting the body of either a man or a woman and, in Gournay's view, 'the demands of propriety required' that God appear as a male. Otherwise Christ could 'not have avoided scandal if he had been born a woman and, as a young person, had mingled with the crowds at all times of the day and night' when preaching. However, if anyone were 'so foolish as to imagine that God is masculine or feminine' they would show clearly 'that they are as incompetent in philosophy as in theology' (p. 72). It may have seemed blasphemous to some people to suggest that God is not male, but it is absurd to assume that God is a sexual being who resembles the bearded men that are often used to depict Christ in paintings.[42] Since God is not a male, that provides another reason for denying that men have a greater resemblance to God than women.

However, despite the plausibility of Gournay's interpretations of biblical passages that were traditionally used by opponents of equality, it is difficult to see how she could have won the public endorsement that she sought. She was not recognized as a theological scholar and, in contrast with van Schurman, her competence in biblical languages was inadequate to the scholarly challenge that she assumed. An even more serious obstacle to Gournay's hermeneutic efforts was that she belonged to a church that claimed for its centralized teaching office in Rome an exclusive authority to interpret the Scriptures. The Council of Trent (Session IV: 8 April 1546) had taught dogmatically that

no one...shall dare to interpret the sacred Scripture either by twisting its text to their own individual meaning in opposition to that which has been and is held by holy mother church, whose function is to pass judgement on the true meaning and interpretation of the sacred Scriptures; or by giving it meanings contrary to the unanimous consent of the fathers,[43]

even if many of those who exercised that office relied on a Latin translation of the original texts. Evidently, Gournay could have argued that there was no universal agreement among the Fathers of the Church about the inferior status of women. However, there had been no unanimity among patristic authors about the Bible's teaching on astronomy, but that did not prevent the Vatican's injunction against Galileo in 1616 concerning heliocentrism.[44]

---

[42] Cf. Poulain, 'When speaking about God, it never occurred to any woman to tell me that she imagined God was like a venerable old man' (p. 135).

[43] *Decrees*, I, 664 (a slightly modified translation).

[44] Galileo commented about the disputed stability of the Earth: 'we may believe that it never so much as entered the thought of the Fathers to debate this.' 'Letter to the Grand Duchess Christina', in *Discoveries and Opinions of Galileo*, trans. S. Drake (New York: Doubleday, 1957), 202.

Gournay therefore was in a situation in which centuries of clerical misogyny had denied equality to women in a church that had stopped short of teaching explicitly that women are inferior to men by nature. Although she was not contradicting a dogmatic teaching of her church, she was claiming to interpret the Scriptures in a novel manner when the church to which she belonged reserved that function exclusively to the pope and the bishops. That was an untenable position in the early seventeenth century.

Of course, Gournay did not depend exclusively on her own scholarship to reinterpret biblical texts that were apparently inimical to women; she also appealed to the traditionally acknowledged authority of 'the Fathers' whom she described as buttresses of the Church. The 'consent of the Fathers' had been accepted by the Church, for centuries, as a guide to interpreting the Scriptures.[45] Since unanimity was often lacking, it was open to disputing theologians to select those Fathers who happened to agree with their own views or to claim that some Fathers (such as Saint Augustine) were more authoritative than others. On the question of women in the Church, however, it was difficult to find any Church Father who disagreed with the apparent implications of Saint Paul's epistles. In fact, it was easy to find misogynistic teachings, such as those of Tertullian, who described women as 'the devil's gateway' and recommended to women: 'submit your head to your husband…busy your hands with spinning; keep your feet at home.'[46] It was equally easy to find praise for women as virgins, as exemplars of modesty, or as submissive to the teachings of the Church. An independent review of patristic theology was therefore likely to buttress the interpretation of Gournay's opponents rather than her novel claim to equality.

One final theme that emerges clearly in Gournay's writing, which is independent of theological disputes and is taken up by her successors, is the effect on women of the inadequate education with which they were generally provided.

If, therefore, women succeed less often than men in achieving various degrees of excellence, it is surprising that the lack of a good education and the preponderance of even patently poor teaching does not make matters worse, and that these factors do not prevent them completely from succeeding…why would the education

---

[45] Many early Church councils appealed to the prior teaching of the 'Fathers' as a criterion of faith, in many cases as a distinct source of faith in parallel with the Scriptures. See for example *Decrees*, I, 83, 107, 175, 220, 314, 496, 663 (and post-Gournay), II, 806.

[46] *On the Apparel of Women*, ANF, IV, 14, 25: PL 1, 1305, 1334.

of women, in literary and social studies, not bridge the gap that is usually found between the minds of men and women ... (pp. 59–60)

The role of education in the *ancien régime* was a very contested issue. The provision of elementary education was almost exclusively monopolized by religious orders of men during Gournay's lifetime, and those involved realized the potentially subversive effect of education on public obedience to the churches and to the absolute power claimed by the monarchy. It was even more obvious that the admission of women to education would affect their acceptance of traditional subservient roles in the home and the churches. The dispute about whether women were 'capable' of study, therefore, masked an underlying concern about the redistribution of power that would result if, as feared, they proved their opponents' assessment of their abilities wrong. Accordingly, women's access to education became central to the arguments proposed by many subsequent authors, including van Schurman and Poulain, and is taken up again in the context of their contributions to the equality debate.

Anna Maria van Schurman and Women's Education

There were at least three reasons that were widely offered for claiming that study or learning was inappropriate for a Christian woman. The most common reason focused on the term 'woman' and argued that *women* lacked the innate capacities or social conditions that are required for study. For example, they suffered from a lack of intelligence, or a lack of motivation, or a lack of other prerequisites (such as free time) for study. The second and equally prevalent reason given, especially among strict Calvinists, relied on the term 'Christian' and argued that it was inappropriate for a *Christian* woman to engage in studies. Finally, there was a third type of objection, which was invoked against van Schurman by the Calvinist theologian André Rivet (1595–1651), to the effect that it was a waste of resources and *irrational* for women to undertake expensive and difficult studies when they were excluded from the public offices or duties for which such studies were allegedly designed. That was a simple and alluring Aristotelian argument: if some activity is intended to achieve a particular objective, it is irrational to embark on the means while knowing that the objective is incapable of realization. I return to Rivet's objection and van Schurman's reply below.

Once van Schurman asked the question, 'is the study of letters appropriate for a Christian woman?' (p. 79), she faced the same challenge as Gournay—to identify a reliable foundation from which to argue for a positive answer. She approached this question initially by qualifying her thesis, and thereby avoided many trivial potential objections. For example, she was not arguing, as Lucrezia Marinella had done, that women were generally superior to men.[47] She replied to one of Rivet's misunderstandings: 'I seem to have supported uncritically an invidious and empty claim about the superiority of our sex in comparison with yours', whereas she was not claiming that 'women are more suited to study than men' (pp. 106–7). She was arguing instead for the equality of men and women, and she explicitly associated her thesis with that of Gournay, with the qualification: 'I would not dare, nor do I wish, to approve it [Gournay's thesis in the *Equality of Men and Women*] fully in every respect' (p. 107).

Secondly, van Schurman was not claiming that all women were equally competent to engage in higher studies, or that all women enjoyed the family circumstances and financial resources necessary for such study. At the outset of the *Dissertation* she limited the scope of her thesis so that it applied to women only in the same general way that equivalent claims applied to men. Accordingly, study would be appropriate only for those women who had a minimum natural capacity for study; those who were exceptionally unintelligent (as were some men) could therefore not be used as counter-examples. Likewise, any advanced study of the kind envisaged presupposed that the person undertaking the study had acquired an elementary education at home or from a tutor, and that the prospective student had enough time at their disposal—free from burdensome work at home, on a farm, and so on—to engage in study. However, in relation to the most contested term in her thesis, van Schurman wrote simply: 'when I say "a Christian woman", I mean someone who both professes to be a Christian and is actually such in practice' (p. 79).

Since all the Christian sects that were relevant to this dispute accepted the same canonical books of the New Testament as being, in some sense, divine

---

[47] *La Nobilità, et l'eccellenza delle donne, co' diffetti et mancamenti de gli Huomini* (Venice, 1601); *The Nobility and Excellence of Women, and the Defects and Vices of Men*, trans. A. Dunhill (Chicago: University of Chicago Press, 1999).

revelation and as binding on the conscience of believers, it was a commonplace for participants in the debate (as in Gournay's *Equality*) to quote Scripture in support of their own position—even those who were diametrically opposed to women's equality, such as Alexis Trousset. However, because of the fundamental disagreement about interpreting biblical texts that had provoked the Reformation, appeals to the authority of the Scriptures were effective only among those who shared the same understanding of those texts and of the authority, or otherwise, of different churches to provide authoritative interpretations of them. Some of van Schurman's arguments were, therefore, subject to the same limitations as those of Gournay: they were likely to persuade only those who shared her belief in the Bible's divine source and who adopted similar interpretations of its various books.

There was a second and potentially more far-reaching objection from any form of religious fundamentalism that denied the significance of all studies for men or women. This kind of anti-intellectualism found its most famous expression in *The Imitation of Christ* by Thomas à Kempis.[48] That book, which rivalled the Bible in popularity and appeared in hundreds of editions, repeatedly invoked a false disjunction between scholarly learning and simple religious faith, and recommended the latter at the expense of the former.

What will it avail thee to dispute learnedly about the Trinity if thou lack humility and thus displease the Trinity? High-sounding words do not make a man holy and righteous; but a virtuous life endeareth him to God. I had rather feel contrition than understand the definition thereof. If thou didst know the whole Bible by heart and the teachings of all the philosophers, what would all this avail thee without the love of God and without his grace?[49]

The conclusion drawn by à Kempis was that 'a humble rustic that serves God is better than a proud philosopher who, neglecting the good life, contemplates the courses of the stars.'[50]

When van Schurman reflected on her earlier studies towards the end of her life, she referred to the 'excellent little book of Thomas à Kempis.'[51] In retrospect, she adopted his pessimistic view of the insignificance of learning and rejected the central thesis of the *Dissertation*:

---

[48] The first printed edition appeared in 1486. I cite the Latin edition *De imitatio Christi, libri quattuor* (Antwerp: Plantinian, 1627), and *Of the Imitation of Christ*, trans. R. Whytford; rev. W. Raynal (London: Chatto and Windus, 1953).

[49] *Imitatio*, 20; *Imitation*, 33.

[50] *Imitatio*, 22; *Imitation*, 34.

[51] *Eukleria*, 22.

I believed at that time that I ought to learn everything that I could know to flee from ignorance and, indeed, I invoked there the words of the Philosopher: '*in order to escape from ignorance*'…Nonetheless, it is clear from what I wrote how far my thoughts had strayed from the warning of our Saviour, that 'one thing is necessary'…My own conviction now, however, is that the slightest experience of God's love can give us a truer and deeper knowledge of sacred Scripture than the most comprehensive science of that sacred language itself. I also think the same judgement should be made about all the other sciences.[52] (pp. 115, 117)

Van Schurman concluded, as had Labadie, that the kind of studies that she had defended in the *Dissertation* were irrelevant to becoming a good Christian. But this retrospective devaluation of study failed to acknowledge the validity of her earlier reply to Rivet, in March 1638, when he objected to a draft version of the *Dissertation* as follows:

The magnificent works of God, about which the Psalmist writes, may be celebrated by everyone, although only a few people know in detail about the rotation of the heavens, the relative positions of the planets, the influence of the stars, and similar phenomena. Thus it often happens that those who are considered to be most knowledgeable about such things are seen to turn away from God and to attribute everything to nature rather than to God. In contrast, those who rely on simple observation are over-awed and celebrate the wonderful works of God; they are completely satisfied with their author, while the very learned tire their brains vainly in such things and, after lengthy disquisitions, are left to dine on fresh air. (p. 106)

All objections along these lines, whether inspired by Thomas à Kempis or articulated by Rivet, miss the point. If one argues that learning is redundant or harmful to a truly Christian life, then that applies equally to men and women. Rivet was a professor of theology, and he was certainly not arguing that his life's work was meaningless; he was trying to defend the claim that theological studies were appropriate for men but not for women. But that thesis could not be demonstrated simply by contrasting the simple faith of rustics with the potentially misleading learning of scholars. The radical choice recommended by Thomas à Kempis implied no distinction between men and women.[53] Van Schurman's original reasoning in the

---

[52] The citation of 'one thing is necessary', which was borrowed from Lk. 10: 41–2, was also reproduced in Latin as an epigraph on the title page of *Eukleria*: '*Unum necessarium. Maria optimam partem elegit.*'

[53] It is worth mentioning that *The Imitation of Christ* was directed to an exclusively male, clerical readership. It recommended that readers not become familiar with any woman but that they should commend all virtuous women in general to God (Bk. I, Ch. 8, s. 1).

Dissertation was therefore correct; even if one agreed that higher studies are unnecessary or irrelevant for Christians, there was no basis (in Scripture) for adopting a version of that conclusion that applied only to women.

Rivet then appealed to a few sentences in letters written by prominent leaders of the early Church. These included Saint Paul's injunction against women teaching or having authority over men, and Saint Peter's allusion to women as 'the weaker vessel'.[54] Such selective quotations failed to address the question that was notoriously disputed among biblical scholars of the seventeenth century: did the Bible recommend the social distinctions to which it alluded as if they were divinely ordained, or did it merely reflect the customs and social arrangements of the period in which the 'epistles' of the early Church were written? That issue had been discussed extensively earlier in the century, most famously by Kepler and Galileo when they rejected Scripture as a criterion for deciding between competing theories in astronomy.[55] Galileo had argued, in 1615, while taking his cue from Augustine's commentary on the book of Genesis, *De Genesi ad Litteram*: 'the Bible…was not written to teach us astronomy'.[56] It was equally arguable that the Bible's doctrinal content did not extend to the role of women in the family or the church, and that references to such matters in the New Testament merely reflected the social conditions of its authors and original readers.

Following the Galileo controversy, seventeenth-century commentators addressed a number of questions that were relevant to the style of argument adopted by Gournay and van Schurman, which involved distinguishing the theological content of Scripture from the historical, social, and linguistic contingencies in which it was expressed. The most fundamental issue concerned the evidence on the basis of which an individual or a church could reasonably accept some ancient book—the original copies of which were all lost—as divine revelation. Since there was no independent confirmation from God that the Scriptures contained divine teaching, those who accepted the Bible as God's word did so by an act of religious faith. While reflecting on that first step, Locke commented on the circularity

---

[54] I Tim. 2:11–15; I Peter 3:7.

[55] J. Kepler, *New Astronomy*, trans. William H. Donahue (Cambridge: Cambridge University Press, 1992), 60; G. Galilei, 'Letter to the Grand Duchess Christina', 203, 212. For Galileo's discussion of the interpretation of the Scriptures, see E. McMullin, *The Church and Galileo* (Notre Dame, IN: University of Notre Dame Press, 2005), 88–116.

[56] 'Letter to the Grand Duchess Christina', 212.

in the reasoning of so-called 'enthusiasts' who lack any independent criterion to decide what is or is not divinely revealed in the Scriptures: 'It is a Revelation because they firmly believe it, and they believe it, because it is a Revelation.'[57] In other words, people first believe that certain texts are divinely inspired and thereby acquire their authoritative status for religious belief; once that step is taken, believers then accept on faith (a second act of faith, or the same act duplicated) the content of what those writings teach.

Secondly, even if believers accepted in some general sense that the New Testament communicated divine revelation, they still had to make sense of how God could speak to them in a human language, and whether all the connotations and implications of the words used were equally part of revealed doctrine. The most obvious prerequisite for understanding revelation was a capacity to read the original languages in which the Bible was written. Saint Augustine had acknowledged that necessity in his treatise on Christian doctrine, with a mild rebuke to those who relied exclusively on Latin translations: 'Users of the Latin language …need two others, Hebrew and Greek, for an understanding of the divine Scriptures, so that recourse may be had to the original versions if any uncertainty arises from the infinite variety of Latin translators.'[58] The required linguistic competence was often lacking among official church teachers in the seventeenth century, who compensated for their inability to read biblical languages by adopting traditional interpretations.[59] Even if readers could understand the original languages in which the Bible was written, however, there was a further issue of distinguishing the doctrinal content of the texts from the inessential cultural features that were associated with its expression.

Galileo was no biblical scholar, but he had recognized clearly that one ought not to adopt a literal interpretation of many words and sentences that occur in the Bible.

Hence in expounding the Bible if one were always to confine oneself to the unadorned grammatical meaning, one might fall into error. Not only contradictions and propositions far from true might thus be made to appear in the Bible, but even grave heresies and follies. Thus it would be necessary to assign to God feet, hands, and eyes, as well as corporeal and human affections, such as anger, repentance,

[57] *An Essay concerning Human Understanding*, ed. Peter J. Nidditch (Oxford: Clarendon Press, 1975), IV. xix. 10.
[58] *De Doctrina Christiana*, ed. and trans. R. P. Green (Oxford: Clarendon Press, 1995), 73.
[59] Among the first to offer extensive analyses of this issue, based on their knowledge of the relevant languages, were Jean Le Clerc (1657–1736) and Richard Simon (1638–1712).

hatred, and sometimes even the forgetting of things past and ignorance of those to come. These propositions uttered by the Holy Ghost were set down in that manner by the sacred scribes in order to accommodate them to the capacities of the common people, who are rude and unlearned.[60]

Locke developed this Augustinian theme in *The Reasonableness of Christianity*; since the gospel was preached to an uneducated people, the core beliefs of the faith should be understood by reference to the language and cultural context in which they were originally expressed. For Locke, the Scriptures are

... a Collection of Writings designed by God for the Instruction of the illiterate bulk of Mankind in the way of Salvation; and therefore generally and in necessary points to be understood in the plain direct meaning of the words and phrases, such as they may be supposed to have had in the mouths of the Speakers, who used them according to the Language of that Time and Country wherein they lived, without such learned, artificial, and forced senses of them, as are sought out, and put upon them in most of the Systems of Divinity.[61]

Locke went further and argued that what he called the 'Fundamental Articles of the Faith' were contained in the four gospels and the Acts, because when Paul and others sent epistles to various churches, they wrote to people who were already Christians and must therefore have accepted the core beliefs of Christianity.[62] Such letters, therefore, should not be understood as containing any essential features of Christian doctrine. If Locke's argument were accepted, it would imply that most of the biblical texts that were unfavourable to women merely reflected the culture of the society in which they were written.

In summary, those (including Rivet and Labadie) who were convinced by Jansenist or radical Calvinist views about the irrelevance of study for a genuine Christian life had to choose within a range of implausible alternatives. One was to claim that they were able to understand the Scriptures without knowing the languages in which they were written. Since that was impossible, they had to devolve the interpretation of the Scriptures to (a) competent scholars or (b) members of a central teaching authority; in the latter case, Christians were expected to accept passively what they were

[60] 'Letter to the Grand Duchess Christina', 181.
[61] *The Reasonableness of Christianity as delivered in the Scriptures*, ed. J. C. Higgins-Biddle (Oxford: Clarendon Press, 1999), 6.
[62] Locke, *Writings on Religion*, ed. V. Nuovo (Oxford: Clarendon Press, 2002), 215.

taught. The Council of Trent forcefully endorsed option (b), but that was completely alien to Rivet and van Schurman. The only remaining alternative, then, for Protestant churches was to distinguish between those who were sufficiently educated in biblical languages to interpret the Scriptures and those (the majority of Christians) who had to rely on others to determine the content of their religious faith.

For those who accepted the Bible as the exclusive source of Christian doctrine, that suggested the question: was there was any basis in the Scriptures for making such a distinction along gendered lines? There was nothing more than tradition or custom to support the claim that women were ineligible to interpret the scriptures or teach the gospel. Any appeal to custom assumed a version of the circular argument that Locke identified. In this case, one refers simply to what had been believed for many centuries to decide which details of the New Testament were taught by God and, once they are accepted as divinely revealed, those details acquire an epistemic or doctrinal status that makes them unchallengeable. By appeal to custom the limited roles to which women were admitted in early Christian Churches—though these were also a matter of empirical dispute—were converted into a doctrine that was supposedly revealed by God. For others, however, such limitations were merely expressions of the social customs of the time and place in which those Churches emerged from their Jewish origins.

Van Schurman rejected the suggestion that Christians, including women, should blindly or uncritically follow the biblical interpretations of others. One reason was that most Christian churches of the period classified at least some of the doctrinal teachings of other churches as heretical, and preached that those who adopted a heresy (knowingly or otherwise) were destined for eternal damnation. Even van Schurman had changed her allegiance from the strict scholastic Calvinism of Voetius to the mystical quietism of Labadie, and neither of those theological positions classified the choice involved as arbitrary, or absolved its adherents from the moral duty of avoiding heresy. Therefore, unless one were to choose arbitrarily any religion that one encountered and to follow it uncritically, Christians (at least those who were capable of benefiting from study) needed appropriate learning to identify and avoid heresy. Van Schurman supported that rationale for study in the tenth argument in the *Dissertation*:

Whatever protects us against heresies and uncovers their traps is appropriate for a Christian woman. But the sciences ... etc. Therefore,

The justification of the major premise is obvious, since no Christian should neglect their duty in this common danger. The minor premise is proved because a more sound philosophy is like a breastplate and (if I may use the words of Clement of Alexandria) it is like the fence of the Lord's vineyard or of the Saviour's teachings; or—to use a simile that pleased Basil the Great—when combined with the gospel, it resembles leaves that provide an ornament and protection for their own fruit. Spurious or corrupt reason, by which heresies are best supported, is certainly refuted more easily by using right reason. (pp. 86–7)

This is confirmed by her fourteenth argument, to the effect that ignorance is 'a blindness and mental darkness' that is conducive to vice and, therefore, is inappropriate for a Christian woman (p. 88). This reflects Gournay's sharp rebuke to those who believed that 'in order to be chaste, a woman should not be educated'. If women were not to be misguided by heretical preachers or to confuse vice and virtue, they should not be excluded from informing themselves as best they could, by study, of the most plausible guides to good living.[63]

Those who opposed women's access to education argued incoherently that all Christians were morally bound to avoid heresy, but that most Christians should be denied the only means by which they could distinguish between heresy and authentic religious doctrine. They then relied on custom to assign women exclusively to the latter category. They might have avoided incoherence temporarily by invoking divine predestination, so that the theological ignorance in which many people would compromise their eternal salvation would also result from God's intentions. The theory of predestination, however, was designed to protect the absolute freedom by which God grants grace to those who are saved, and it presupposed that mere human beings could never know God's mind. To convert that theory of grace into a rationalization for women's ignorance would imply an incoherent and gendered version of predestination, defended by male theologians who claimed officially that the mind of God was inaccessible.

In relation to the second issue addressed by van Schurman—the natural capacity of women to undertake studies—the *Dissertation* argued that 'women are endowed by nature with the principles of all arts and sciences or with a capacity to acquire them' (p. 82) and replied to various objections. If such arguments and objections were to avoid an infinite regress,

---

[63] Compare Mary Wollstonecraft, *A Vindication of the Rights of Woman*, ed. J. Todd (Oxford World's Classics, 1994/2008), 84: 'it should seem, allowing them [women] to have souls, that there is but one way appointed by Providence to lead *mankind* to either virtue or happiness.'

they had to begin with propositions that were beyond dispute or, if they aimed merely to refute opponents, with premises that were accepted by such opponents. Van Schurman adopted both alternatives and, in doing so, addressed the claim that women's nature is inferior to that of men.

The fundamental argument was that women have the same natural capacities that men exercise in study. This was implied by the commonplace assumption that had been exploited previously by Gournay: namely, women have the same form as men, where 'form' was understood as scholastic philosophers (including Calvinist theologians at Utrecht or Leiden) used it.[64] The conclusion about women's innate abilities was inferred from empirical evidence and the scholastic axiom that 'acts cannot occur without the corresponding principles' (p. 82). Since at least some women had succeeded in studying as successfully as some men, their *nature* must be such that it is capable of those achievements.

Despite the exceptional learning of van Schurman, however, it was evident to all who engaged in this controversy that there were very few learned women in the seventeenth century. Many women could not read or write even in their vernacular,[65] and this uncontested evidence was exploited by opponents of women's equality to argue that, in general, women lacked the natural ability to engage in study. This clearly begged the question about the provision of education to girls or women. To test the comparative natural abilities of men and women, it would be necessary to provide them both with similar educational opportunities and then determine if they were equally successful. Van Schurman had emphasized at the beginning of the *Dissertation* that she was not claiming that all women were suited to higher studies, no more than all men. Her thesis, rather, was that there was no evidence to support a gender-based distinction between the capacities of women and men to engage in higher studies, and that the disputed issue

---

[64] The commitment of Calvinist theologians to scholastic philosophy is evident in the seventeenth-century debates, in The Netherlands, between supporters and opponents of Cartesianism. See for example Theo Verbeek, *Descartes and the Dutch* (Carbondale and Edwardsville, IL: Southern Illinois University Press, 1992); G. Voetius, *Disputationes theologicae selectae*, 5 vols. (Utrecht: J. à Waesberge, 1648–69); J. W. Beardslee, ed. *Reformed Dogmatics* (New York: Oxford University Press, 1965). The widespread reliance on Aristotelianism extended to other Christian churches; see for example Philip Melanchthon, *Orations on Philosophy and Education*, ed. S. Kusukawa (Cambridge: Cambridge University Press, 1999).

[65] Illiteracy was not confined to women. One hundred years after van Schurman's *Dissertation*, 86% of brides and 71% of grooms in France could not even sign their wedding contracts. See P. Ariès, *Histoire de la vie privée* Vol. 3: *De la Renaissance aux Lumières* (Paris: Éditions du Seuil, 1986), 76.

of women's native ability could be decided only if they enjoyed the same educational opportunities as men.

Rivet's proposal grudgingly acknowledged the logic of this argument, but he then claimed that van Schurman's thesis, while it was true, was inapplicable until suitable academies for women's education were founded.

You yourself would readily admit that they [young women] could not all be self-taught, or that they would all have parents who would arrange for them in their homes the kind of education that you happened to enjoy. Nor would it be appropriate for them to attend schools for males, integrated with the boys. (p. 105)

The same counter-argument could have been made with equal validity about men, by substituting the word 'men' for 'women', so that not all men could be self-taught, and so on.

At this point, Rivet changed direction to focus on the objectives or ends of study and assumed that their only objective was to prepare students for the specific offices or employments in which many were subsequently employed. For example, someone who studied geometry might become an artillery officer, or those who studied law might work as tax officials to implement royal decrees effectively in a population that was reluctantly tax-compliant. The traditional exclusion of women from all such offices, including priestly offices in Christian churches, thus gave Rivet the opportunity to argue as follows:

Now since it is undisputed that the female sex is not suited for political or ecclesiastical offices, and especially for teaching publicly, why would young women labour to acquire learning that is designed for those objectives from which they are excluded, unless perhaps you make an exception for a few who, in some nations, are allowed to succeed to the throne when male heirs are unavailable? 'But I suffer not a woman to teach' (says the Apostle), 'nor to usurp authority over the man, but to be in silence.'[66] If women are bound by this, then it is particularly appropriate that young women not be involved in it. It follows that they do not need the specific learning that is concerned with speaking well, if you consider how that learning is used ... (pp. 103–4)

This was another transparent case of begging the question. Rivet assumed (i) that the custom of excluding women from civil offices did not require any justification and that there were biblical grounds for excluding them from ecclesiastical offices; (ii) that all studies are justified only by some

---

[66] I Tim. 2: 11–15.

utilitarian objective. Van Schurman had to consider how best to deny both assumptions as diplomatically as possible.

She conceded that men might continue to assume exclusive responsibility for preaching within the reformed churches. However, such a division of duties within Calvinism—which had significantly reduced the number of sacraments that were previously recognized within Christianity from seven to two, and consequently reduced the status and role of the priesthood[67]—failed to address two fundamental issues. One was that the exclusion of women from study breached the laws of equity:

> But those of us who seek the voice of reason rather than of received custom do not accept this Lesbian rule. By what law, I ask, did this fall to our lot: by divine law or human law? They will never prove that these restrictions, by which we are certainly forced into line, are determined by fate or prescribed *by God*. (p. 97)

Van Schurman was willing to respect the customs of the society and church to which she belonged, but she refused to accept them as if they were God's law. The epistles of the early church, already discussed above, merely reflected the customs or social expectations of the period in which they were written. There was therefore no divine authority for excluding women from those studies that, as a matter of custom, prepared young men for offices in the church or the state.

Accordingly, at the beginning of the *Dissertation*, she listed the studies that are appropriate for young women: grammar, logic, rhetoric, physics, metaphysics, history, and knowledge of languages—especially the languages in which the Bible was written. Her only reservation applied to studies that were exclusively directed to public offices from which women were excluded; however, even while accepting that limitation, she defended the appropriateness for women of a 'theoretical' knowledge of those disciplines:

---

[67] Calvin's *Institutes* increased very significantly in size from one edition to another. I quote the 1541 French edition, translated by E. A. McKee as *Institutes of the Christian Religion* (Grand Rapids, MI: William B. Eedermans, 2009). Calvin rejected the traditional teaching that celebrants of the Eucharist are priests (p. 578), and reduced the sacraments to Baptism and the Eucharist. He also distinguished between human laws designed 'to preserve public decency' and those required for salvation, and understood the limitations on women's role in the early church as a mere local accommodation to custom. 'We have [biblical] examples of the first kind of law in St Paul when he forbids women to teach publicly or to show themselves with uncovered heads (I Cor. 14:34...I Timothy 2:12). What, is there such a great mystery about a woman's hair style that it would be a great fault to go out in the street with a bare head? Is silence so much commanded that she cannot speak without great offence?' (pp. 653–54).

I do not recommend as strongly those studies that pertain to the practice of law, to military affairs, or to the art of public speaking in a temple, court, or academy, because they are less appropriate or necessary. However, we do not concede at all that a woman should be excluded from a scholastic or, as it is called, a theoretical knowledge of those things, especially the very noble discipline of politics. (p. 81)

The thesis of the *Dissertation*, therefore, was not that some kind of limited curriculum of studies should be established for young women, but that all studies were equally appropriate for men and women, even if some were less highly recommended as long as the custom prevailed of excluding women from most public offices.

Having challenged Rivet's assumption that the exclusion of women from study required no justification, van Schurman rejected his second assumption that study was merely a training for specific offices or employments by quoting an Aristotelian principle that appeared famously in the opening line of the *Metaphysics*: 'All men [human beings] by nature desire to know.'[68]

There are others who seem not to acknowledge that study has any objective other than riches or empty fame, or as training for employment in some public office, which is a *fundamental* and rather shameful *falsehood*, as if it were a complete waste of time to philosophize '*in order to escape from ignorance*'. (pp. 89–90)[69]

In contrast, many of the arguments deployed in the *Dissertation* assumed that study was one way for human beings to fulfil their natural potential and to realize objectives that were intrinsic to the activity of study itself. According to Aristotle, there are moral and intellectual virtues, both of which are acquired only by appropriate training. Study was the recognized practice or training necessary to acquire intellectual virtues. 'Virtue, then, is of two kinds: that of the intellect and that of character. Intellectual virtue owes its origin and development mainly to teaching, for which reason its attainment requires experience and time.'[70] Thus study perfects the mind (argument viii) and fills it with a natural pleasure that is worthy of human beings (argument xiii). Study also makes it possible for women to achieve other extrinsic objectives apart from offices or employments;

---

[68] AR II, 1552 (980ª22).

[69] The phrase quoted from Aristotle is from *Metaphysics*, Book I, Ch. 2: 'therefore since they [the earliest philosophers] philosophized in order to escape ignorance, evidently they were pursuing science in order to know, and not for any utilitarian end' (AR II, 982ᵇ20).

[70] NE, 1103ª5.

for example, it provides a way of knowing God through his creation (argument ix), and of avoiding idleness and its alleged temptations to vice (argument iv).

The circularity of Rivet's objections to women's study, which was exposed by van Schurman's analysis, was aptly summarized a century later in the anonymous tract attributed to 'Sophia': 'Why is *learning* useless to us? Because we have no share in public offices. And why have we no share in public offices? Because we have no *learning*.'[71]

Van Schurman's defence of the educational rights of women was developed in the form of a scholastic disputation, in which participants were expected to defend their theses by using syllogisms and by appealing to recognized authorities. The *Dissertation* was simply arguing in accordance with the standards of the time and appealing to principles that were accepted by critics within the Reformed Church. Van Schurman applied to women the views about study that were widely attributed to the most famous Greek philosophers, on whom the theologians of all the Christian churches relied to justify their prolix and misogynistic objections to women's study: that the acquisition of knowledge is a cultivation of one of the most characteristic features of human nature, and that it is impossible to live a good life or a Christian life without having the knowledge required to identify either one.[72] While her arguments could not have convinced those who did not share those assumptions, they were an effective response to those within the Reformed Church who relied merely on tradition to exclude women from education and the civil and ecclesiastical offices for which education was a necessary training.

To address a wider audience of opponents, however, it would have been necessary to step outside those shared theological assumptions, and to question the authority of the Bible and ancient authors to decide the factual and moral issues associated with women's equality. That challenge was assumed by Poulain de la Barre.

---

[71] *Woman Not Inferior to Man* (p. 12 above), 27.

[72] She wrote to Princess Elizabeth of Bohemia: 'It is true that I have great respect for the scholastic doctors' (p. 109). Most of the Calvinist theologians against whom she was likely to defend women's education, in 1641, were equally sympathetic to scholastic philosophy.

Poulain de la Barre: Equality and Reason

In the 'Afterward' to *A Physical and Moral Discourse concerning the Equality of Both Sexes* (henceforth, the *Discourse*), Poulain identified two authorities to which opponents of women's equality appealed: the writings of famous male authors, and the Bible. He challenged them as follows:

> As regards the first of these, I think they may be answered satisfactorily by saying that I recognize no authority here apart from the authority of reason and sound judgement. As regards Scripture, it is not in any way contrary to the aim of this work, on condition that one understands each of them correctly...Scripture does not say a single word about inequality; and since its only function is to provide a rule of conduct for people in accordance with the ideas of justice that it advocates, it allows everyone the freedom to judge as they wish about the natural and true state of things. (p. 200)

Whereas Gournay and van Schurman had accepted the authority of the Bible but rejected interpretations of particular texts that discriminated against women, Poulain repudiates Scripture completely as irrelevant for deciding whether men and women are equal. He consciously appeals to the precedent of Galileo by citing geocentrism as a naïve prejudice: 'Apart from a few scholars, everyone thinks that it is indubitable that the Sun moves around the Earth, despite the fact that what we observe in the revolution of the days and the years leads those who examine it to believe that it is the Earth that moves around the Sun' (p. 122). Although he was still a member of the Catholic Church when he wrote the *Discourse*, Poulain supported Galileo's general principle about what the Scriptures do not teach; he then ventured into the theological minefield of clarifying their genuine doctrinal content.

The *Discourse* suggests that it is no more difficult to interpret the New Testament than to read 'the Greek and Latin authors' (p. 166), and it is therefore open to anyone who can read those languages to contribute to this hermeneutic task. By the time Poulain published *The Doctrine of Protestants* (1720), long after his defection from Rome, he had identified three ways of interpreting biblical texts: by deferring to tradition, by adopting the authoritative teaching of some church, or by using reason. He argued in favour of the third option:

> Sound reason, good philosophy, and criticism are the genuine and natural interpreters of Holy Scripture ... right reason also tells us: (1) to read the Holy Scriptures at least in the same spirit and with the same attitude, and according to the same rules,

by which one reads and ought to read all good books; (2) to examine and weigh up everything as if no one else had read or understood it before us.[73]

This theory of interpretation coincided with a view expressed by many liberal Calvinist theologians of the period. For example, the Saumur theologian, Moise Amyraut, addressed this question from a perspective that was subsequently adopted by Locke and even more radically by Toland: that is, by first asking about the potentially competing contributions of reason and faith in determining the content of one's religious beliefs.[74] Amyraut argued that it is not possible to believe propositions that are inconsistent with reason, and he identified the Catholic doctrine of transubstantiation as a prime example of the latter (as Poulain later did).[75] He also examined the scope of the senses and intellect as cognitive faculties by which we can know some things with relative certainty. While acknowledging that there are some 'mysteries', such as the Trinity, that are proper objects of religious faith, the Saumur theologian concluded that there are many knowledge-claims that are within the scope of our senses and reason and, in those cases, religious faith cannot override the clear evidence for what is naturally known. Thus reason and sensory observation set *a priori* limits for what should be believed as an object of religious faith, as Poulain assumed in his *Conversations concerning the Education of Ladies*.[76]

The equality or otherwise of the sexes was a question that, according to Poulain, fell within the scope of human reason and empirical investigation, and it was both irrelevant and inappropriate to invoke Scripture to decide it. 'For whatever falls within the scope of reason should be known by reason' (p. 204). In contrast with Gournay's reservations about the capacity of reason to 'prove' the equality thesis, he was confident that reason was competent to address questions about sexual equality. However, one of the central issues in dispute was not about something that could be observed in any ordinary

[73] *La doctrine des Protestans* (Geneva: Fabri & Barrillot, 1720), 267, 274–5.

[74] John Toland's views are most famously expressed in *Christianity Not Mysterious* (London, 1696).

[75] *De l'élévation de la foy et de l'abaissement de la raison en la créance des mystères de la Religion* (Saumur: Jean Lesnier, 1641). Amyraut's views about faith and reason are summarized in D. M. Clarke, 'Faith and Reason in the Thought of Moise Amyraut,' in A. P. Coudert, *et al.* eds. *Judaeo-Christian Intellectual Culture in the Seventeenth Century* (Dordrecht: Kluwer, 1999), 145–59.

[76] 'For how could one persuade an idolater or a Mohammedan of the falsity of their religion and the truth of our own without reasoning with them to show them that one is contrary to reason and the other is consistent with it.' *De l'éducation des dames*, PO, 214.

sense of that term, because it concerned the capacities (or an alleged lack of capacity) of women. Whether they realized it or not, therefore, all contributors to the discussion were involved in identifying relevant evidence about women's abilities and then making inferences from that evidence to their disparate conclusions. In doing so, many contributors argued fallaciously.

Scholastics often appealed to the Latin axiom, *ab esse ad posse valet illatio*: from the fact that something is the case, it is valid to conclude that it is possible. It seems, in retrospect, that many opponents of women's education and equality relied on a logically invalid counterpart of that scholastic axiom: *ab non-esse ad non-posse valet illatio*, or one may validly conclude what is not possible from what is not the case. Since this logical mistake does not currently have a special name, it may be called the 'incapacity fallacy'. It was evidently true that in the seventeenth century most women were not educated and were unable to engage in philosophical and theological discussions (as were most men). This fact about women led many opponents of equality to conclude that women's 'nature' explained this situation. That conclusion, however, involved an invalid inference with the same logical structure as the incapacity fallacy. It is illogical to argue from the fact that some people do not do something to the conclusion that they are incapable of doing so. In addition to being fallacious, such an inference was also subject to a number of specifically Cartesian objections, which were borrowed by Poulain from (a) Descartes' distrust of what are apparently 'facts', (b) his rejection of scholastic-style explanations, and (c) his novel account of how realities may be known, with a qualified certainty, by constructing hypotheses about how they appear to us in observations.

Descartes had often emphasized a distinction between the spontaneous judgements we tend to make on the basis of observation—which he called prejudices—and the reflective judgements we ought to make about matters that fall within the scope of our cognitive faculties. Poulain adopted the same distinction; he defined prejudices as 'judgements that are made about things without examining them' (p. 119).[77] He also added a rather prescient anticipation of what later became a familiar theme in Marx: that the interests of those who hold certain beliefs may provide a stronger motivation for their convictions than the evidence that supports them objectively.

I realize that this discourse will make many people unhappy, and that those whose interests... are opposed to what is defended here will not miss an opportunity to

---

[77] Compare Wollstonecraft, *A Vindication of the Rights of Woman*, 189: 'A prejudice is a fond obstinate persuasion for which we can give no reason.'

criticize it...If one examines the foundations of all these various beliefs [about women], one finds that they are based only on self-interest or custom...Thus one should be suspicious of everything that men have said about women because they are both judges and litigants.[78] (pp. 121, 123, 151)

Critics might have replied that men's interests just happen to coincide with a 'fact' that is independently confirmed by the evidence, and that it was premature to offer an ideological explanation of a belief before it is shown to be false. To avoid that objection, Poulain had to provide evidence on the basis of which his equality thesis could be confirmed. He did so by using a distinction between appearance and reality that was borrowed from Descartes and contemporary Cartesians in Paris, such as Jacques Rohault.[79]

One of the fundamental principles of Descartes' natural philosophy is that the real world may not, in fact, be as it appears to us in sensory perceptions. This reservation was not inspired by scepticism, but by the opposite—by his great (some might say unjustified) confidence in our ability to speculate, beyond appearances, about the underlying or unobservable structures of natural phenomena. Descartes introduced this distinction in the first sentence of The World (which was published posthumously in Paris in 1664): 'the first thing that I want to bring to your attention is that there may be a difference between our sensation of light... and whatever it is in the objects that produces that sensation in us.'[80] He repeated the same reservation in the Principles of Philosophy, when he advised against making hasty, mistaken judgements based on our external or internal sensations (such as pain): 'all of us have judged from our childhood that all the things that we sense are things existing outside our minds, and are exactly similar to our sensations, that is, to the perceptions that we have of them.'[81]

[78] Cf. 'women depend on men only because of the laws that men have made for their own particular advantage' De l'excellence des hommes, PO, 314.

[79] Poulain's spokesman in The Education of Ladies spoke about his attendance at a Cartesian conference: 'I allowed one of my friends to bring me to a discussion in which a Cartesian talked to us about some issue that concerned the human body'; De l'éducation des dames, PO, 281. Jacques Rohault (1618–72) had begun to hold conferences on Cartesianism in Paris as early as 1659; his main work appeared as Traité de physique (Paris, 1671); Engl. trans. A System of Natural Philosophy, trans. J. and S. Clarke, 2 vols. (London, 1723). The distinction between apparent and real qualities is expounded at length in vol. II, 151–83.

[80] AT XI, 3: Discourse on Method and Related Writings, trans. D. M. Clarke (London: Penguin, 2003), 85.

[81] AT VIII-1, 32: Meditations and Other Metaphysical Writings, trans. D. M. Clarke (London: Penguin, 2003), 138.

If sensory experiences are not accurate reflections of the real world, what other options are available?

Descartes argued that we acquire a more trustworthy understanding of the actual world by constructing hypothetical explanations of the ways in which it appears in our sensations than by projecting onto natural phenomena the qualitative experiences that those phenomena evoke in our minds. For example, we cannot understand the nature of light simply by examining our sensations of light, nor can we determine whether the Sun or the Earth moves by merely observing how they appear to us. In general, we have no 'argument that guarantees' that 'the ideas we have in our thought are completely similar to the objects from which they originate.'[82] Poulain repeats almost verbatim the same caution: 'It would be a mistake to accept the way things occur in people's minds as the way they occur in nature, because the former does not always give us an idea of the latter.'[83] The only way to know or understand the objective realities from which our perceptions originate is, in Poulain's words, by hypothesizing 'what particular internal or external disposition of each object produces the thoughts or sensations that we have of it' (p. 155).

Poulain then applies this general principle about appearance and reality to the *perception* of a reality that is both natural and social: that is, the condition of men and women in society. He adopts almost casually an attitude of counterfactual confidence that allows him to claim that, contrary to the almost universal belief of people and the apparent differences between the sexes, men and women in general have the same natural abilities. This conclusion is based on an 'historical conjecture' that explains how women came to occupy the inferior roles in society to which they had become accustomed, which is introduced by the phrase: 'it happened more or less as follows' (p. 127).

This hypothesis involved a speculative reconstruction of how, at the beginning of history, men were superior to women in physical strength; how societies were formed; how they went to war and relied on the strength of male warriors; how the role of women was limited to child-rearing and how, over centuries, the prejudice about women's inequality corresponded to what people actually observed in almost every society. Since the inferior condition of women is readily explained by such an historical hypothesis,

---

[82] AT XI, 3: *Discourse on Method and Related Writings*, 85.
[83] *De l'éducation des dames*, PO, 216.

there is no more reason to claim that women are naturally inferior to men than to assume that sensations of light resemble the reality of which they are sensations. Here as elsewhere we acquire reliable knowledge of a complex social reality, not simply by consulting our sensations (though we must begin there), but by speculating about the underlying and, for the most part, unobservable structures that cause our perceptions of it.

If we cannot avoid speculating about such unobservable structures, we need to distinguish between speculations that *explain* natural phenomena and those that do not do so.[84] There was a well-known Cartesian objection to a style of metaphysical explanation that was popular among scholastics. Cartesian natural philosophers argued that one makes no progress in explaining any phenomenon simply by postulating a 'form' or 'nature' that corresponds to each reality that needs to be explained. Thus, in relation to women's status in society, one explains nothing by inferring a so-called 'nature of women' from the manner in which women lived and behaved in the seventeenth century (or previously). What people observed in that period was the end result of generations of custom, social influence, and a lack of education. Any inference to an underlying nature, therefore, would require distinguishing between (a) the effects of custom and education and (b) some underlying reality that may be significantly different from how it appears. We cannot 'make a judgement about corrupted nature unless we know perfectly what nature is in ourselves or, to express it more clearly, what nature has given us and what we have acquired from education, example, and custom.'[85] According to Poulain, it was necessary to distinguish between women's nature, as it must have been when first created, and the condition in which women's nature appeared after centuries of adverse custom.

In addition to these general reservations about the non-explanatory character of scholastic forms or natures, Cartesians had another reason not to rely on the theory of the soul as a distinct substance that was officially taught by the Fifth Lateran Council.[86] Descartes argued consistently that

---

[84] Poulain hints at how to construct genuine explanations of natural phenomena in his discussion of liquidity, which was consistent with the type of explanation proposed by contemporary Cartesian natural philosophers (p. 155).

[85] *De l'éducation*, PO, 258: see also 266.

[86] In his letter dedicating the *Meditations* to the Sorbonne, Descartes acknowledged the Lateran Council's invitation to Christian philosophers to develop arguments in support of its teaching about the soul (AT VII, 3). However, the Sorbonne failed to provide the endorsement that he requested for his book and, in the second edition, he resiled from his original plan and changed the title of the *Meditations* so that it aimed to demonstrate merely the 'distinction' of the soul from the body rather than its 'immortality'.

we have no direct knowledge of substances, and that our knowledge of them is limited to knowledge of their properties.[87] Thus, we cannot begin with knowledge of a substance and then draw conclusions about its properties, because the inference must go in the opposite direction. Accordingly, if we notice certain features of women's condition that require an explanation, we make no progress by talking about a corresponding woman's 'nature' (understood as a substance), about which nothing is known apart from the very features that it is meant to explain.[88]

One of the corollaries of Poulain's historical hypothesis was that women's bodies are not relevantly different from those of men with respect to most of the social functions from which they are excluded. He claims that, with the obvious exception of bodily functions that are specific to generation, 'men and women are similar in almost everything that pertains to the external and internal constitution of the human body' (p. 184). He also assumes that one's head is the most important bodily organ for learning, and that women's brains work in the same way as those of men (pp. 158, 180). Evidently, there are differences between some men and some women in bodily strength but, for the same reasons as those offered by Gournay and Van Schurman, Poulain rejects physical strength as a criterion for deciding if men are superior to women.[89] All such superficial differences between the sexes are secondary if used to justify excluding women from offices or social functions that were traditionally reserved for men.

Despite Cartesian objections to natures or forms, it is also true that, like many other feminists of the period, Poulain claimed that 'the mind has no sex'. Therefore, if there were any natural inequalities between men and women, they could not result from the sexuality of the minds with which women were endowed. However, Poulain was not assuming a radical dualism of mind and body, or that the functioning of human minds is

---

[87] AT VII, 176; VII 222; VII, 360; VIII-1, 25. In contrast, Gournay's argument (p. 66) assumed knowledge of the spirituality of the human soul from revelation.

[88] Cf. John Stuart Mill, *Three Essays on Religion* (1874), in M. M. Robson, ed. *Collected Works of John Stuart Mill*, vol. x (Toronto and London: University of Toronto Press, 1969), 373: 'Nature, natural, and the group of words derived from them ...[provide] one of the most copious sources of false taste, false philosophy, false morality, and even bad law.'

[89] While admitting, in general, a difference in physical strength, Poulain points to the same implications as Gournay had done: 'sheer physical strength should not be used to distinguish between human beings; otherwise brute animals would be superior to humans and, among men, those who are more robust would be superior' (p. 185). See also *De l'excellence des hommes*, PO, 319: 'Experience shows us ...that those who are stronger do not always possess more intelligence, natural genius, or skill.'

unaffected by the body. That kind of metaphysical dualism was less prominent in Descartes' later work, and was mitigated by the mind–body interaction defended by the Cartesians whom Poulain was likely to have heard in
Paris, such as Jacques Rohault, Gerauld de Cordemoy, or Louis de La Forge.
The union of the body and soul and their reciprocal interdependence was
a more fundamental datum of human experience than the speculative distinction of the soul as a scholastic substance. Besides, if the soul were as
separable from the body as scholastics had assumed, it would undermine
one of the primary supports of Poulain's whole thesis: namely, the extent
to which custom and habit, and the 'passion' of self-interest, facilitate the
false beliefs that we hold about sexual equality. If gender[90] is understood as
a cultural construct, as the sum total of the ways in which men and women
are thought of and treated in a given culture, then the primary issue to be
addressed when discussing the equality of men and women is neither their
souls (understood as separate, immaterial substances) nor their sexual differences, but the entrenched misogynistic traditions that supported spurious philosophical explanations of inequalities that resulted merely from
custom rather than from nature.

While developing this theme about the moral or political conclusions
that may be drawn validly from the universality of women's subjection,
Poulain comes close to stating the principle with which David Hume is
widely credited: namely, that it is invalid to draw a moral conclusion from
exclusively factual premises. Poulain commented that 'if some practice is
well established, then we think that it must be right' (p. 125). When the
anonymous tract by 'Sophia' was published in 1739, its author made explicit
the inferential gap between statements of fact and moral conclusions:

It is enough for the *Men* to find a thing establish'd to make them believe it well
grounded. In all countries we are seen in subjection and absolute dependence on
the *Men*, without being admitted to the advantages of sciences, or the opportunity
of exerting our capacity in a public station. Hence the *Men*, according to their usual
talent of arguing from seemings, conclude that we ought to be so. But supposing it
to be true, that *Women* had ever been excluded from *public offices*, is it therefore necessarily true that they ought to be so? God has always been more or less resisted by

---

[90] The term 'gender' was not used in this sense in the seventeenth century. However, one of
the most important of Poulain's claims was that the social understanding of men and women
was the primary factor in explaining their differential treatment; he therefore had our distinction between sex and gender before the corresponding linguistic conventions developed.

ungrateful man, a fine conclusion it wou'd be then to infer, that therefore he ought to be so. [91]

'Sophia', inspired by Poulain, anticipated the more well known caution about such inferences that David Hume published, the following year, in *A Treatise of Human Nature*.[92]

In summary, Poulain challenged the perception of women's condition in society as if it revealed natural rather than social 'facts' about them. He rejected as invalid and as a spontaneous mistaken judgement the inference that women are incapable of being other than they appear to be. Furthermore, he described as non-explanatory the suggestion that one could understand women's condition in terms of their 'nature': 'Lawyers... attributed to nature a distinction that results only from custom... They would be hard pressed if they were required to explain intelligibly what they mean by "nature" in this context' (p. 152). Finally, he was reluctant to base the equality thesis on a radical substance dualism that presupposes sexless equal souls that are infused mysteriously into each body by God. That merely shifts the locus of inferiority from a woman's soul to her body and, for example, to the assumption that women's brains inhibit the operation of souls that would otherwise be as rational and competent as those of men. Malebranche adopted that conclusion, despite being a committed Cartesian dualist.

The delicacy of the brain fibers is one of the principal causes impeding our efforts to apply ourselves to discovering truths that are slightly hidden...This delicacy of the brain fibers is usually found in women...normally they [women] are incapable of penetrating to truths that are slightly difficult to discover. Everything abstract is incomprehensible to them...They consider only the surface of things... a trifle is enough to distract them, the slightest cry frightens them, the least motion fascinates them. [93]

---

[91] *Woman Not Inferior to Man: or, A short and modest Vindication of the Natural Rights of the FAIR-SEX to a perfect Equality of Power, Dignity, and Esteem, with the Men. By Sophia, a Person of Quality* (London: John Hawkins, 1739), 35. The 1751 edition substitutes 'usual paralogism' for 'usual talent of arguing from seemings'.

[92] *A Treatise of Human Nature*, ed. David Fate Norton and Mary J. Norton, 2 vols. (Oxford: Clarendon Press, 2007), I, 302.

[93] *The Search after Truth*, Bk. II, Part II, ch.1 (ST, 130). Malebranche acknowledges that there are exceptions to the general rule: 'if it is certain that this delicacy of the brain fibers is the principal cause of all these effects, it is not at all certain that it is found in all women...In short, when we attribute certain defects to a sex, to certain ages, to certain stations, we mean only that it is ordinarily true, always assuming there is no general rule without exceptions' (ST, 130).

Having rejected scholastic theories of mind and styles of explanation, Poulain offered instead an historical hypothesis about how women's inferior social condition developed over time. That hypothesis was simple to test, at least in principle: it required a large-scale social experiment over a long period of time, in which women would be given access to all the same educational opportunities as men. A credible decision about women's natural ability could be made only when that experiment was completed.

Poulain's more famous contemporary, Molière, had written a number of comedies, in the 1660s and 1670s, in which he mocked the aspirations of contemporary women to enjoy the same education as men. The most explicit of these plays was Les femmes savantes, which was first produced in Paris in May 1672—as Poulain was writing his book on equality—and in which Molière mocks Philaminte's suggestion that women could make scientific discoveries. He even attributes to her the apparently absurd claim that she had seen men on the Moon.[94] Molière caricatured such women as rejecting marriage and traditional female roles, and as aspiring instead to join the academies from which they were excluded.[95] Molière's farcical stage representations of the educational ambitions of 'polite' ladies merely exploited a growing awareness that women's access to education was central to discussions of equality.

Poulain shared with Descartes and with Montaigne (half a century earlier) a generally negative assessment of the formal education that was then provided in exclusively male schools and colleges, in which students were trained to memorize and repeat in Latin the contents of a scholastic curriculum. Descartes concluded that, on balance, women were lucky not to have had their minds contaminated by scholastic learning; they could therefore approach questions with an open mind and could understand novel discoveries more easily than men. Poulain endorsed the same assessment:

... one would consider women lucky rather than despise them because they are not involved in the sciences. For if, on the one hand, they are thereby deprived of the opportunity to develop their talents and their characteristic advantages, on the other hand they have no opportunity to ruin or lose them. Despite this privation, they develop intellectually, in virtue and in grace, as they get older. (p. 134)

---

[94] Les femmes savantes, ed. Hubert Carrier (Paris: Hachette, 1992), Act III, Sc. 2, ll. 889-90.
[95] Another character in the same play says: 'Il n'est pas bien honnête, et pour des causes, / Qu'une femme étudie et sache tant de choses' (Act. II, Sc. 7, ll. 571-2).

Poulain reports, through his spokesman in the *Conversations*, that his own studies had equipped him merely to speak in Latin about matters that he did not
genuinely understand: 'having studied from the age of nine to the age of twenty
with much dedication and success as a student, I had hardly made any more
progress than if I had never begun, and I had to begin all over again.'[96] That
suggested that the education of men needed fundamental reform and, once
reformed, that the revised curriculum should be made available to women.

It is not surprising that, on this issue, Poulain borrowed and adapted
various proposals about education that were current in Cartesian circles.
He endorsed Descartes' suggestion that there is only one science and one
method, which is applied to different subjects (p. 168). Secondly, the logic
of his proposed social experiment was (as van Schurman had argued) that
women must be admitted to exactly the same educational opportunities as
men, and that there is no subject from which they should be barred. There
is no distinct type of women's education or women's subjects, as recommended by Jean Luis Vives in the sixteenth century or by Poulain's contemporary, François Fénelon.[97] Poulain recommended exactly the same studies
and the same authors for men and women. These included the *Port-Royal
Logic*, Descartes' *Discourse on Method, Meditations,* and his *Treatise on Man*;
Cordemoy's *Discourse on the Distinction and Union of the Soul and the Body*; La
Forge's *Treatise on the Human Mind*, and Rohault's *Treatise on Physics*.[98]

Evidently, education is not confined to reading books, and women
should use their good judgement or common sense to evaluate and judge
all matters for themselves. 'Examine everything, make judgements about
everything, reason about everything.'[99] Poulain even offers the same advice
that Descartes had implemented consistently in his own life, namely, not to
read many books. Accordingly, if women wished to choose one philosopher
among those who were accessible in French, 'I cannot think of one that is
more appropriate for you than Descartes.'[100] However, Poulain reminded

[96] *De l'éducation des dames*, PO, 281.

[97] Juan Luis Vives, *De institutione feminae Christianae* (Basel, 1524/1538); *The Education
of a Christian Woman*, trans. Charles Fantazzi (Chicago: University of Chicago Press,
2000); *Fénelon on Education*, trans. H. C. Barnard (Cambridge: Cambridge University
Press, 1966).

[98] *De l'éducation*, PO, 272. Gerauld de Cordemoy, *Le discernement du corps et de l'âme, en six
discours* (Paris, 1670); A. Armauld and P. Nicole, *La Logique ou l'art de penser* (Paris, 1662); for
further titles, see note 26.

[99] *De l'éducation*, 273.

[100] *De l'éducation*, 277.

his readers (p. 10 above) that Descartes was no more infallible than other authors and that they should all be read critically, although some were not strongly recommended. 'Books on rhetoric …are not much use [for learning how to think and speak well].'[101] This reflects the negative assessment found in *Equality*, where rhetoric is described as a kind of 'verbal optics' (p. 148) that can be used to deceive listeners, like the tricks of a magician.

For exactly the same reasons as those mentioned by van Schurman, Poulain does not claim that all women are equally capable of benefiting from education, no more than all men.

I do not claim that they [women] are all suited to the sciences and to public office, or that each woman is capable of doing everything. No one claims that about men either. I ask only that, considering the two sexes in general, we recognize that there is as much aptitude in one as in the other. (p. 132)

The proposal, then, was to admit women on an equal basis with men to all kinds of study and, once educated, to allow them to compete for admission to all offices and professions.

The admission of women to most professions, including that of a professor or judge, was a revolutionary thesis in the seventeenth century, although it is taken for granted in many societies today. However, Poulain also included on his list of professions that of a pastor or minister in a church, which continues to be a bridge too far for many religious traditions. This, then, is possibly the most relevant and realistic example today of Poulain's fundamental claim—that the exclusion of women, which is based only on custom, becomes transformed into something else that is unchangeable, such as 'nature' or 'God's command'.

The profession that comes closest to that of a teacher is being a pastor or minister in the Church, and nothing other than custom can be shown to exclude women from this. They have a mind just like ours, which is capable of knowing and loving God, and thus of leading others to know and love Him. They share the same faith as us; the gospel and its promises are addressed equally to them…If men got used to seeing women presiding in church, they would be no more disturbed by it than women are when they see men in the same office. (p. 175)

According to this argument, there is no basis other than custom for excluding women from any position of leadership in a church.

---

[101] *De l'éducation*, 276.

That might seem to run counter to various sayings of Saint Paul: that wives should submit to their husbands (Col. 3:18), that the head of the woman is the man and the head of Christ is God (I Cor. 11:3), or that women should be silent in church (I Timothy 2: 11). Although Poulain was not attempting to justify his equality thesis by appeal to the Scriptures, as a Christian he had to reconcile his proposals about women in the Church with apparently contrary biblical passages. He argued that the New Testament does not say that women should submit to men 'because of their sex or of divine law' and there 'is not a word about inequality and natural dependence' in Paul's injunctions.[102] Paul was not *recommending* the subjection of women, no more than he was endorsing slavery for those who happened to be slaves when he wrote to the Colossians: 'Servants, obey in all things your masters according to the flesh; not with eyeservice, as menpleasers; but in singleness of heart, fearing God' (Col. 3: 22). His message was rather that, even for those who happen to be subject to others—such as women or slaves in first-century society—they should still be Christian in whatever civil or social status they occupied. What Saint Paul meant was that 'there is neither male nor female, neither Jew, Gentile, nor slave in relation to God.'[103]

One final objection to this version of the equality thesis was that it is based on speculation, and that it lacks the certainty that results from what opponents claimed to have observed. Poulain had two replies to this: one, that we know very few things with certainty. He complimented one of the interlocutors, in *Conversations on the Education of Ladies*, with the acknowledgement: 'I am pleased that you are convinced that you know nothing with certainty, except that you have a firm and unwavering desire to know things in the best way possible' (p. 211). The second response was that the belief held by opponents of women's equality was equally speculative: it involved an invalid inference from the cultural conditions to which women were historically subject to a conclusion about their underlying 'nature' or lack of ability. The only way to decide between the rival hypotheses was by conducting some version of the educational and social experiment that Poulain suggested. The evidence to date from that experiment suggests that Poulain, rather than his critics, was correct.

---

[102] *De l'excellence des hommes*, PO, 315.
[103] *De l'excellence des hommes*, 315, in reference to Col. 3:11.

Equality and Difference

Gournay, van Schurman, and Poulain argued for the equality of men and women, although they stopped short of defining the term 'equality'. Nonetheless, there are enough clues in their supporting arguments, despite the diversity of the authorities on which they relied, to identify some features of their common objective. First and foremost, none of these authors denied the following obvious truth: that if we consider those observable features of human beings to which the concept of equality may be applied most readily with an agreed metric—such as their size, strength, intelligence, virtue, linguistic ability, and so on—it is not true that all human beings are equal. Likewise, there are as many differences, observable or otherwise, among women as there are among men. These concessions anticipated a widely acknowledged conclusion of discussions of equality today: that the plausibility of any claim about human equality seems (at least initially) to vary inversely with the specificity with which it is expressed. Undisputed statements of equality at a very abstract level—such as, that all human beings are equally human—seem to be trivial or uninformative, while those that are specific seem to be disconfirmed by familiar counterexamples.

This persuaded many modern proponents of equality to argue for equality of opportunity, which is a moral or political claim to the effect that all persons should enjoy equal access to certain human goods. Even that proposal, however, assumes that the people in question already share relevant factual characteristics in virtue of which they ought to enjoy whatever equal opportunities are claimed for them: they ought to be treated equally because they are equal in some sense. The seventeenth-century proponents of gender equality struggled with these interrelated dimensions of the demand for equality: (1) a factual claim about human beings, which is difficult to articulate satisfactorily and which seems to vary between apparent metaphysical triviality and empirical falsifiability, and (2) a moral or political claim about how human beings ought to be treated, which assumes a satisfactory resolution of the issue identified in (1).[104]

---

[104] Article 1 of the United Nations Universal Declaration of Human Rights (1948) illustrates the challenges involved in combining specific factual and moral claims: 'All human beings are born free and equal in dignity and rights. They are endowed with reason and conscience and should act towards one another in a spirit of brotherhood.'

In respect of the factual claim, all three proponents of equality in this collection argued for the equality of men and women as human persons. Gournay and van Schurman adopted the metaphysical account of people that was inherited from Aristotle and was almost universally accepted in Western Christianity—about the mind or reason as a substantial form that defines what it means to be human—and challenged opponents to say how women's minds could be less rational, immaterial or immortal than those of men. For Gournay, this metaphysical equality was also confirmed by the Genesis account of creation; God created a single species called 'man', and some patristic commentaries on Genesis confirmed that the term 'man' applied equally to male and female people.

Nonetheless, this metaphysical equality, if focused exclusively on souls or minds, was compatible with an equally general claim about the inferiority of women's bodies or even Aristotle's infamous suggestion that women were defective men. For example, if women's brains function less well than those of men—as Malebranche assumed with no supporting evidence—then the innate abilities that accompany a human soul could be systematically frustrated in their operation by the natural infirmities of female bodies. The relevant biological sciences that could have addressed that empirical question were not adequately developed, in the early modern period, to resolve it in favour of either opponents or proponents of equality. At the same time, all the available evidence confirmed that some women were as able, in every respect, as some men, and that the observable differences in capacity between men and women corresponded in degree and frequency to similar differences between men. Therefore the mere assertion of the inferiority of women's bodies was, as Poulain argued, a projection onto nature of a difference that probably resulted merely from custom.

This helped to refocus the factual claim about the equality of the sexes on capacities and dispositions rather than actual achievements, and on moral or intellectual features of human beings rather than their bodily characteristics. In particular, the protagonists of equality argued that women have the same capacity for moral judgement as men, and therefore an equal capacity to acquire and practise moral virtues. The Christian tradition to which all three authors belonged had almost universally taught that women could excel in virtue and be recognized as saints or exemplary Christians. Indeed, even the ancient pagans who provided the philosophical basis for Christian culture acknowledged that women were as capable as men of intellectual and moral virtues. Plutarch had especially helped to identify which human features were relevant to the equality debate. He argued, in *Isis and Osiris*, that 'having a beard and wearing a coarse cloak does not make philosophers', and he reminded readers in *The Education of Children* that, if physical strength were chosen as a criterion for comparison, human beings would be surpassed by elephants and lions.

Strength is much admired, but it falls an easy prey to disease and old age. And, in general, if anybody prides himself wholly upon the strength of his body, let him know that he is sadly mistaken in judgement. For how small is man's strength compared with the power of other living creatures! I mean, for instance, elephants and bulls or lions. But learning, of all things in this world, is alone immortal and divine. Two elements in man's nature are supreme over all—mind and reason.[105]

Thus the factual dimension of egalitarianism was inspired by an almost uniform tradition of Greek culture and Christian writing, to the effect that the worth of human beings should not be assessed by wealth, beauty, health, or physical strength, and that the merit and dignity of people derive from characteristically human features that are not shared with other animals.

As Poulain emphasized, these human capacities were not features merely of an incorporeal, sexless soul. They were features of an embodied self that relied necessarily on appropriate conditions to facilitate their development and expression. For the same reason, Gournay remarked ironically, in the opening sentences of *The Ladies' Complaint*, that it was not enough to congratulate women on their natural capacities if they were denied all relevant opportunities for developing them. Therefore, the factual claim about women's natural abilities supported a moral and political demand for equality of opportunity. Besides, any dispute about the reality of women's natural capacities (which were not fully realized) could not be decided without first implementing equality of opportunity.

The concept of equality of opportunity generates a range of moral and political issues today that depend not only on some implicit concept of justice, but on the extent to which modern states provide many of the opportunities to which citizens claim a right. They include questions about the extent to which some or all opportunities should be equalized between competing individuals, about who should pay the costs involved, and whether full equality of opportunity is compatible with choices made by individuals that result in unequal outcomes. The equality thesis in the

---

[105] *Isis and Osiris*, LCL 306, 353, and *The Education of Children*, LCL 197, 5 D–E.

seventeenth century was very much a first chapter in this debate. Early modern proponents of gender equality drew attention to the circularity of excluding women from offices and professions because they were inadequately educated to engage in them, and of excluding them from the relevant education because they were not admitted to the corresponding professions or offices in the churches and in civil society.

They also drew attention—especially van Schurman—to the fundamental principle that supports equality of opportunity: namely, a concept of fairness or distributive justice in the allocation of resources when there is not an adequate supply to satisfy all those who desire them. When some group or class of people is treated differently from another, it is a basic principle of equity that one must justify the differential treatment by reference to some general principle. Many of the irrational candidates for such a principle are well-known, such as skin colour, the postal code of one's residence, or ethnicity. One of the major successes of the seventeenth-century feminists was to add *sexual identity* to the list of irrelevant criteria by which the unequal treatment of classes of people may be justified. They did that by challenging those who defended the unequal treatment of women to explain the rationality of their principles, so that the burden of proof was shifted to those who supported a less favourable treatment of women. For example, if women are systematically excluded from access to education, one can avoid the charge of irrationality or unfairness only by giving a plausible reason for their exclusion. Gournay and Poulain realized that there was no reason for excluding women from education, except to preserve the privileges and power of men. Evidently, that is not a reason that could ever appear plausible or acceptable to women, no more than the financial gain of slave-owners could persuade slaves to accept their condition voluntarily. Since that underlying reason could not be articulated without the risk of self-refutation, proponents of inequality appealed instead to custom or to traditional interpretations of the Bible (which also relied on custom). That manoeuvre, however, involved converting an arbitrary human arrangement into an equally arbitrary but allegedly incontestable decision by God.

As in other more recent debates about racial or religious equality, the very challenge by early modern feminists to traditional orthodoxies involved a significant element of consciousness-raising. It was not the responsibility of the early proponents of gender equality, as Gournay had assumed, to 'prove' some thesis that straddled the boundaries of the moral, political, and factual. It was enough to demand a justification for the less favourable treatment of women and to examine critically the reasons given for excluding women from offices and positions that were reserved for men. That challenge, once articulated, acquired a perennial relevance. One asks, not why women cannot do something, but why they should be prevented from trying to do it. Egalitarianism thus becomes a moral and political demand for equality of access to opportunities for developing capacities which, until proven otherwise, must be assumed to be equally distributed between men and women, even if their random distribution among individuals of both genders is unequal.

Marie le Jars de Gournay
The Equality of Men and Women[1]

Most of those who defend the cause of women against the arrogant superiority that men claim for themselves adopt the completely opposite view by claiming superiority for women. For my part, since I avoid all extremes, I am content to make women equal to men, for nature is also as opposed to superiority as to inferiority in this respect. What, then, am I claiming? For some people, it is not enough to discriminate in favour of the male sex; they also want to restrict women to the distaff, and even exclusively to the distaff, by a necessary and unbreakable decree. Nonetheless, women may find some consolation by realizing that this kind of contempt is found only among men whom they would least wish to resemble; such men, if they were female, would confer some plausibility on any complaints one could spew out about the feminine sex, and they feel in their hearts that they have nothing to recommend them except what follows from the mere fact of being male. They have heard it trumpeted in the streets very often that women lack respect and also the capacity and even the temperament and physical constitution necessary to acquire that respect. Their rhetoric delights in preaching these maxims, which they do much more successfully to the extent that 'respect', 'capacity', 'physical constitution', and 'temperament' are all positive terms. They have also failed to realize that to endorse hearsay and what is commonly believed is the first sign of a fool.

Listen to how these wits compare the two sexes, while spinning their condescending comments: the highest achievement that women can accomplish, in their opinion, is to resemble the average man, and they no

[1] *A la Reyne, l'Égalité des hommes et des femmes* (Paris: 1622/1641); see Note on the Texts and Translations.

more imagine that a great woman might resemble a great man, by simply changing the sex involved in the comparison, than they would grant that a man could elevate himself to the status of a god. These folk are truly braver than Hercules, who challenged only twelve monsters in twelve combats, while they defeat half the world with a single word!

Is it credible, however, that those who wish to exalt and strengthen themselves by the weakness of others claim, at the same time, that they can do so by their own power? They find this attractive because they think they are excused from the effrontery of reviling the female sex by using a similar effrontery to praise themselves or, rather, to gild themselves—sometimes, I say, individually and sometimes collectively, and also by using whatever false or mistaken criteria they wish—as if the truth of their boasting were confirmed and clarified by their impudence. God knows that I am familiar with some of those happy braggarts, whose boasting has become almost a proverb among those who are most vociferous in their contempt of women. But, if they self-righteously claim to be gallant and superior men because they declare themselves to be such by their own edict, why would they not reduce women to beasts with a complementrary edict that says the opposite? It is reasonable to follow their claims to their logical conclusions. Good God! Do those who claim such superiority never imagine that they need to provide appropriate and relevant examples and a relevant law of perfection for that unfortunate sex?

If I offer a favourable opinion about the dignity or ability of ladies,[2] I do not claim to be able to prove it here with reasons (because those who are tenacious will be able to dispute them) or by examples (because they are too familiar), but only by the authority of God himself and of the Fathers who were buttresses of his Church, and of those great philosophers who have enlightened the universe. Let us introduce some of these glorious witnesses at the outset, and reserve God and subsequently the holy Fathers of his church until the conclusion, as the most valuable witnesses.

---

[2] The French term 'dame' had a wide range of meanings in the seventeenth century. It usually had connotations of noble birth or social distinction, such as the wife of a nobleman in contrast with bourgeois or common people. More widely, it applied to any woman who exercised a high office or a distinguished role in society, including women in religious life. It was used in some contexts, however, to mean simply a woman. I have translated 'dame' throughout as 'lady' on the assumption that the English term has similar shades of meaning.

Plato, whose title 'divine' has never been challenged,[3] and consequently Socrates, who was his spokesman and interpreter in Plato's writings—unless Plato is the spokesman in the same writings for Socrates, his most divine tutor, since they always held the same opinion and expressed it in similar terms—both assign to women the same rights, faculties, and offices in their republics and everywhere else.[4] They also maintain that women have surpassed all the men of their own nation on many occasions, since in fact women discovered elements of the fine arts, especially the alphabet of the Latin language.[5] They excelled and taught officially and indisputably better than men in all kinds of disciplines and virtues, in the most famous ancient cities, including Alexandria, which, apart from Rome, was the premier city of the empire. Hypatia held this high position in that celebrated seat of learning.[6] But was Themistoclea, the sister of Pythagoras, any less accomplished in Samothrace, not to mention the wife of Pythagoras, the wise Theano?[7] We are told that Theano taught philosophy as Pythagoras had done, and that she had as a disciple even her brother who could hardly find any disciples worthy of his tutoring in the whole of Greece. What of Damo, the daughter of Pythagoras, who delivered his *Commentaries* into her hands as he lay dying, and to whom he entrusted responsibility for cultivating his teaching, with the mysteries and gravity that he exhibited all his life?[8] We read even in Cicero, the prince of orators, about the fame and popularity achieved in Rome and its environs by the eloquence of Cornelia, the mother of the Gracchi, and also of the

---

[3] Montaigne, *Essais*, I: 51, 307A: *Essays*, 'On the vanity of words', 344: 'By universal acclaim Plato bore the name *divine*, and nobody thought to dispute it with him.'

[4] Plato, *The Republic*, 451C–457C.

[5] Christine de Pizan, *The Book of the City of Ladies*, I: 33, I: 37, I: 38 and II: 5, reports the legend about Nicostrata (or Carmentis) inventing the Latin language.

[6] Hypatia (*c*.370–415 BC) was head of a platonic school at Alexandria, and is reported to have written commentaries on the *Arithmetic* of Diophantus and on astronomy. The circumstances of her death, when she was stripped and murdered by a mob of religious zealots, made her a symbol of men's lack of toleration of educated women and a martyr for women's liberation. See *The Ecclesiastical History of Socrates Scholasticus* (Cambridge: 1680), 376.

[7] Diogenes Laertius, *Lives of Eminent Philosophers: Pythagoras*, LCL 185, 8.21: 'the same authority [Aristoxenus]... asserts that Pythagoras took his doctrines from the Delphic priestess Themistoclea.'

[8] Diogenes Laertius, *Lives of Eminent Philosophers: Pythagoras*, LCL 185, 8.42: 'He [Pythagoras] had a daughter, Damo... according to a letter of Lysis to Hippasus... when he entrusted his daughter Damo with the custody of his memoirs, he solemnly charged her never to give them to anyone outside his house.'

eloquence of Laelia, the daughter of Caius, who in my view was Sylla.[9] Neither the daughter of Laelia, no more than the daughter of Hortensius, fails to receive from Quintillian a well-known eulogy about that exquisite virtue [of eloquence].[10] What then? If Tycho Brahe, the famous astronomer and Danish baron, had lived today, would he not have celebrated the new star that was recently discovered near the place where he lived? That is how we refer to Miss van Schurman, who emulates these illustrious women in eloquence, in their lyrical poetry, and even in their native Latin language, and who also knows all other languages, both ancient and modern, and all the liberal and noble arts.[11]

But will Athens, the august queen of Greece and of the sciences, be unique among leading cities by not seeing women reach the highest levels as teachers of the human race, both orally and in their illustrious and fertile writings? Arete, the daughter of Aristippus, acquired one hundred and ten philosophers as disciples in that glorious city, and publicly held the chair that her father had vacated on his death. Since she also composed a number of excellent writings, the Greeks honoured her with the following eulogy: 'She had her father's pen, the soul of Socrates, and the language of

---

[9] Cornelia (c.189–110 BC) was the mother of the two Gracchi brothers, Caius Sempronious Gracchus and Titus Sempronious Gracchus. Laelia (185–115 BC) was daughter of Caius Laelius Sapiens, and (despite Gourney's comment) was not the same as Sylla (c.138–78 BC). Cicero refers to Cornelia in *Brutus*, LCL 342, XXVII, 104, and to both Cornelia and Laelia at LVIII, 211: 'We have read the letters of Cornelia, mother of the Gracchi; they make it plain that her sons were nursed not less by their mother's speech than at her breast. It was my good fortune more than once to hear Laelia, the daughter of Gaius, speak, and it was apparent that her careful usage was coloured by her father's habit, and the same was true of her two daughters Muciae, with both of whom I have talked, and of her granddaughters the Liciniae, both of whom I have heard.'

[10] Hortensia, the daughter of Hortensius, was reputed to be an eloquent speaker. See Quintillian, *The Orator's Education*, LCL 124, I.1, 6: 'As to parents, I should wish them to be as highly educated as possible. (I do not mean only the fathers.) We are told that the eloquence of the Gracchi owed much to their mother Cornelia, whose highly cultivated style is known also to posterity from her letters. Laelia, Gaius Laelius' daughter, is said to have echoed her father's elegance in her own conversation; and the speech delivered before the triumvirs by Hortensia, the daughter of Quintus Hortensius, is still read—and not just because it is by a woman.'

[11] This comment was added in the 1641 edition; van Schurman was only fifteen years old when the first edition was published in 1622. Tycho Brahe (1546–1601) was famous for the accuracy of his astronomical observations, and in particular for his observation of a new star or *supernova* in 1572. He was born in Scania, which is in modern Sweden, and conducted his astronomical research nearby on the island of Hven and later in Prague; when compared with the distance of stars from the Earth, both are very close to The Netherlands, where van Schurman lived.

Homer.'[12] I mention here only those who taught publicly and with great prestige in the most famous places, because the number of other great and learned women is almost infinite and it would therefore be tedious to list all of them.

Why was the Queen of Sheba the only one who went to worship the wisdom of Solomon, even crossing so many seas and lands that separated them, unless she recognized it better than anyone else in that whole age?[13] Or, how did she recognize it better than others unless she possessed a corresponding wisdom, which was equal or closer to that of Solomon than the wisdom of all other minds of that era? The dual miracle of nature—the teacher and disciple mentioned at the beginning of this section [Plato and Socrates]—believed that they were acknowledging the esteem and respect that these women deserved and giving extra authority to their own more significant discourses by expressing them, in their books, through the mouths of Aspasia and Diotema[14]—the same Diotema whom Plato was not afraid to call his guide and teacher in some of the higher sciences, though he himself was the teacher and master of all nations under the Sun. Given what Theodoret very willingly acknowledges in his *Prayer of Faith*, he seems to have thought it was very plausible to hold a favourable opinion of women.[15] See also the long and magnificent comparison that the famous philosopher, Maximus of Tyre, made between the method of loving of the

[12] Arete was the daughter of Aristippus of Cyrene (*c*.425–350 BC). She is reputed to have written many philosophical works, none of which survives. See Diogenes Laertius, *The Lives of Eminent Philosophers: Aristippus*, LCL 185, 2.72: 'He gave his daughter Arete the best advice, training her up to despise excess'; 2.86: 'The pupil of Arete was Aristippus, who went by the name of mother-taught, and his pupil was Theodorus, known as the atheist, subsequently as "god".'

[13] I Kings 10: 1–13.

[14] Diotema of Mantinea is acknowledged in Plato's dialogue, *The Symposium*, 201D, as inspiring his ideas about love: 'Now I shall recount to you all a discourse about Love which I once heard given by a woman from Mantinea, who was called Diotema': trans. M. C. Howatson (Cambridge: Cambridge University Press, 2008). Aspasia was the companion of Pericles; Plutarch, *Life of Pericles*, LCL 65, xxiv.

[15] Theodoret (*c*.393–466), was bishop of Cyrrhus (Syria); Gournay's citation does not correspond to the title of any of his works. She most likely referred to *Graecarum affectionum curatio seu Evangelicae veritatis ex gentilium philosophica cognitio* (*The Cure of Hellenic Maladies*), PG 83, 775 at 943, the first chapter of which is entitled '*La Foi*' in French translation. The relevant text is quoted in the Introduction above (pp. 17–18). There is a modern edition and French translation in *Théodoret de Cyr: Thérapeutique des Maladies Helléniques*, trans. P. Canivet, 2 vols. (Paris: Editions du Cerf, 1958). There are similar sentiments in *Theodoret of Cyrus*, trans. I. Pásztori-Kupán (London: Routledge, 2006), *On the Inhumanation of the Lord*, 139, 171.

same Socrates and that of the great Sappho.[16] How much does this king of sages [Socrates] also flatter himself with the hope of engaging in the after-life with the many great men and women who were born through the centuries, and what pleasure does he anticipate enjoying in those conversations when his great disciple reports his final discussions in the divine *Apology*?[17]

Following all these testimonies from Socrates on the subject of ladies, it is easy to see that, if he lets slip a few words in Xenophon's *Symposium* that are critical of women's judgement when compared with that of men, he considers them in relation to the ignorance and inexperience in which they are reared or, at least, he considers them in general terms while leaving plenty of room for frequent exceptions, which the quibblers involved in this debate fail to understand.[18] In the case of Plato, we are also told that he did not wish to begin teaching before Lastheneia (I read that version of the name) and Axiothea had arrived at his auditorium, and that he described the former as the understanding and the latter as the memory that could understand and remember what he had to say.[19]

If, therefore, women succeed less often than men in achieving various degrees of excellence, it is surprising that the lack of a good education and the preponderance of even patently poor teaching does not make matters worse, and that these factors do not prevent them completely from succeeding. If one needs proof: is there any greater difference between women and men than that between different groups of women, which depends on

---

[16] Maximus of Tyre (c.125–85 BC), *The Philosophical Orations*, trans. M. B. Trapp (Oxford: Clarendon Press, 1997), Discourse 18, 167–8; Sappho (born c. 612/30 BC) was a famous Greek poet, though only some fragments of her work survive.

[17] Plato's *Apology* reports the final discussions between Socrates and some of his friends before his death in prison. At 41B–C Socrates refers to the posthumous pleasure he hoped to experience by discussing the question of who is truly wise with 'other men and women'.

[18] In Xenophon's *Symposium*, II: 9, Socrates comments as follows about a girl who had danced: 'It is clear, then, that in many other things as well as in what this girl is doing, the feminine nature is not at all inferior to the man's, but it lacks judgement and strength. As a result, if someone among you has a wife, let him be confident in teaching her whatever he might want her to know ...'. Following an exhibition of great courage by the same dancer, Socrates adds that 'at least those who see this will no longer dispute that even courage is teachable, when she, though a woman, throws herself so daringly into the swords.' *The Shorter Socratic Writings*, trans. R. C. Bartlett (Ithaca and London: Cornell University Press, 1996), 138, 139.

[19] Diogenes Laertius, *Lives of Eminent Philosophers: Plato*, LCL 184, 3.46: 'His [Plato's] disciples were ... and many others, among them two women, Lastheneia of Mantinea and Axiothea of Phlius, who is reported by Dicaearthus to have worn men's clothes'; 4.2: '... among those who attended his lectures [those of Speusippus] were the two women who had been pupils of Plato, Lastheneia of Mantinea and Axiothea of Phlius.'

the education they received, whether they were reared in a city or a village, and whether they came from one nation or another?[20] Consequently, why would the education of women, in literary and social studies, not bridge the gap that is usually found between the minds of men and women, since education is so important that when only one part of it—namely, the experience of social interaction—is well developed among French and English women and is lacking among Italian women, the latter are by and large surpassed very much by the former? I say 'by and large' because, when considered individually, Italian women excel sometimes, and we have acquired some princesses and queens from among their number who were not lacking in intelligence.[21] Why would a genuinely good education not succeed in bridging the gap between the intellectual powers of men and women since, in the example that I have just mentioned, those who are born in less favourable conditions surpass those who are more favourably born with only the simple help of engagement and conversation with society, since the Italian air is more subtle and more suitable for making the mind subtle than that found in France or England—something that is obvious from the capacity of men in that climate when compared in general with that of the French or the English? However, I have discussed this issue elsewhere.[22]

Plutarch, in his work *The Bravery of Women*, maintains that man's virtue and women's virtue are one and the same.[23] Seneca, on the other hand, wrote in his *Consolations* that one must believe that nature did not treat ladies ungenerously, nor does it restrain or limit their virtues or their minds any more than the virtues and minds of men. On the contrary, nature has endowed them with the same strength and an equal capacity for everything honourable and praiseworthy.[24] Following those two authors, let us see what the third member [i.e. Montaigne] of the triumvirate of human wisdom and morals

---

[20] Cf. Montaigne, *Essais*, II: 12, 466A: *Essays*, 'Apology for Raymond Sebond', 520: 'there is a greater difference between one man and another than between some men and some beasts.'

[21] The first and second editions had the phrase 'two queens' rather than the indeterminate 'some princesses and queens'; the original phrase referred to Marie de' Medici and Catherine de' Medici.

[22] In her treatise *De l'éducation de Messeigneurs les enfants de France*, GO, I, 580.

[23] Plutarch, *Moralia*, vol. III: *Bravery of Women*, LCL 245, 242F: 'man's virtues and woman's virtues are one and the same.'

[24] *Consolation to Marcia*, xvi: 'But who has stated that Nature has been ungenerous to women's natures, and has tightly restricted their virtues? They have just as much energy, believe me, just as much aptitude for noble actions, should they wish; they endure pain and toil as well as we do, if they have grown accustomed to them' (S, 68).

thinks about this question in his *Essays*.[25] It seems to him, he says, although he knows not why, that one rarely finds women who deserve to command men.[26] Is that not equivalent to making them equal to men as individuals and acknowledging that, if he fails to make the same claim in general terms, he is afraid of being mistaken (even though he could have excused his reservation by reference to the poor and objectionable way in which women are reared)? Besides, we should not forget that he mentions favourably, in another place in the same book, the authority that Plato attributes to women in the *Republic*, and that Antisthenes denied all differences of virtue and ability between the sexes.[27] As for the philosopher Aristotle, although he remodelled the heavens and the earth, he did not contradict the opinion that is favourable to ladies, unless he contradicted it in general terms because of their poor education and without denying that there are exceptions.[28] Consequently, he confirmed that opinion, probably by adopting the view of both his spiritual father and grandfather, Plato and Socrates, as a stable and permanent conclusion based on the authority of those sages, by whose writings one must acknowledge that the judgement of the whole human race and reason itself has been expressed.

Is it necessary to invoke an infinite number of other ancient and modern minds with illustrious reputations or, among the latter, Erasmus, Politian, Boccaccio, Tasso in his prose works, Agrippa, the honourable and wise teacher of courtesans, and so many famous poets—all of whom completely oppose those who despise the female sex and support the abilities, advantages, and capacity of women for every office, every honourable activity

[25] In the 1594 edition of the *Promenade*, Gournay addresses Montaigne as follows: 'In your *Essays*, father (which amount to the third member of the Triumvirate that includes Plutarch and Seneca)', GO, II, 1297, note 8.

[26] Montaigne, *Essais*, II: 8, 398A; *Essays*, 'On the affection of fathers for their children', 447: 'It seems to me right, somehow, that women should have no mastery over men save only the natural one of motherhood—unless it be for the chastisement of those who have wilfully submitted to them out of some feverish humour.'

[27] Montaigne, *Essais*, III: 5, 897C; *Essays*, 'On some lines of Virgil', 1016: 'In *The Republic* Plato summons both men and women indifferently to a community of all studies, administrations, offices and vocations both in peace and war; and Antisthenes the philosopher removed any distinction between their virtue and our own.' This text refers to *Republic* 455e. Antisthenes (*c*.445–*c*.365 BC) was a pupil of Socrates; see Diogenes Laertius, *Lives of Eminent Philosophers*, vol. II, LCL 185: *Antisthenes*, 6.12: 'Virtue is the same for women as for men.'

[28] This is a very charitable interpretation of Aristotle, who compared women to slaves in *Politics* I, Ch. 2, and the *Nicomachean Ethics*, VIII, Ch. 10.

and noble undertaking?[29] Ladies may genuinely console themselves by the fact that those who despise their merits cannot prove that they themselves are competent, if all those ancient and modern authors are such. Besides, an intelligent person would not say (even if they believed it) that the merits and advantages of the female sex are insignificant in comparison with those of men, because—if indeed anyone dared to express such a view—it would amount to characterizing all those writers [mentioned above] as dreamers for the sole purpose of undermining their testimony, which is completely opposed to such a claim.

It would also be necessary to characterize as dreamers whole nations, including some of the most subtle, such as those of Smyrna (according to Tacitus). Long ago, in order to gain precedence in nobility in Rome, they claimed to have descended from Tantalus, the son of Jupiter, or from Theseus, the grandson of Neptune, or from an amazon whom they therefore compared in dignity to those gods.[30] Citizens of Lesbos seek no less glory in the birth of Sappho, because one finds everywhere today, even in Holland, that the only engraving on their coins was the figure of a young lady with a lyre in her hand, together with the name 'Lesbos'. Is that not equivalent to acknowledging that the greatest honour that they and their island could ever have had was to have cradled the infancy of that heroine? Since we have stumbled accidentally into discussing women poets, we learn that Corina publicly outshone Pindar in their shared art, and at the age of

---

[29] Some of the relevant works of Erasmus are in the *Colloquies*, trans. C. R. Thompson, *Collected Works of Erasmus* (Toronto and London: University of Toronto Press, 1997), vols. 39 and 40: 'The Girl with no Interest in Marriage' (39: 279), 'The Abbot and the Learned Lady' (39: 499), and 'The Council of Women' (40: 905); Politian, born Angelo Ambrogini (1454–1494), was an Italian humanist and author of *Angelus Politianus Cassandrae fideli Venetae puellae doctissimae* in *Opera Omnia* (Venice: A. Romanus, 1498), diiii (3–4); Giovanni Boccaccio (1313–1375) was the author of the *Decameron* and of *De mulieribus claris* [*Concerning Famous Women*], from which many authors, including Gournay, borrowed; Torquato Tasso (1544–1595) was most famous for his poem, *La Gerusalemme liberata*, but also published a number of essays in 1582, including his *Discorso della virtù feminile, e donnesca* [*A Discourse on Feminine and Womanly Virtue*] (Venice: B. Giunti, 1582); 'the teacher of courtesans' was Baldassare Castiglione (1478–1529), the author of *Il Cortegiano*. Heinrich Cornelius Agrippa (1486–1535) was the author of books on occult philosophy and of the *Declamatio de nobilitate et praecellentia foeminei sexus* (1529); Eng. trans., *Declamation on the Nobility and Preeminence of the Female Sex* (University of Chicago Press, 1996).

[30] Tacitus, *Annals*, LCL 312, IV. 56: 'The deputies from Smyrna, on the other hand, after retracing the antiquity of their town—whether founded by Tantalus, the seed of Jove; by Theseus, also of celestial stock; or by one of the Amazons—passed on to the arguments in which they rested most confidence: their good offices towards the Roman people ...'

nineteen (which coincides with the age at which she died) Erinna[31] wrote a poem of three hundred verses which was so excellent that it compared with the majesty of Homer's poems, and provoked Alexander to entertain the following doubt: should he have valued more highly the happiness of Achilles for having been associated as a hero with this great poet [Homer], or that of the same poet for having such a great heroine as a rival?[32] Did ladies know to choose, among these two poets, the one to whom they would attribute the glorious victory or, at least, equality?

As regards Salic law, which excluded women from the throne, it was in force only in France and was instituted during the age of Pharamond exclusively in response to the wars against the empire, the shackles of which our forefathers cast off, because the female sex was probably less suited physically for battle, given the necessity of bearing and nourishing their children.[33] One should also mention, however, that once peers of the realm were created in France, primarily as vassals for the king (which is implied by their title), the lady peers of rulers had the same role, privileges, and voting rights everywhere, and with the same scope, as their male equivalents.[34] One may consult Hotman for the etymology of peers, and du Tillet and Matthieu in the *History of the King* for lady peers.[35] It is also worth considering that, according to Plutarch, the Lacedaemonians, that brave and generous people, consulted their wives about all matters, both public and private; and Pausanius, Suidus, Fulgose, and Laertius, will confirm most of the other authorities or testimonies that

[31] Corina of Boeotia was a lyric poet who is believed to have flourished in the fifth century BC and, if so, was a contemporary of Pindar. Erinna (fourth century BC) was also a Greek poet from the island of Telos, who is reputed to have died at the age of nineteen.

[32] Achilles is the hero of Homer's narration of the Trojan War in the *Iliad*; Alexander the Great (356–323 BC) became a legendary hero by comparison with Achilles.

[33] Salic law became codified in the early sixth century and, from the fifteenth century, was understood in hereditary monarchies as excluding women and descendants in the female line from succeeding to the throne. Pharamond (c.370–427) was a legendary early king of the Franks.

[34] Montaigne, *Essais*, I: 41, 256C; *Essays*, 'On not sharing one's fame', 287: 'Just as, despite their sex, women who succeeded to peerages had the right to attend and give their opinion in cases falling within the jurisdiction of the peers of the realm ...'

[35] See François Hotman, *Francogallia*, 3rd edn. (J. Bertulphi, 1576) Ch. xiiii: 'De comestabulo, & Paribus Franciae', 165–181; Jean du Tillet, *Recueil des Roys de France, leurs couronne et maison* (Paris: Adrian Perier, 1607), 362–78: 'Des Pairs de France'; Pierre Matthieu, *Histoire de France et des choses memorables advenues aux Provinces estrangeres durant sept annees de Paix* (Paris: I. Metayer, 1606), vol. II, Bk.V, 297 ff. The title used above by Gournay does not correspond to that of any book by these authors.

I gathered above.[36] To those I might add that the *Theatre of Human Life* and *The Clock of Princes*, to which I can appeal in this context, recount a number of other similar testimonies and provide the names of their authors.[37] Nonetheless, French people have been well served by accepting the institution of regents as equivalent to kings during the minority of the latter; for, without it, how seriously would their state have collapsed? The Germans, those bellicose peoples who, as Tacitus says, were proclaimed victorious more often than defeated during more than two hundred years of war,[38] used to bring a dowry to their wives (rather than the opposite), and they also included nations that were always ruled exclusively by women. And when Aeneas presents to Dido the crown and sceptre of Troy, commentators say that this results from the fact that women who were eldest daughters—as this princess was—used to rule over royal households in ancient times.[39]

Could one wish for two more favourable infringements of Salic law (if it can cope with two)? Nevertheless, the fact is that our ancient Gauls, and also the Cathaginians, did not despise women because, when they joined forces in Hannibal's army to cross the Alps, they assigned responsibility for arbitrating their disputes to the women of Gaul.[40] If in many places men rob women of their share of the most important benefits, they are mistaken when they convert their usurpation and tyranny into an entitlement, because inequality in physical rather than in spiritual strength or in other meritorious qualities obviously explains this theft and is the reason why it is tolerated. Moreover,

---

[36] Plutarch, *Lives: Lycurghus*, LCL 46, 14, 1–3, 3.5; Pausanias (*c.*115–180), was an ancient geographer and the author of *Description of Greee*, 5 vols., LCL 93, 188, 272, 297, 298; 'Suidas' refers to a tenth-century Greek encyclopedia that was re-issued in various editions, including a complete Latin translation as ΣΟΨΙΔΑΣ: *Suidas hunc primum integer latinitate donatus*, 2 vols. (Geneva: Peter de la Roviere, 1619/30); Battista Fregosa (1452–1504), or 'Fulgose', was doge of Genoa, and the author of *Factorum dictorumque memorabilium libri IX* (Paris: Peter Caveilat, 1584); Bk.VIII, Ch. 3: 'Women who excelled in learning', mentioned some of the women cited by Gournay.

[37] Antonio de Guevara, *Relox de principes o Libro aureo des Emperador Marco Aurelio* (1529), was translated into French as *L'Horloge des princes* (1531), and I have translated that French title here as *The Clock of Princes*. Theodor Zwinger's *Theatre of Human Life* appeared in Latin as *Theatrum vitae humanae* (1565) and in some subsequent editions as *Theatrum humanae vitae*; it included historical examples 'of all good and bad things that can happen to human beings.'

[38] Tacitus, *Germania*, LCL 35, §37: 'the total amounts to about two hundred and ten years; for that length of time has the conquest of Germany been in process.'

[39] Refers to the *Aeneid*, I, 653.

[40] Plutarch, *Moralia*, vol. III: *Bravery of Women*, LCL 245, 246C–D: 'The women, however, put themselves between the armed forces and, taking up the controversies, arbitrated and decided them...if the Carthaginians complained against the Celts, the judges should be the Celtic women.'

physical strength is such a lowly virtue that when beasts, men, and women are compared, beasts outperform men more than men outperform women.[41] Since the same historian, Tacitus, teaches us that when force prevails, equity, integrity, and even modesty become the virtues of the conqueror, will anyone be surprised that prudence, wisdom, and all good qualities in general are the attributes of our men to the exclusion of women, in addition to their exclusion from all worldly privileges?[42]

Besides, the human animal, if understood correctly, is neither a man nor a woman because the sexes were not created unconditionally or in such a way that they constitute different species, but exclusively for the purpose of propagation.[43] The unique form and specific characteristic of this animal consists only in the rational soul;[44] and if we are allowed to laugh in the course of this argument, it would not be inappropriate to jest that there is nothing more like the male cat on the windowsill than a female cat. Man and woman are so much one that, if man is more than woman, then woman is more than man. Mankind was created male and female, according to Scripture, while counting the two of them as only one creation.[45] Jesus Christ is called the 'Son of Man' even though he is the son only of a woman, which is a complete and definitive perfection of the proof of this unity of the two sexes. Saint Basil the Great speaks as follows in his first homily on the Hexaemeron: 'The virtues of man

[41] Plutarch, *The Education of Children*, LCL 197, 5 D–E, was one source of this common-place: 'if anybody prides himself wholly upon the strength of his body, let him know that he is sadly mistaken in judgement. For how small is man's strength compared with the power of other living creatures! I mean, for instance, elephants and bulls and lions.' See also Boethius, *The Consolation of Philosophy*, III, 8.7, trans. P. G. Walsh (Oxford World's Classics, 1999), 52.

[42] Tacitus, *Germania*, LCL 35, §§35, 36, suggests merely that one of the German peoples happened to have been both victorious and just. 'The special strength of their sterling strength [i.e. the Chauci, a German tribe] is, indeed, just this, that they do not depend for their superior position on injustice…where might is right, self-control and righteousness are titles reserved for the stronger.' However, it would be a logical mistake to conclude that there is any universal connection between being victorious and exercising justice or other virtues, and Gournay is presumably being ironic here.

[43] The 1622 edition used a more scholastic expression of the same idea: 'the sexes were made not unconditionally, but *secundum quid*, as they say in the Schools; that is to say, exclusively for the purpose of propagation.' GO, I, 978, note 12.

[44] It was a commonplace in the philosophy taught almost universally in Europe in the seventeenth century that the defining feature (or, in Aristotelian language, the form) of a human being was the possession of a rational soul or mind.

[45] Gournay uses the term '*l'homme*' here to mean mankind rather than a male, and alludes to Gen. I: 27: 'And God created man to his own image: to the image of God he created him: male and female he created them.'

and of woman are the same because God bestowed on them the same creation and the same honour; *male and female he created them*.[46] Now, in those whose nature is one and the same, one must conclude that their actions are also the same, and that their esteem and praise are therefore equal when their works are equal. That, therefore, is the declaration of this powerful champion and venerable witness of the Church.

It is a good idea to be mindful, at this point, that certain quibblers in ancient times went so far in their idiotic arrogance as to deny the image of God to women, in contrast with men; according to that argument, they should have identified the beard as the characteristic feature of that image.[47] It was also necessary, therefore, to deny that women were made in man's image, because they could not resemble man without resembling Him whose image men bore. God himself distributed the gifts of prophecy indifferently between women and men, and also established women as judges, teachers, and leaders of his faithful people, in peacetime and in war, in the persons of Huldah and Deborah.[48] Moreover, He made them triumphant with this people in some great victories, in testimony of which their songs have the distinction of a place in the holy Bible, as have likewise the canticles of Mary, the sister of Moses, and of Ann the daughter of Phanuel.[49] Besides, women have been

---

[46] This does not refer to the first of Basil's nine homilies on the Hexaemeron (to which van Schurman refers in note 20), but to the first of two supplementary homilies that were attributed alternatively to Saint Basil or to his brother, Saint Gregory of Nyssa. It is found in PG, vol. 30, col. 33, under the title *De Hominis structura*, which offers a commentary on Gen. 1:27: 'God created man to his own image'. The scope of the term 'man' is explained as follows: 'Lest anyone through ignorance misunderstand the word "man" as referring exclusively to the male sex, he adds: "male and female he created them", so that it is understood that the woman as much as the man was created in the image of God…both sexes were created with the same dignity; their actions are equal, as are their rewards and punishments.' The final phrase quoted by Gournay in the text is given in Latin, from the Vulgate version of Mk. 10: 6: '*masculum et feminam fecit eos*'. There is a similar commentary on the same text in Saint Gregory of Nyssa, *De hominis opificio*, PG, 44: 178–9; Eng. trans. *On the Making of Man*, NPNF, vol. 5, 406: 'In saying that "God created man" the text indicates, by the indefinite character of the term, all mankind.'

[47] Plutarch, *Isis and Osiris*, LCL 306, 353, was the first to deny the significance of a beard: 'It is a fact, Clea, that having a beard and wearing a course cloak does not make philosophers…'. Cf. Philo, *On the Account of the World's Creation given by Moses*, LCL 226, XXIII (p. 55): 'Moses tells us that man was created after the image of God and after his likeness…Let no one represent the likeness as one to a bodily form; for neither is God in human form, nor is the human body God-like. No, it is in respect of the Mind, the sovereign element of the soul, that the word "image" is used.'

[48] Huldah (II Kings 22:14) and Deborah (Judges 4:4) were prophetesses in the Old Testament.

[49] Miriam, the sister of Moses (Exodus 15:20) and Anna (Lk. 2:36) were described as prophetesses.

victorious and crowned as such in many regions of the world. But, one might ask, over whom were they victorious? Over Cyrus and Theseus; to whom we may add Hercules, against whom they at least fought well even if they did not achieve victory.[50] Likewise, the fall of Penthesilia was the crowning achievement of Achilles' glory.[51] Listen to how Seneca and Ronsard speak of him:

> He vanquished the Amazons, the ultimate terror of the Greeks.
> He reduced Penthesilia to dust.[52]

Nor was Virgil able to accept the death of Camilla (when she was surrounded by a furious army that seemed not to fear anyone other than her), except by recourse to an ambush and a surprise shot from a distance.[53] Epicharis, Leaena, Porcia, and the mother of the Maccabees—could they provide us with a proof that women are capable of another kind of victory, namely, the magnanimous strength that consists in constancy and the endurance of the most harsh suffering?[54] Moreover, have they excelled less

---

[50] Cyrus died in battle against Thamyris, the queen of Scythia: *Herodotus*, LCL 117, I: 214. Theseus fought against the amazons; Plutarch, *Lives*, vol. I: *Theseus*, XXVII (LCL 46). The third example alludes to the resistance of the amazons to Hercules, who was sent to fetch the royal girdle of Hippolyte; this is probably borrowed from the amended version of the legend in Boccaccio, *Concerning Famous Women*, Ch. 18.

[51] Virgil's *Aeneid*, I, 490–94; *The Aeneid*, trans. Edward McCrorie (Ann Arbor, MI: University of Michigan Press, 1995), p. 30: 'and crazed Penthesilea, the Amazon leader,/blazing among crescent shields, surrounded by thousands./One breast bared, a gold girdle beneath it,/the war-queen dared to charge into men though a virgin.' Gournay translated several books of the *Aeneid*; her version of these lines is found in GO, II, 1158.

[52] Seneca, *Tragedies*, vol. I: *Trojan Women*, LCL 62, 243: 'Then fell the fierce Amazon, our latest dread.' Gournay had a special interest in the poetry of Pierre de Ronsard (1524–1585); Ronsard refers briefly to Penthesilia in his *Institution pour l'adolescence du roy Tres-chrestien Charles IX* de ce nom, in *Oeuvres complètes*, ed. J. Céard et al. (Paris: Gallimard, 1994), 2: 1007, l. 45.

[53] Camilla was the queen of the Volscians and was killed in battle against the army of Aeneas: *Aeneid*, VII: 932.

[54] Epicharis committed suicide rather than betray those involved in a conspiracy against Nero. See Montaigne, *Essais* II: 32, 724C; *Essays*, 'In defence of Seneca and Plutarch', 820; Leaena was a woman who endured torture rather than betray others: Pliny, *Natural History*, LCL 352, VII. 23: 'Bodily endurance ... has produced many examples, the most famous in the case of women being that of the harlot Leaena who on the rack refused to betray the tyrannicides, Harmodius and Aristogiton.' Portia or Porcia, the wife of Marcus Brutus, is mentioned in Plutarch, *Lives*, vol. VI: *Brutus*, XIII. 2–6, LCL 98, where she is reported to have inflicted a knife wound in her own thigh to share her husband's suffering. See also *Brutus*, LII. 4. Finally, the mother of the Maccabees refers to a mother whose seven sons were martyred for their faith in 117 BC and whose story is told in the apocryphal books known as II Maccabees (Ch. 6:18–8:41). They gained fame in the Christian tradition through the homilies of Saint John Chrysostom, *In sanctos Maccabaeos et in matrem eorum*, PG, 50: 617–24; *Homilies on the Maccabees*, in *St. John Chrysostom: The Cult of the Saints*, trans. W. Mayer (New York: Saint Vladimir's Seminary Press, 2006).

in faith, which includes all the principal virtues, than in strength in all its manifestations? Paterculus tells us that, when the Romans were proscribing men, the fidelity of children was non-existent, that of freed slaves was slight, and that of women was very great.[55]

To continue with my list of testimonies from the saints: if Saint Paul excludes women from ecclesiastical ministry and commands them to be silent in church, it is obvious that this is not because of any contempt on his part. It is rather that, since they are more beautiful and graceful than men, he was afraid that they might arouse temptations in others during the open and public displays in which they would participate while preaching and ministering. I claim that contempt is obviously out of the question here, because this apostle speaks of Thesbe as his assistant in the work of Our Lord;[56] besides, Saint Thecla and Saint Appia were included among his cherished children and disciples.[57] I shall omit mentioning the great respect that Saint Peter had for Saint Petronilla, or adding that Mary Magdalene is named in the Church as equal to the apostles (the phrase used in Latin is 'par apostolis'), among other places in the calendar of the Greek Church that was published by Génébrard.[58] Indeed the Church and the apostles themselves excused her from the rule of silence, since she preached for thirty years in the grotto of Marseilles, as reported by the whole of Provence.[59] If anyone rejects this testimony about Mary Magdalene, we will ask them what else the Sibyls were doing, if they were not preaching to the whole universe, by

---

[55] Velleius Paterculus (c.19 BC–31 AD), *Compendium of Roman History*, LCL 152, II. 67: 'One thing, however, demands comment, that towards the proscribed their wives showed the greatest loyalty, their freedmen not a little, their slaves some, their sons none.'

[56] Gournay probably meant Phoebe, whom Paul recommends in Rom. 16:1–2 as a deaconess in the church.

[57] Saint Francis de Sales (1567–1622) refers to Saints Thecla and Appia as being guided by Saint Paul, in the Preface to his *Introduction to the Devout Life*, trans. M. Day (London: Burns & Oates, 1956), 3.

[58] Petronilla was a first-century martyr and, according to a later legend, was the daughter of Saint Peter. Her remains were transferred to Saint Peter's Basilica during its reconstruction in the sixteenth century. Gilbert Génébrard (1535–97), a Benedictine monk and later bishop of Aix, translated a number of Greek and Latin books. He includes *Maria Magdalena* among the saints in the Greek Calendar (22 July), in *Psalterium Davidis Graecolatin.m cui ad fidem vulgatae et multorum exemplarium restituto, Calendarium Hebraeum, Syrum, Graecum, et Latinum, cum Genebrardi argumentis accessit* (Paris: Oliver de Varennes, 1605).

[59] There were many inconsistent traditions about where Mary Magdalene died or was buried; one tradition suggested that she spent thirty years doing penance and preaching at the grotto of Sainte Baume (the Holy Balm) near Marseille. See Susan Haskins, *Mary Magdalen: Myth and Metaphor* (London: Harper Collins, 1993).

divine inspiration, about the future arrival of Jesus Christ?[60] They would then have to tell us if it is possible to deny the preaching of Saint Catherine of Siena, about which the good and saintly bishop of Geneva has recently informed me.[61]

Finally, all nations used to admit women and men without distinction to the priesthood, and Christians are required to believe that women are at least capable of administering the sacrament of baptism.[62] But how can it be just to deny them a faculty for administering the other sacraments if they are justly granted the capacity to administer baptism? If one says that the early Fathers of the Church were forced to adopt this practice, despite their own convictions, by the needs of young children who were dying without baptism, it is certain that they would never have believed that necessity could excuse them from prevarication to such an extent that they would grant permission to violate and profane the administration of a sacrament. Consequently, it is clear that, by conceding to women this faculty for administering baptism, they considered them worthy of that office, and that they forbade them to administer the other sacraments simply to maintain the scope of men's authority for all time, either because they themselves were male or, rightly or wrongly, in order to maintain peace between the two sexes by the incapacity and repression of one of them.

Saint Jerome certainly wrote wisely in his *Letters* that, in matters pertaining to the service of God, one should take account of what is spiritual and of the church's teaching, and not of the sex of the minister.[63] It is even more reasonable to generalize that opinion, and to allow women access to all

---

[60] Sibyls were women who claimed to have the power of prophecy; Saint Jerome, *Against Jovinianus*, 1.41, reported that 'there were ten [Sibyls] whose ornament was virginity, and divination the reward of their virginity' (NPNF, 6: 379*b*).

[61] Saint Francis de Sales, who had died in 1622 as this book was being written, had recommended to Gournay that she read the writings of Saint Catherine of Siena (1347–1380). There were many French and Latin translations available of Catherine of Siena's works, including *La Doctrine spirituelle, escrite par forme de dialogue de l'excellente vierge S. Catherine de Siene* (Paris: R. Chaudière, 1602).

[62] The administration of the sacraments (except for baptism) was reserved to priests in those Christian churches that distinguished ordained priests from lay members. Baptism was an exception, insofar as any Christian could baptize a child in case of necessity, for example, if a child was in danger of dying without being baptized because no ordained minister was available. The belief that baptism was necessary for salvation was disputed by Christian churches following the Council of Trent; *Decrees*, I, 665–7, 685–6.

[63] Saint Jerome expressed sentiments like that in various letters. For example, in letter 127, §5, he wrote: 'we judge of people's virtue not by their sex but by their character' (NPNF, VI, 255a).

sciences and all the most excellent and worthwhile activities or, in a word, to those that are classified as the best. That would also be consistent with the intentions of that same Saint who, in all his writings, honoured and very strongly recommended women, to such an extent that he dedicated to the virgin Eustochium his commentaries on Ezekiel, despite the fact that priests were forbidden to study this prophet before the age of thirty.[64] Whoever reads what Saint Gregory also wrote about his sister will not find that he is any less favourable to women than Saint Jerome.[65]

I was reading the other day a quibbler[66] who was ranting against the authority that protestants commonly attribute to the alleged inability of women to read the Scriptures, in which I found that he had the best reason in the world if he had applied the same exclusion to the inability of men in respect of such a common permission—an inability, however, that he was unable to notice because men have the honour of wearing a beard like him. Furthermore, Saint John, the eagle and most cherished of the evangelists,[67] did not despise women, any more than Saint Peter and Saint Paul, or more than the three Fathers of the church (Saint Basil, Saint Jerome, and Saint Gregory), because he addresses his epistles especially to them. That does not include an infinite number of other saints or Fathers of the Church, who adopt the same view in their writings.

As regards Judith's achievement, I would not dare to mention it if it were unique—in other words, if it depended only on the action and will of the agent involved—no more than I speak of other similar deeds [by women], although there are very many of them and they are as heroic in every way as those that crown the most illustrious men.[68] I do not record private actions, for fear that they might seem to be mere ebullient results of personal

---

[64]   The Prologue to *Commentariorum in Hiezechielem libri xiv*, CCSL, vol. 75 (1964), 3.

[65]   Allusion to Saint Gorgonia, sister of Saint Gregory of Nazianzus (329–390), who composed a 'Funeral Oration on his Sister Gorgonia' (NPNF,VII, 238–45).

[66]   This comment was added in the 1626 edition. It may refer to the Jesuit, François Garasse, *La doctrine curieuse des beaux esprits de ce temps, ou pretendus tels* (Paris: Sebastien Chappelet, 1623), which claimed that 'women and girls, no matter how learned they may be, should not read the books of Scripture as they wish and without skill' (p. 498). His reason why 'it is neither appropriate nor permissible for women and girls to read the Bible is because of the difficulty of the Scriptures or ... the depth of the mysteries' they contain (p. 499).

[67]   Saint John, the author of one of the four gospels, was often symbolized as an eagle.

[68]   Judith, 10–13, reports the story of how, when Holofernes was laying siege to the Jewish city of Bethulia, Judith persuaded him to become inebriated; when he fell asleep, she decapitated him and thereby delivered her people from certain defeat.

energy rather than general advantages and endowments of the female sex. However, the accomplishment of Judith deserves to be mentioned here, because it is very true that her plan appears to have been an inspired favour and a gift of God's special grace to women rather than a purely human and voluntary event. It emerged in the heart of a young lady among so many pusillanimous men, at a time when it was so much needed and involved a very challenging task, the purpose of which was the salvation of a people and a city that was faithful to God. The action of the maid of Orleans [Joan of Arc] seems to have been similar, and was accompanied by many similar circumstances; it had a greater impact, however, because the circumstances in this case extended to the salvation of a great kingdom and its prince:

> This illustrious Amazon, instructed with the help of Mars
> Mows down squadrons of troops and braves dangers
> Wearing a hard breastplate on her round breast
> Whose red nipple sparkles with graces.
> To crown her head with glory and laurels
> She, a virgin, dares to confront the most famous warriors.[69]

Let us add that Mary Magdalene was the only one to whom the Redeemer said the following words and promised this magnificent favour: 'They will talk about you in every place where the gospel is preached.'[70] Besides, Jesus Christ declared his most joyful and glorious resurrection in the first instance to ladies, so as to make them apostles of the original apostles (according to the famous saying of Saint Jerome in the *Prologue to the Prophet Zephaniah*)[71] and, as we know, with a definite mission: 'Go', he said to this lady, 'and relate what you have seen to the Apostles and to Peter.'[72] One should notice, in this context, that on the occasion of his circumcision he revealed his spiritual rebirth at the same time and in the same way to women as to men: in the person of

---

[69] This is Gournay's adaptation of lines from the *Aeneid* (see note 51 above), in which Joan of Arc is cast in the role of an amazon. Gournay had done a number of translations of various books of the *Aeneid*.

[70] Matt. 26:13: 'Wheresoever this gospel shall be preached in the whole world, that also which she hath done shall be told for a memory of her.'

[71] Saint Jerome, *Commentariorum in Sophoniam Prophetam: Prologus*, CCSL. vol. 76A (1970), 655, where he refers to the women to whom the risen Christ appeared as 'apostolae apostolorum' [female apostles of the apostles].

[72] Mk. 16:7: 'But go, tell his disciples and Peter that he goeth before you into Galilee. There you shall see him, as he told you.'

Anna, the daughter of Phanuel, who was mentioned above and who recognized him by means of her prophetic gift; to the venerable old man, Saint Simeon; and, before them, to Saint Elizabeth when he was still enveloped in the secrecy of the virgin's womb.[73] That birth, moreover, was predicted among the gentiles only by the Sibyls that I mentioned above, which was a superlative privilege for the female sex. How greatly were women also honoured by the dream that occurred in Pilate's house, which was experienced by one woman in preference to all men and on such a significant occasion?[74]

If men boast that Jesus Christ was born a man, one can only reply that the demands of propriety required it. He could not have avoided scandal if he had been born a woman and, as a young person, had mingled with the crowds at all times of the day and night in order to convert, support, and save the human race, especially when facing the malice of the Jews.[75] If, however, anyone is so foolish as to imagine that God is masculine or feminine (even though his name sounds as if it were masculine), or that he had to choose one sex rather than the other to honour and exalt the Incarnation of his Son, they show clearly that they are as incompetent in philosophy as they are in theology.

On the other hand, the advantage that men enjoy by the fact of God's Incarnation in their sex—if they can draw any advantage from it, given what was just said about the necessity involved—is balanced by his very precious conception in a woman's body, by the unqualified perfection of that woman, who was the only one called perfect among all purely human creatures since the fall of our first parents, and by her assumption into heaven, which is also unique among human beings.[76] Besides, one could

---

[73] Lk. 2:25–38 tells of the encounter of Jesus Christ, on the day of his circumcision, with Anna and Simeon; Lk. 1: 41–2 relates the story of Mary the mother of Jesus meeting her cousin, Elizabeth, when both women were pregnant, and Elizabeth's foetus moving in her womb when greeted by her pregnant cousin.

[74] Matt. 27: 19, where the wife of Pilate dreamed about the baneful consequences of the conviction of Jesus: 'And as he [Pilate] was sitting in the place of judgment, his wife sent to him, saying: Have thou nothing to do with that just man; for I have suffered many things this day in a dream because of him.'

[75] Gournay had applied a similar argument to justify Saint Paul's preaching, in the 1594 edn. of *The Promenade of M. de Montaigne*, GO, II, 1358, note 9.

[76] According to traditional Christian theology, Jesus Christ was both man and God, and therefore not 'purely human;' hence the unique status attributed to his mother. Although the doctrine that Mary was assumed bodily into heaven after her death was not promulgated as a defined teaching of the Catholic Church until 1950, it had been widely accepted as a theologically sound doctrine for many centuries prior to that.

perhaps say that her humanity is superior to that of Jesus Christ, because he did not need his humanity for his passion, resurrection, and the redemption of human beings, which were his characteristic responsibilities, whereas her sex was necessary for her maternity, which was also her exclusive responsibility.

Finally, if the Scriptures declared that the husband is the head of his wife,[77] it would be the greatest folly for men to understand that as an entitlement to dignity. For, given the examples, authorities, and arguments cited in this discourse, by which the equality of God's graces and favours to both sexes is proved—let us even say the unity of the sexes—and given the fact that God says: 'The two shall be one' and then announces: 'A man shall leave his father and mother to give himself to his wife',[78] it seems as if that declaration of the gospel[79] [about the headship of the man] was made only because of the explicit need to foster peace within marriages. This need for peace would require undoubtedly one of the conjugal partners to yield to the other, because the common frailty of human minds would not allow agreement to emerge merely from rational discussions, as it should have done in a fair balance of reciprocal authority, nor would the superiority of man's strength have allowed submission on his part.

However true it may be, as some maintain, that this submission was imposed on women as punishment for the sin of eating the apple, it is still a long way from showing the claimed superior dignity of men. If one believed that Scripture commanded women to yield to men, as if it were unworthy on their part to oppose them, look at the absurdity of what that would imply: woman would find herself worthy of being made in the image of the Creator, of benefiting from the most holy Eucharist and the mysteries of redemption and of paradise, and of the vision—indeed, the possession—of God, but not worthy of possessing the advantages or privileges of man.

Would that not be equivalent to declaring that man is more precious and more exalted than all these things and, therefore, to committing the most serious blasphemy?

---

[77] Ephesians 5: 21–22: 'Let women be subject to their husbands, as to the Lord. Because the husband is the head of the wife, as Christ is the head of the Church.' See also I Cor. 11: 3, Gen. 3: 16.

[78] Gen. 2: 24: 'Wherefore a man shall leave father and mother, and shall cleave to his wife: and they shall be two in one flesh.'

[79] Technically, this injunction is found in a letter of Saint Paul rather than in one of the four gospels.

The Ladies' Complaint[80]

Blessed are you, reader, if you do not belong to the sex of those who are precluded from all blessings and are deprived of their freedom, and who are even deprived of almost all virtues by being excluded from public duties, offices, and functions—in a word, if you are not deprived of the power by the moderate exercise of which most virtues are acquired, so that ignorance, slavery, and the capacity to play the fool are established as women's only happiness (if they like that game) and as their supreme and only virtues.[81] Blessed are you, a second time, who can be wise without guilt, since your masculinity allows you—to the same extent that all these things are forbidden to women—every well-meaning action, every noble judgement, and every expression of exquisite speculation. But, while remaining silent temporarily about the other complaints of our sex, I ask you: how unjust is the way in which women are usually treated in conversations, insofar as they are included in them at all? I am so little (or, more accurately, so greatly) satisfied with my own situation that I am not afraid to admit that I know this from my own personal experience. If women possessed the reasoning and thoughts of Carneades,[82] there is no man, no matter how puny he may be, who would not put them in their place with the approval of most of their company when, with merely a smile or a slight nod of the head, his silent eloquence would communicate: 'It's only a woman speaking.'

---

[80] *La Grief des dames* (Paris: Jean Libert, 1626). See Note on the Texts and Translations, and note 2 above about the term *dame* in French.

[81] This sentence has sarcastic connotations of the paradoxical beatitudes in Matt. 5: 3–10; e.g. 'Blessed are the poor in spirit: for theirs is the kingdom of heaven.' Those who are deprived of all goods (*biens*) are described as 'blessed' (*bienheureux*).

[82] Carneades (214–129/8 BC), born in Cyrene (North Africa) went to Athens and became head of the academy founded by Plato. He was renowned for his skill in argument. Cf. *Essais*, I: 26, 164C; *Essays*, 'On Educating Children,' 184: 'And how many men have I known in my time made as stupid as beasts by an indiscreet hunger for knowledge! Carneades was turned so mad by it that he could not find time to tend to his hair or his nails.'

Such a man rejects objections of every kind that women could make against the decrees of his judgement, no matter how discreetly they are made, as merely bitter prickliness or at least as stubbornness, either because he does not believe that they could strike his precious head with any response apart from that of bitterness or obstinacy, or because he feels in the depths of his heart that he is poorly prepared for combat and has to pretend that it is a trivial quarrel in order to avoid the blows that might strike him. Is that not too stupid a strategy to rely on, namely, to avoid engagement with certain minds that one may find difficult to defeat by reasoning?

Another man who is stopped in his tracks by his own feebleness and pretends that he would not wish to disturb anyone who dresses like us will be declared both victorious and courteous at the same time. Another still, despite accepting that a woman is capable of participating in a debate, thinks that his sense of propriety prevents him from engaging in a fair contest with a female mind, because he borrows his understanding of propriety from what is commonly believed—which is to despise women in this respect. When all is said and done, there is a big difference between leading some common person by the nose and being vain about the fact that they lead us by the nose!

Let us continue. This vulgar man, uttering many silly remarks, will always win the contest either because he has a beard or displays a proud simulated ability that he and his companions measure according to what is fashionable or useful, without realizing that his silly remarks occur to him quite often because he is more of a buffoon or flatterer than his companions, or because they result from cowardly submission, some other vice, or from the good grace and favour of someone who would not grant a place in their affections or their company to people who are more capable than himself.

The first kind of man mentioned above will be struck, because he lacks the intelligence required to recognize a blow delivered by a female hand. The second one mentioned recognizes the blow and feels it; then, in order to evade it, he turns the discourse into either a joke or a whirlwind of incessant cackling. Alternatively, he unravels it and diverts it in some other direction, and begins to spew out pedantically many learned things that no one asked him about or, by means of this ostentation, confuses and complicates the discussion with logical tricks while believing that flashes of learning, if scattered willy-nilly in every direction, will be enough to confuse his opponent.

These people know that, by acting in that way, it is easy to deceive bystanders who cannot decide if such displays of gallantry amount to victory or defeat, since they can very rarely judge the structure and content of a conversation and the relative strength of those engaged in it. They are also very seldom capable of not succumbing to the effect of the pseudo-science that presumptuous vanity spews out as if it were an exercise in reciting one's homework for school. Thus, to win the argument, it is enough for these men to dodge the challenge, and their gain in glory is proportionate to their wish to avoid the effort involved in a genuine contest. Let these few words suffice about conversation, insofar as the participation of ladies is concerned; for, in relation to the art of conversation in general and its defects and perfections, the *Essays* provide an excellent treatment of that.[83]

Let us notice, in this discourse, that it is not only those who are uneducated who stumble at this hurdle against the female sex. Even among those, living or dead, who have acquired a reputation for learning in our own day—sometimes, I would say, while clothed in official robes—there are some who have been known to despise completely the writings of women without deigning to take the trouble to read them and get acquainted with their content, without accepting any advice or suggestions they might find in such readings and, above all, without wishing to know if they themselves could produce something that all kinds of women would find worth reading. That makes me suspect that, even when they read men's writings, they perceive the shape of their authors' beards better than the structure of their arguments.

These expressions of contempt from teachers with moustaches are truly very convenient, according to popular opinion, for highlighting the lustre of their wisdom because, if a man is to win the esteem of the common people—that many-headed monster—especially at the Court, all he needs to do is despise one person after another and to swear that, in his own estimation, he is the best in the world,[84] just like that unfortunate woman who thought she could make herself a model of beauty by going about the streets of Paris, crying out with her hands on her hips: 'Come and see how beautiful I am.'

I would wish, however, in keeping with the demands of charity, that these people would add only one more mark of subtlety to the one just mentioned, by showing us that their intellectual ability always surpasses that of the female sex, when they are compared one to one, or alternatively— as a second best option—that it is equal to that of their neighbours, even those neighbours, I say, who are less than outstanding. As a result, among

[83] *Essais*, III: 8, 922B; *Essays*, 'On the Art of Conversation', 1045: 'To my taste the most fruitful and most natural exercise of our minds is conversation. I find the practice of it the most delightful activity in our lives.'

[84] *Essais*, II: 36, 756A; *Essays*, 'On the most excellent men', 855–6: 'to be the first among the Greeks is to be easily the best in the world.'

the lists of those of their ilk who dare to write, we would not read appalling translations when they dabble in translating some worthwhile author, or feeble and infantile ideas if they get involved in lecturing. We would avoid frequent contradictions, innumerable lapses, and a judgement that is blind to choice and to the succession of things, in works whose only seasoning is a light linguistic dressing on top of stolen material, like whipped egg whites.

In this context, I stumbled the other day on a prefatory letter by a well-known person among those who claim never to bother reading anything that is written by a woman. Good God! What gems, what glory, what oriental treasure, what splendour, what a gift from Palestine recovered from a hundred leagues beyond Mount Lebanon! Good God! What crawl-marks of flies, masquerading as phoenixes in the opinion of their authors! How far removed from genuine stylistic embellishments are those who look for them in excessive and ostentatious verbosity, especially in prose! 'Those to whom nature has given a skinny body,' according to a man of great merit, 'pad it out with stuffing; and those whose imaginations conceive of dry or insignificant material expand them with words.'[85] Besides, what a shame that France evaluates the merit of writers with such defective vision and dubious criteria that it has bestowed a reputation for excellent writing on an author, such as the author of this letter, who has never had any quality to recommend him other than a cosmetic camouflage, assisted by a bit of scholastic learning. I am inclined not to name him out of respect for the dead.[86]

Finally, to return to the charitable attitude of wishing my neighbour well, I would also hope that any member of that swarm of writers or intellectuals, who despise the unfortunate and much criticized female sex, would cease using the services of printing companies and thereby at least leave us in doubt about whether or not they are capable of writing a book. For they show that they are incapable of doing so when they enhance their own writings by exploiting the labour of others—enhancing them, I say, in matters of detail and sometimes even in their totality, so that the respectable man whom the *Essays* mocked for the same vice, when their author was still alive, will not end up as the only example of this practice.[87]

[85] This is a loose quotation from *Essais*, I: 26, 157C; *Essays*, 'On Educating Children', 176: 'People whose bodies are too thin pad them out: those whose matter is too slender pad it out too, with words.'

[86] The anonymous author remains unidentified.

[87] In the *Essais* I: 26, 151B: *Essays*, 'On Educating Children', 170, Montaigne wrote about meeting, in Pisa, 'a decent man who is such an Aristotelian that the most basic of his doctrines is that the touchstone and the measuring-scale of all sound ideas and of each and every truth

If I deigned to bother defending ladies against these learned men, I would have found supporters quickly in Socrates, Plato, Plutarch, Seneca, Antisthenes, or also in Saint Basil, Saint Jerome, and such minds, whom they so freely deny and reject when they establish a distinction—especially a universal distinction—between the merits and capacities of the two sexes.[88] But they are adequately conquered and penalized for displaying their stupidity when they refute the particular by the general[89]—if one could assume that, in general, the ability of women is inferior. They also display their stupidity in the audacity of despising the judgement of such famous people as those mentioned above (apart from some modern authors), and the eternal decree of God Himself, who produced no more than a single creation of two sexes and who, moreover, honours women in His sacred history with all the gifts and graces that he shares with men, as I have argued more fully in the *Equality of Men and Women*.

Besides, men like that should surely be willing to be informed that we do not know if they are capable of defeating women by the sovereign law of their own arbitrary choice, which condemns women and restricts them to inadequacy, or whether they can achieve any glory in their attempts to erase women by their scorn, from which they draw their weapons with such self-satisfaction. But we know some women who would never seek glory in something as insignificant as erasing men, either in the same way [as men behave, by scorn] or by comparing themselves with men. Furthermore, they will know that, by relying on the same subtlety with which men try to scorn women without listening to them or reading their writings, women in contrast will aim to win the battle because they have heard what men have said and will have read what they wrote. They will also manage to remember a dangerous maxim that has a very good pedigree: that only the most inept are content with their own ability while glancing over their shoulder at the ability of others, and that ignorance is the mother of presumption.

---

lie in their conformity with the teachings of Aristotle, outside of which all is inane and chimerical.' The author in question was Girolamo Borro, who published on various topics in Aristotelian natural philosophy, including the tides and gravity: *Del flusso e reflusso del mare & dell'inondatione del Nilo* (Florence, 1577), and *De motu gravium et levium* (Florence, 1575).

[88] For Antisthenes, see note 27 above.

[89] Gournay assumes the standard epistemic account of the relation between universal and particular knowledge-claims—that we know the truth-value of propositions about individuals first, by experience, and that universal propositions are known only by induction from particular cases. It would be a fundamental mistake, therefore, to assume that we know the truth of universal claims about women independently, and to use those universal claims to refute the very evidence on which they are based, namely, evidence about particulars.

Anna Maria van Schurman

A Dissertation on the Natural Capacity of Women for Study and Learning[1]

A moral question: is the study of letters appropriate for a Christian woman?[2]
We shall try to defend an affirmative answer. We preface the discussion
with the following presuppositions, first in relation to the subject, and
then also concerning the predicate.[3]

The words used in the subject [of the thesis] are free of all ambiguity
because, when I say 'a Christian woman', I mean someone who both professes to be a Christian and is actually such in practice.

The words used in the predicate [of the thesis] are, first, the 'study of
letters'. 'Study', I claim, is understood here (if I omit its other meanings)
as a diligent and eager application of the mind. By the word 'letters' we
understand a knowledge of languages, history, and all disciplines—both
the higher disciplines that are called faculties, and the lower ones that are
called philosophical sciences.[4] The only discipline that we do not include

---

[1] *Dissertatio de Ingenii muliebris ad Doctrinam, & meliores Litteras aptitudine*
(Leiden: Elsevier, 1641).

[2] Van Schurman calls this, in Latin, a '*problema practicum*'. Since scholastic Latin distinguished
between theoretical and practical disciplines and identified the latter with ethics and politics,
it seems appropriate to translate it as a question of morals or what is in keeping with appropriate standards for a Christian woman. The study in question is identified in Latin as '*studium
Litterarum*'; *Litterae* is wider in scope than literature in the modern sense or the liberal arts, and
includes all the subjects that were available in various academies, colleges or schools. For that
reason I have adopted the somewhat obsolete term 'letters' to include the extensive range of
subjects intended by the author.

[3] 'Christian woman' appears as the subject of the thesis in Latin throughout the following
arguments, and 'the study of letters is appropriate' appears as the predicate.

[4] For the translation of the Latin term '*scientia*', see Note on the Texts and Translations.

is scriptural theology, properly so-called, because we think it is beyond dispute that scriptural theology is appropriate for all Christians.

Secondly, I use the word 'appropriate', which is equivalent to asking whether it is necessary, fitting, and proper. Having thus defined the words, we need to distinguish the realities to which they apply.

Among women, some are naturally talented while others, indeed, are less so; again, some are poor and others are wealthier. Finally, some are more involved in household cares or duties, while others are less so.

The 'study of letters' is divided into either universal studies, that is, when we work at all disciplines simultaneously, or particular studies, when we apply some faculty to learn a single language or a particular science.

We shall therefore limit the scope of the thesis as follows. First, in relation to the subject: we shall assume that the woman to whom the thesis refers is endowed with at least a mediocre natural intelligence, and that she is not absolutely inept at learning.[a] Secondly, we assume that she is instructed by using whatever means are necessary, and that the resources of her household are not so meagre that she is completely obstructed [in her attempts to study]. I introduce this exception because few women are fortunate enough to have parents who are willing or able to provide them with that education themselves, and it is impossible to hire tutors in this region without incurring significant expenses.[5]

Thirdly, we assume that the time and resources available to her are such that there are some periods when she is free from any general or special vocation, which undoubtedly includes devotional exercises and her household duties. There are two factors, each of which would partly facilitate that: if she enjoyed immunity and freedom from cares and duties in her childhood years and then, when she is older, if she were celibate or else had

---

[a] Concerning the education of girls who, in wealthy families, are taught partly at home and partly outside the home, consult Titus Livius, *Ab urbe condita*, Book 3, section 3.44 ff.; Pliny, *Letters*, Bk. I, letter 16, Bk. III, letter 3, Bk. IV, letter 19; St Athanasius, *Contra Gentes and De Incarnatione*, ed. and trans. R. W. Thomson (Oxford: Clarendon Press, 1971), 163, 275–6; Plutarch, *The Education of Children*, LCL 197, 5–69; Emperor Gordianus, *Codex* of Justinian, II, 18, 15, '*De negotiis gestis*'; Magnus Aurelius Cassiodorus Senator, *Variarum librii XII*, ed. with notes by Gulielmus Fornerius (Lyon: J. Chouët, 1595), Bk. IX, letter xxiii, 540–42, and *Institutes of Divine and Secular Learning*, trans. James W. Halporn (Liverpool: University of Liverpool Press, 2004).

[5] In her autobiography, *Eukleria* (1673), van Schurman acknowledges that her parents had hired a tutor to educate her at home because they lived in the country (Chap. II §2).

the support of servants who usually free more wealthy women to a great extent from domestic duties.

Fourthly, her objective will not be vainglory and boasting, or any useless curiosity. Her aim will rather be, apart from the general objective of God's glory and the salvation of her soul, to become better and happier, and to educate and guide her family (if that is one of her duties) and benefit all women as much as possible.

Limitations on the scope of the predicate

I limit 'the study of letters' as follows: I consider that all genuine disciplines or, as it is called, the whole *encyclopaedia*,[6] would be completely appropriate for a Christian woman (as a proper and universally applicable good or enhancement of a human being). This study should be such, however, that it corresponds to the dignity and nature of each science or art, and to the ability and resources of each girl or woman, and the individual disciplines to be learned should be presented in an appropriate order, place, and time and be related to each other properly. The sciences or arts that are most closely related to sacred Scripture and the moral virtues, and that are most helpful to them, should be considered most important. We think that grammar, logic, and rhetoric fall into that category, although logic should be included among the first on our list, since many people have rightly thought of it as the key to all sciences. Next in order are physics, metaphysics, and history, etc., and knowledge of languages, especially Hebrew and Greek, all of which can help us achieve a more complete and better understanding of sacred Scripture (to say nothing of other authors). Other subjects, such as mathematics (which also includes music), poetry, etc., painting, and similar liberal arts may be pursued as recreations or as enhancements of one's natural abilities. Finally, I do not recommend as strongly those studies that pertain to the practice of law, to military affairs, or to the art of public speaking in a temple, court, or academy, because they are less appropriate or necessary.[7]

---

[6] Van Schurman uses this Greek term a number of times, to refer to a general education which precedes professional or higher studies.

[7] This may reflect van Schurman's reading of Vives when she corresponded with Rivet (see below, p. 108). '"But in what kind of literature should a woman be versed?" someone may ask, "and in what reading will she immerse herself?"...the study of wisdom, which forms morals in the way of virtue, the study of wisdom, which teaches the best and holiest way of life. I am not at all concerned with eloquence. A woman has no need of that; she needs rectitude and wisdom ... in the education of a woman the principal and, I might also say, the only concern should be the preservation of chastity.' *The Education of a Christian Woman*, trans. Charles Fantazzi (Chicago: University of Chicago Press, 2000), 71.

However, we do not concede at all that a woman should be excluded from a scholastic or, as it is called, a theoretical knowledge of those things, especially the very noble discipline of politics.

We qualify the phrase that a study of letters is 'appropriate' or 'expedient' as follows. It is not as if such study were specifically required or needed, or as if it were literally necessary, for eternal salvation, or indeed as if it were a good that contributes to the very essence of blessedness in this life. Study is rather an occupation or means that could contribute most to the integrity of one's life and thereby lead us much more easily to the love of God and to eternal salvation by contemplating very beautiful things.

Our thesis, therefore, is the following: the study of letters is appropriate for a Christian woman. To confirm this, we offer the following arguments, the first of which are concerned with the subject [of the thesis], while the subsequent ones concern the predicate [of the thesis].

1) An Argument derived from the Subject of the Thesis

All arts and sciences are suitable for anyone who is endowed by nature with the principles of all arts and sciences, or with a capacity to acquire those principles. But women are endowed by nature with the principles of all arts and sciences or with a capacity to acquire them. Therefore, all arts and sciences are suitable for women.

The proposition [i.e. the major premise] is proved because, if principles or a capacity to acquire principles are appropriate for someone, then knowledge of the conclusions that follow naturally from those principles is also appropriate.

The assumption [about women's ability] may be proved both by what is characteristic of the form of this subject—i.e. human reason[8]—and also by its acts or effects, since it is obvious that women in fact learn various arts and sciences, and acts cannot occur without the corresponding principles.[9]

---

[8] According to the scholastic theory of matter and form, inherited from Aristotle, the defining feature (or form) of human beings is the possession of reason.

[9] Alludes to the scholastic axiom '*agere sequitur esse*' (that actions follow from the nature of the agent); thus the act of knowing on the part of (at least some) women presupposes that their natures are such that they are capable of knowing.

2) An Argument based on the Subject of the Thesis

The arts and sciences are suitable for whoever has a natural desire for the sciences and arts. But women have a natural desire for the sciences and arts. Therefore,[10]

The justification of the major premise is obvious, since nature does nothing in vain. The minor premise is proved because whatever is innate in a whole species is also innate in its individual members. However, every human being (as the Philosopher stated clearly in *Metaphysics*: Book I, Chapter 2) has a natural desire to know.[11]

3) An Argument based on a characteristic or associated external feature

The contemplation and knowledge of sublime and heavenly things is appropriate for anyone whom God created with a sublime countenance that is raised towards heaven. But God created woman with a sublime countenance that looks up towards heaven. Therefore,

'While other animals look downwards at the earth, He gave a sublime countenance to human beings, etc.'[12]

4) Argument

The study of letters is most appropriate for whoever has the greatest need for a sound and enduring occupation. But a woman has the greatest need for a sound and enduring occupation. Therefore,

The consequent clause[13] in the major premise is proved because nothing other than study provides a comparable focus for all mental activities and, as the great Erasmus says, nothing so occupies all the affections of a girl as completely as study, to which she may flee at any time as if it were a refuge.[b]

---

[b] In his letter to Budé, in which he discussed the education of Thomas More's daughters. Erasmus to Guillaume Budé (1467–1540), in *The Correspondence of Erasmus* (Toronto and London: University of Toronto Press, 1988), vol. 8, 297: 'Scarcely any mortal man was not under the conviction that, for the female sex, education had nothing to offer in the way of either virtue or reputation. Nor was I myself in the old days completely free of this opinion, but More has quite put it out of my head. For two things in particular are perilous to a girl's virtue, idleness and improper amusements, and against both of these the love of literature is a protection.'

[10] Here and in subsequent syllogisms, van Schurman omits completing a sentence when it is obvious.

[11] The first sentence of the *Metaphysics* reads (980ª22): 'All men by nature desire to know' (AR II, 1552).

[12] Ovid, *Metamorphoses*, LCL 42: I, ll. 84–86: 'And, though all other animals are prone, and fix their gaze upon the earth, he gave to man an uplifted face and bade him stand erect and turn his eyes to heaven.'

[13] In the Latin text, the consequent clause is 'the study of letters is most appropriate.'

The minor premise is proved by this two-fold argument.

1. Whoever is most in danger of vanity because of the feebleness or fickleness of their native intelligence or temperament, and because of the innumerable attractions of the world, has the greatest need for a sound and enduring occupation. But women, because of the feebleness etc...Therefore,

The major premise of this argument, in turn, may be proved by the fact that opposites are best cured by their opposites, and because nothing resists vanity more effectively than a serious and enduring occupation.

We think that the minor premise is beyond dispute, because scarcely any virtue, however heroic, can overcome the temptations of youth and of the times that one lives in, unless it is applied to issues that are serious and significant.

2. The reasoning by which the assumption (or the minor premise of the fourth argument) is proved: whoever has plenty of free time has the greatest need for a sound and enduring occupation. But those women who have most [financial etc.] resources also have most free time. Therefore,

The consequent clause in the major premise here is also proved, first because free time of its very nature is tedious and therefore burdensome. Accordingly, St Gregory of Nazianzus rightly said that '*no work is the hardest work*'.[14] Secondly, because leisure gives rise to vices, for 'when human beings are doing nothing they learn to do evil.'[15]

5) Argument

The study of letters is appropriate for anyone who happens to enjoy a more tranquil and free life. But women generally enjoy a more tranquil and free life. Therefore, the study of letters is generally appropriate for women.

The justification for the major premise is obvious, for nothing is more conducive to study than tranquillity and freedom.

We prove the minor premise by this argument: whoever happens to have most free time and not to be involved in the distractions and burdens of

---

[14] St Gregory Nazianzen (329–390 AD), one of the Cappadocian Fathers of the Church who was involved in theological discussions of Arianism at the Council of Constantinople (381).

[15] This is a maxim attributed to Publilius Syrus, a first-century BC author, whose maxims were collected in various editions under the title *Sententiae*.

public life has a more tranquil and free life. But women, especially if they are celibate, happen to have more free time, etc. Therefore,

6) Argument

If the study of the principal sciences is appropriate for someone, then the study of instrumental or auxiliary sciences is also appropriate for them. But the study of the principal sciences is appropriate for a Christian woman. Therefore,

The consequent of the major premise is validly inferred, because if some objective is appropriate for someone, then the proper means by which they could more easily achieve that objective are also appropriate for them. But instrumental or auxiliary sciences are proper means. Therefore,

The minor premise is proved by the fact that study is appropriate for a Christian woman—that is, a diligent and serious meditation on the word of God, knowledge of God, and contemplation of his most beautiful works, which are equally relevant to all Christians.

The study of letters is appropriate for whoever ought to seek recreation at home, by themselves, rather than outside the home among other people. But women should seek recreation at home alone, rather than outside the home among other people. Therefore,

The major premise [of this supplementary argument] is very true, because studies have the advantage of being always accompanied by pleasure, even if those who are studying are not accompanied by anyone else. Thus, according to the Greek proverb, wise people are described as 'self-acting and speaking from their own experience.'

The justification of the minor premise could not be clearer, for the Apostle wishes women to be *keepers of the home* (Titus 2:5).[16] Besides, experience shows that many people doubt the faith, diligence, and even the modesty of women if their tongues, ears, and eyes are accustomed to wander more often and to focus on external delights.

7) Argument based on the nature of the Predicate or of Science

The sciences and arts are appropriate for anyone for whom, in general, every virtue is appropriate. But, in general, every virtue is appropriate for a woman. Therefore, the sciences and arts are appropriate for a woman.

---

[16] In Titus 2:4–5, St. Paul encouraged young women to be 'sober, to love their husbands, to love their children, [to be] discreet, chaste, keepers at home, good, obedient to their own husbands, that the word of God be not blasphemed.'

The major premise is apparent from the distinction between two types of virtue, intellectual and moral, within which—namely, the first—the Philosopher includes the sciences and arts.[17]

The minor premise does not require any justification, since virtue (as Seneca says) does not discriminate between different social classes or between the sexes.[18]

8) Argument based on the Objective of the Sciences

Whatever perfects and adorns the human intellect is appropriate for a Christian woman. But the sciences and arts perfect and adorn the human intellect. Therefore,

The major premise is justified because, in the case of all creatures, their own final and supreme perfection is appropriate for them and is something towards which they ought to strive with all their strength.

The minor premise is proved because the sciences and arts are habits by which the natural powers of the human intellect are perfected.[c]

9) Argument

Whatever contributes, by its nature, to stimulating in us a greater love of and reverence for God is appropriate for a Christian woman. But the sciences and arts, by their nature, contribute towards stimulating a greater love of and reverence for God. Therefore,

The truth of the major premise is clearer than light, because the most perfect love of God and the greatest reverence for Him are appropriate for all human beings, to such an extent that it is impossible to sin by excess in this respect.

The minor premise is proved by this argument: whatever reveals God and his works so that they are observed and known by us to a greater extent also contributes, by its nature, to stimulating in us a greater love of and

---

[c] When some good is added to another good (as the Philosopher says in the Topics), it makes a greater good; Aristotle, Topics, Book III, Chapter 3: 'Again, a thing is more desirable if, when added to a lesser thing, it makes the whole a greater good' (AR, 118[b]17).

[17] 'Virtue, then, is of two kinds: that of the intellect and that of character. Intellectual virtue owes its origin and development mainly to teaching, for which reason its attainment requires experience and time; virtue of character (ēthos) is a result of habituation (ethos), for which reason it has acquired its name through a small variation on "ethos"' (NE, 1103[a]5).

[18] On Anger, Bk. 3, §8: 'they [virtues] exert a good influence on all they are in contact with'; Consolation to Marcia, §7: 'They [the virtues] have been given their strength by nature, which draws no distinction between persons;' (S, 24, 60).

reverence for God. But the sciences and arts reveal God and his works, to be observed and known better by us. Therefore,

We prove the major premise of the subsequent auxiliary argument as follows: if something is genuinely most beautiful, best, and most perfect, then it is loved more and is considered worthy of reverence to the extent that it is better known. But God and all his works are the most beautiful, best, etc. Therefore,

The minor premise can also be proved by reference to the objective or effects of the sciences, none of which fails to contribute greatly towards an easier and more distinct knowledge of God and his works.

10) Argument

Whatever protects us against heresies and uncovers their traps is appropriate for a Christian woman. But the sciences, etc. Therefore,

The justification of the major premise is obvious, since no Christian should neglect their duty in relation to this common danger.

The minor premise is proved because a more sound philosophy is like a breastplate and (if I may use the words of Clement of Alexandria) it is like the protective fence of the Lord's vineyard or of the Saviour's teachings;[19] or—to use a simile that pleased Basil the Great—a sound philosophy, when combined with the gospel, resembles leaves that provide an ornament and protection for their own fruit.[20] Spurious or corrupt reason, by which heresies are best supported, is certainly refuted more easily by using right reason.

11) Argument

Whatever teaches prudence without any detriment to one's reputation and modesty is appropriate for a Christian woman. But the study of letters teaches prudence, without any detriment, etc. Therefore,

The major premise is generally accepted, since everyone knows that the honour of the female sex is very fragile and that there is almost nothing that it needs more than prudence. Besides, they know how difficult and how risky (as they say) it is to acquire prudence by relying only on one's own practice and experience.

---

[19] *The Stromata or Miscellanies,* Bk I, Ch. 20, ANF, vol. 2, 323: 'the Hellenic philosophy does not, by its approach, make the truth more powerful; but rendering powerless the assault of sophistry against it, and frustrating the treacherous plots laid against the truth, is said to be the proper "fence and wall of the vineyard".'

[20] St Basil the Great (*c.*330–379): *Homilies on the Hexaemeron,* Homily V, § 8, in *Saint Basil: Exegetical Homilies,* trans. A. C. Way, in *The Fathers of the Church,* vol. 46 (Washington, DC: Catholic University of America Press, 1963), 79.

The minor premise is proved, because the writings of learned men[21] provide not only outstanding precepts but also the most excellent models of virtue, and they lead us to virtue as if they held us by the hand.

12) Argument

Whatever is conducive to a genuine magnanimity of the soul is appropriate for a Christian woman. But the study of letters is conducive to a genuine magnanimity of the soul. Therefore,

I prove the major premise because, to the extent that someone is more inclined by nature to the vice of pusillanimity, they have a greater need for the opposite virtue. But a woman by her nature, etc...Therefore,

The minor premise is proved because science lifts up the human soul and dispels from things those shadowy appearances that are generally feared or ineffectively pursued.

13) Argument

Whatever fills the human mind with an exceptional and virtuous pleasure is appropriate for a Christian woman. But the study of letters fills the mind with an exceptional and virtuous pleasure. Therefore,

The rationale for the major premise is that nothing is more agreeable to human nature than an exceptional and virtuous pleasure, which represents in human beings an image, of some kind, of divine joy. That was described magnificently by Aristotle as follows (Ethics 7:13): 'Pleasure is something divine that is innate in mortal beings.'[22]

The minor premise is proved because no pleasure (except only the supernatural pleasure of Christians) is greater or more worthy of a noble mind than the pleasure that usually results from a study of letters; this can be established easily by examples and reasons.

14) An Argument from the Contrary

The study of letters is appropriate for anyone for whom ignorance or a lack of understanding is inappropriate. However, ignorance etc. is inappropriate for a Christian woman. Therefore,

---

[21] The text uses the exclusive term 'vir' in Latin to refer to men rather than to learned authors.
[22] Van Schurman quotes a Latin version of the Nicomachean Ethics: 'everything by nature has something divine in it' (NE, 1153ᵇ32).

The major premise is confirmed by this argument. Whatever, by its nature, causes not only error in the intellect but also vice in the will or in one's actions, is not appropriate for a Christian woman. But ignorance or a lack of understanding, by its nature, causes error, etc. Therefore,

The justification of the major premise in this argument is demonstrated, first in respect of error in the intellect, because ignorance or a lack of understanding in the intellect (which is said to be the eye of the soul)[d] is nothing other than a blindness and mental darkness that proves to be the cause of all error. Secondly, it is demonstrated in respect of vice in the will or in one's actions, because whatever by its nature makes people proud, uncivilized, etc. also causes vice in the will or in one's actions. But ignorance or a lack of understanding by its nature makes people proud, etc. Therefore,

The justification of the major premise here is obvious. The minor premise is proved because, to the extent that people know themselves less well, they are more pleased with themselves and despise others; and those who do not know the extent to which they do not know will think that their own condition is excellent. Then (to say something about being uncivilized) there is nothing more intractable than ignorance, which Erasmus acknowledges having experienced more than once.[23] And to refer to the opinion of the divine Plato: '*Human beings [as we are saying, are tame animals, but they] tend to become the most godlike and the tamest animals [only] if they obtain a proper education [and a fortunate nature]. But if they are not reared well or adequately, they tend to become the wildest of all animals that live on the earth*' (*Laws*, Book 6).[24] Besides, learning the noble arts faithfully refines one's moral character and prevents people from becoming uncivilized. Finally, one can show the danger of ignorance in relation to vice from the very nature of vice and virtue. Since every virtuous act requires so much *precision* to comply fully with the norm of right reason, even the slightest *lack of precision*, which arises spontaneously from ignorance, may be sufficient for an act to satisfy fully the conditions of a vice.[25]

I omit here, for the sake of brevity, examples and testimonials.

---

[d] Matt. 6:13: '*If the light that is in thee be darkness, how great is that darkness?*'

[23] Erasmus, *The Praise of Folly*, trans. J. H. Hudson (Princeton, NJ: Princeton University Press, 1941), 109.

[24] 766A; van Schurman omits some phrases from the original text, which are indicated in square brackets above.

[25] Cf. NE, 1106[b]29–35: 'Again, one can miss the mark in many ways... but one can get things right in only one way.' The second term used by van Schurman, *ataxia*, does not occur in Aristotle's text. Different versions of this principle were common in scholastic theology: that an act is morally right only if it satisfies all the relevant criteria for a good act, and that it becomes morally defective by failing to satisfy even one criterion.

A Refutation of Opponents

We think that the following should be mentioned at the outset, as items that are already known.

First, there are some opponents who, blinded by unknown prejudices, do not limit the scope of our thesis. Instead, they think it implies that there are no women who are less naturally gifted or whose resources are less adequate than others and, as a result, that what we have argued above is less applicable to them. There are others who seem not to acknowledge that study has any objective other than riches or empty fame, or as training for employment in some public office, which is a *fundamental* and rather shameful *falsehood*, as if it were a complete waste of time to philosophize '*in order to escape from ignorance.*'[e] Finally, there are those who at least do not deny that studies are appropriate for a woman, but they deny only that the higher sciences are appropriate for them. Perhaps they are distracted by jealousy or, undoubtedly, by fear that it may happen that '*many students are more accomplished than their teachers.*'[26] There is also the saying of the ancient poet: 'You youths display effeminate minds, while a heroic woman has the mind of a man.'[27]

The Thesis of Opponents

The study of letters is not appropriate for a Christian woman, unless perhaps she was motivated to study by some special divine impulse or instinct.[28]

1) An Argument [i.e. by opponents] based on the Subject

The study of letters is not appropriate for anyone whose natural ability is weaker. But a woman's natural ability is weaker. Therefore,

Opponents will prove the major premise because a reliable and strong natural ability is required for the study of letters, unless we wish to labour

---

[e] Aristotle, *Metaphysics*, Book I, Ch. 2: 'therefore since they (the earliest philosophers) philosophized in order to escape ignorance, evidently they were pursuing science in order to know, and not for any utilitarian end' (AR, 982ᵇ20).

[26] Quoted in the original language from a Greek proverb.

[27] Cicero quotes a slightly different version of this line from an unknown poet in *De Officiis*, Bk I, Ch. 18, §61: '*Vos enim iuvenes animum geritis muliebrem, illa virgo viri.*'

[28] This was one of the objections made by André Rivet; see p. 102–3 below.

in vain or to risk lapsing into *weakness in one's reasoning ability*.[29] They claim that the minor premise is widely accepted.

We reply to the major premise that, given what we said above about the scope of our thesis, those who are completely unsuited to studies (because their natural ability is limited) are exceptional cases, since we specified that a mediocre natural ability is the minimum required for that purpose. We also say that an outstanding natural ability is not always necessary for studies, because we also see that mediocre minds are included indiscriminately in the ranks of learned men.

I reply to the minor premise that it is not absolutely true but is true only in comparison with the male sex. For even if the natural ability of women were not comparable to that of the most excellent men (who are like '*eagles in the clouds*'),[30] nonetheless there are quite a number of women who, in fact, may benefit by being admitted to studies.

In contrast, we infer the opposite conclusion: the study of letters is most appropriate for those whose natural ability is less able. But a woman's natural ability is less able. Therefore,

We prove the major premise because the means and supports by which such deficiencies may be corrected are most suitable for those who are provided with fewer natural gifts. But studies of letters are those means and supports. Therefore,

2) Second Objection

If someone's mind is not inclined to study, then studies are not appropriate for that person. But the mind of a woman is not inclined to study. Therefore,

They prove the major premise because nothing should be done against the will of Minerva (as they claim).[31] They will prove the minor premise from custom alone, since women very rarely apply their minds to study.

We reply to the major premise, that it should have said: studies are not suitable for anyone whose mind is not inclined to study even when all appropriate means have been attempted. Otherwise, the consequent clause in the major is denied.

---

[29] Quoted from *Physics* 253ª33, where Aristotle argued that to claim that everything is at rest implies a defect in one's ability to reason.

[30] Quoted in Greek from Aristophanes, *Birds:* LCL 43, 987; it may also have been a proverb prior to its use by Aristophanes.

[31] Minerva was the Roman goddess of poetry, medicine, and wisdom.

We say, in reply to the minor premise, that it is impossible to draw any valid conclusion about our inclination to study before encouraging us to embark on studies by the best means and reasons available, and also before we have had any experience of how enjoyable they are. Meanwhile, we are not lacking examples that show that the opposite is true.

3) Third Objection

The study of letters is not appropriate for anyone who lacks the necessary means for studying letters. But women lack the necessary means, etc. Therefore,

There is no dispute about the major premise. Opponents try to prove the minor premise because there are no academies or colleges today in which women can study.[32] We deny this conclusion, however, because it would be sufficient [for our thesis] if women were taught at home under the direction of their parents or by a private tutor.

4) Fourth Objection

Those whose studies frustrate the characteristic objective of studies are not well suited to them. But the studies in which women engage frustrate the characteristic objective of study. Therefore,

The major premise can be proved, because the reason why we do anything that is undertaken freely is to achieve some objective. The proponents of this objection prove the minor premise by the fact that women are very rarely, if ever, appointed to public offices, whether they are political, ecclesiastical, academic, etc.

We reply to the major premise that women never frustrate the proper objective of speculative sciences. In the practical sciences, however (which we have just mentioned), although they do not realize their primary or public objective, they do achieve the secondary and, I would say, the more private objective of those sciences.

5) Fifth Objection

If a little knowledge is enough for someone to pursue their vocation, then neither the *encyclopaedia* nor the higher sciences are appropriate for them. But women need only a little knowledge to pursue their vocation, etc. Therefore,

---

[32] This was also one of Rivet's objections; see below p. 105.

Opponents prove the consequent of the major premise because it is not appropriate for anyone to do something that is superfluous or foreign to their vocation. They will prove the minor premise because they restrict a woman's vocation within very narrow boundaries, namely, those of her private or domestic life.

If we leave aside the major premise, we reply to the minor premise that the terms used are ambiguous. First, the term 'vocation': if they understand this word to mean the vocation of a private life in contrast with public offices, we say that, by the same reasoning, the *encyclopaedia* and the higher sciences should also be denied to all men who live a private life. However, the most authoritative opinion of Plutarch about all human beings individually, of whatever social status, is that '*a perfect human being must be able to perceive the things that are and to do the things that ought to be*'.[33]

If they understand the word 'vocation' to mean a special vocation that applies to family matters or household duties, we say that it does not in any way exclude the universal vocation that applies to all of us, in the first place, insofar as we are Christians or at least human beings. Thus I dare to assert that an unmarried woman can and ought to make time for this latter [i.e. universal vocation], insofar as she is usually very free from the obstacles of the former [i.e. household duties]. '*The unmarried woman careth for the things of the Lord*' (I Cor. 7: 34).

Secondly, the phrase 'is enough' is ambiguous. What we said above about qualifying the phrase 'is it appropriate?' (in respect of the necessity of studying letters), is sufficient to remove that ambiguity.

Our thesis, therefore, stands: that the study of letters is appropriate for a Christian woman.

Hence we draw the following conclusion: that women can and should be encouraged to embrace this kind of life by the best and strongest arguments, by the testimonies of the wise, and finally by the examples of illustrious women. This applies above all to those women who enjoy, more than others, the leisure and other means and supports [that are required] for the study of letters; and since it is helpful to imbue the mind with better studies even from infancy, we therefore think that parents should be the first to be encouraged and advised seriously about their duty.

---

[33] Pseudo-Plutarch, *Placita philosophorum*, 874F3: *Plutarch: Oeuvres morales*, trans. G. Lachenaud (Paris: Les Belles Lettres, 1993), vol. XII², 70.

Excerpts from the Correspondence[34]

Van Schurman to Rivet

To the most distinguished man and venerable father in Christ, Mr André Rivet, Doctor of Theology:

Reverend Sir and venerable father in Christ: Nothing could please me more than knowing the benevolent attitude with which you accepted the gift, however small, that my mediocre talents were able to give your granddaughter. If you decide to evaluate the gift in question on its own merits, it was small indeed. If, however, you consider my affection for her, to which I think you are fully entitled because of our long friendship, I think it would be impossible to donate anything better.

I received with great pleasure, as was appropriate, the books with which you wished to enhance my library. I was very pleased with that gift when I considered both the donor and also the subject matter, that is, the issue about which you have achieved your victory. What shall I send in reply? There is nothing immediately at hand with which I might compensate you, even though I would very much like to do so, unless it is possible for someone to have already repaid their debts simply by feeling gratitude. Besides, I do not consider as a smaller benefit the fact that you agree to offer your assistance by helping me in all my studies and resolving other more serious doubts. I certainly acknowledge your advice, as I should do, because where I do not understand something sufficiently I am in two minds and am forced, as it were, to hop along with one foot

---

34 *Opuscula Hebraea, Graeca, Gallica, Prosaica & Metrica* (Leiden: Elzevier, 1648).

in the air. I have desired your opinion avidly, however, for some time about a serious issue (something that is most important to the status and condition of young women), and I think that nothing would be more important or wonderful than if your opinion—almost like a rescript[35]—confirmed my own view. If however you do not agree, I will not feel ashamed to sound a retreat, once you have instructed me.

Nonetheless, you gave me an opportunity to doubt what you proposed as if it were a universally true proposition in the letter you previously sent me and in which, having praised me and my studies in your customary fashion, lovingly and respectfully, you wrote as follows: 'It may not be appropriate for many to choose this kind of life; it may be enough that some people, who are called to it by a special inspiration, become outstanding now and again.' If that refers to married women who are involved in managing a household or others who are necessarily involved in family matters, I readily agree.

If, however, it applies to girls who are endowed with natural ability, which our age produces so abundantly and who are to be educated more liberally, I find it more difficult to agree. A great admiration for the sciences or the equality of the common law encourages me to reject the view that something is rarely found among women although its pursuit is very commendable for all people. For since wisdom is such an adornment of the human race that it ought to extend by right to all and to each person (to the extent, indeed, that each individual happens to deserve it), I do not see why this particular adornment, which is by far the most beautiful of all, is not appropriate for young women, in whom we acknowledge a zeal to adorn and improve themselves.

Nor is there any reason why such a change should be a cause of concern to any commonwealth, since the glory of studies does nothing to obstruct the light of those who rule. On the contrary, there is universal agreement about the following: that a state in which many subjects are guided by wisdom rather than by laws will eventually flourish best. Besides, it will be impossible to show respect and honour to virtue and even to the chorus of the learned unless their more influential members know how to respect the

---

[35] A rescript in Roman times was an official reply to a private request or petition to the civil authorities; the same term is used in the Catholic Church for replies from Rome to private petitions.

glory and splendour of literary works with a genuine appreciation rather than a blind admiration.

But, to avoid delaying further in the preliminaries, I come to the very core of the controversy in which, if it is properly set out, the whole truth of the issue will become clear. The principal question, therefore, is this: whether the study of letters and the fine arts, above all else, is appropriate for young women. I am persuaded by strong arguments that the affirmative answer is more convincing. For, to begin the discussion with civil law, I remember reading somewhere that, according to Ulpian, women were excluded from civil and public offices.[36] I shall not inquire laboriously here by what rule of equity this was decreed, except that I think it implies clearly that the leisure in which we pass our time is legitimate and praiseworthy.

Evidently, we enjoy plenty of free time, and a peace that is receptive to the muses. Most of all, however, we enjoy as a special advantage a greater freedom from necessary work and immunity from domestic cares and duties. It is true indeed that this ample and unoccupied section of our lives, if it is frittered away in excess and carelessness and not put to good use, becomes an occasion for all the vices. Basil said admirably: 'Idleness is the beginning of evil-doing.'[37] However we succeed in avoiding this Charybdis, is it not the case that the mind is gradually enervated and reduced to a likeness of the idleness and indolence that it experiences? What follows from this, then? See how Seneca, as someone who cultivates a more sublime mind, opens up a path between the rocks when he says that only the leisurely (that is, those who use their leisure well) have time for wisdom, and they alone are alive. They not only take care of their own generation, but they bring every other era to bear on their own.[38] One should not seek leisure independently of what is best, but should seek what is best while at leisure. Thus we will not be bothered or disappointed by a greater tranquillity in a

---

[36] Ulpian was a Roman jurist who died c.228 BC. 'Women are excluded from all civil or public employments; therefore they cannot be judges, or perform the duties of magistrates, or bring suits in court, or become sureties for others, or act as attorneys.' Justinian, Digest, trans. S. P. Scott (Cincinnati, OH: 1932), Bk. 50, title 17.2, which is borrowed from Ulpian, Ad Sabinam, Book I.

[37] St Basil, Homilies on the Hexaemeron (note 20 above), Homily VII, § 5 (p. 113): 'idleness is the beginning of evil-doing. Natural reason which teaches us an attraction for the good and an aversion for the harmful is implanted in us.'

[38] Seneca, On the Shortness of Life, §14: 'Of all men only those who find time for philosophy are at leisure, only they are truly alive; for it is not only their own lifetime they guard well; they add every age to their own; all the years that have passed before them they requisition for their store' (S, 155).

place of retreat. Indeed, there are two things (as Cicero says)—leisure and solitude—that cause listlessness in others, but are a source of stimulation for someone who is wise.[39]

But it is customary to object that spinning and sewing constitute an adequate schooling for women. I admit that many have indeed been convinced of this and, in our own time, those who are *malicious* have generally agreed with them. But those of us who seek the voice of reason rather than of received custom do not accept this Lesbian rule. By what law, I ask, did this fall to our lot: by divine law or human law? They will never prove that these restrictions, by which we are certainly forced into line, are determined by fate or prescribed *by God*. For if we look for testimony from antiquity, both the examples of every age and the authority of the greatest men demonstrate the opposite. That is shown with no less learning and charm by the most noble glory of the Gournay family, in the book she wrote entitled *The Equality of Men and Women*.

To avoid having people say that I repeat what others have already done, however, I shall refrain from recounting these testimonies here. It is enough to add to those very clear words that the higher disciplines are not only appropriate for us, but that we should expect them in the kind of life that we enjoy. The most magnanimous among the leisured do not allow themselves to be coerced within such narrow limits, nor do all those who are endowed with greater natural ability allow themselves to be reduced below their nature. It seems clear to me that if these draconian laws should prevail, it cannot seem so surprising that some people are drawn in by the flattering blandishments of the world as a result of this worthless thought. What happens is that no honour, dignity, or reward for virtue, by which morally upright souls are usually encouraged to pursue praiseworthy objectives, offers any hope in that situation. We vainly discard the nobility that we received from our ancestors when it is quickly enveloped by an idle obscurity. Thus it happens that when one reads history, often over a very long period of time, the monuments of our glory are like the trace of a ship that passes through the sea.

'But', they ask, 'where does your glory come from? Whence your immortality? Is it ever from leisure?' Why not? But it is from leisure illuminated

---

[39] *On Duties*, Bk. 3, Chap. I.i, LCL 30: 'The two conditions, then, that prompt others to idleness—leisure and solitude—only spurred him on.'

by the light of wisdom. It is appropriate for us to be illustrious with the aid of Minerva—however, not as if we appeared in armour but rather dressed as citizens. Besides, where a true philosophy is dominant in one's mind, it allows no access to the vain and distracting activities of a vacillating mind. Erasmus, the distinguished patron of all higher studies in humanism, clearly expressed it in these words when he discussed the education of the daughters of Thomas More: 'Nothing' he said 'so occupies the whole heart of a young woman as much as study.'[40] Is it not the case that we shall spurn completely the chorus of this world, the specious authority of examples, and the vanity of an impotent age when we survey these worldly things from the lofty heights of wisdom?

Besides, since it pertains not only to duty but also to the happiness of all to strive towards the perfection of our pristine origin (from which we have all fallen short), we should try by every means possible to have the image of Him who is the light and the truth begin to shine more and more dominantly in our minds. Although I do not deny that theology (insofar as it is the best way to perfect the intellect) can provide everything that is required for that purpose, nonetheless I do not understand how those who wish theology to walk alone and unaccompanied seem to have understood inadequately the majesty of such a great queen.[41] For when we examine the book of natural things, is there anyone who fails to see how parts of these sciences combine in a beautiful harmony and how much support and light one provides to the other? Nor should we be hindered at all by the fact that some people restrict this study within narrow parameters, by thinking that we have little interest in knowing whether this machine of the world came together from atoms; whether it emerged from a formless chaos; whether some bodies happen to have a celestial nature while others are terrestrial; whether the upper masses of the earth revolve in a circle or whether those that tend to turn around the lowest rather than the highest masses are spinning; whether the setting Sun is immersed in the ocean and whether it owes its light also to the antipodes; whether the shape of the Earth is round or square; or, finally, whether it is the universe itself or merely the range of our eyesight that is bounded by the earth's horizon. If we listened to such opinions, which are commonly tossed about at the expense of our dignity,

[40] See footnote b above concerning Erasmus to Budé.
[41] Alludes to the medieval metaphor of philosophy and other disciplines as handmaidens to theology, which was described as the queen of the sciences.

then God, the creator of all things—who introduced us to this theatre so that his most beautiful works could be shown to us, to be known and celebrated—would be frustrated in His objective. Nature is not the kind of stepmother who would forbid us to inspect her. Why else would God have endowed us with what the Philosopher claims is innate in all human beings, namely, a desire to know?[42] Why would He have given us an erect posture except to enable us to lift up our eyes and minds to contemplate Him?

We would certainly be tree-trunks rather than human, we would be guests in this world rather than its inhabitants, if we did not bring a mind excited and, as it were, fired up by divine love to such beautiful, august things in which the majesty of the eternal divinity shines forth. Nor may we think that we fulfil our duty admirably by merely looking at these things intermittently, as if peering through a net. If we did that, we would not look at things in order to know, but we would show instead that we do not see and that we do not wish to know any more. There is nothing that our eyes can behold that is more marvellous than a human being, and nothing more beautiful than the home of a human soul [i.e. the human body]. But how small is something that is judged only by its cover or merely by its external appearance? How miserably should we blush at the wonderful hymns of pagans, in which they examine nature in such depth and, by thus probing, get closer to the first cause of all things and become more accustomed to singing the praises of the noblest artisan? Furthermore, when we turn our minds to the sacred Scriptures, as if to a star, who will deny that we are driven to the same expression of gratitude by so many examples of holy people who learned from the Scriptures what they needed to celebrate their God?

Moreover, without saying anything in general terms about the study of history as it is practised today, for the most part, in women's salons and in the halls of the mighty, we shall review only in passing whether knowledge of public affairs is appropriate for a private individual. I concede readily that a study of history is directly relevant to the practice and needs of a commonwealth. Nonetheless, we think it should not be neglected by anyone, because of the theoretical knowledge and special benefits that it confers on individuals. The sacred Scriptures anticipate us on this issue; they not only anticipate us, but they lead us by the hand. In the Scriptures the

---

[42] Aristotle, *Metaphysics*, 980ª22: 'All men [human beings] by nature desire to know' (AR II, 1552).

divisions of temporal periods are related to the reigns of monarchs; both the rise and fall of the greatest peoples are described or foretold. Nor is that surprising, because the stunning judgements of God, which we should observe constantly, appear more splendidly when they are expressed in the natural world. If God wished that all people should participate in this study and if these universal judgements cannot be expressed in the life of any one individual, would the contemplation of his admirable government [of nature] not stimulate our lyres? In this context, the royal psalmist, completely spell-bound, exclaims always: 'O Lord, how great are thy works! thy thoughts are very deep.'[43]

Someone may object at this point that what I have written amounts to nothing more than recommending the monastic life or limiting our duties to speculation alone. In fact, however, reason seems to imply that we look after ourselves first, to determine what is sufficient for our own happiness, and that we consider our neighbour only then. If people have never properly had time for themselves, they are vain to want to look after the affairs of others. It is vain to try to help others with advice or good deeds if one fails to help oneself. Finally, someone who is a stranger in their own home will in vain encourage others towards a civil community or the bond of a *superior commonwealth* of Christians. For, I ask, would it not be temerity to wish to build the whole *economy* of moral virtues on ignorance and commonly held opinions? Thus, except when chance intrudes, the examples available from every age teach us that no one appeases great gods successfully unless they have been instructed with a great and sound knowledge before approaching them. That knowledge surely prepares us, disposes us, and makes us ready to act well, and it raises the mind to accomplish outstanding deeds.

Besides, there is nothing more useful for a young woman, and nothing more necessary, than to distinguish between right and wrong, between what is harmless and harmful, between the appropriate and the inappropriate. But does that not require much more expert knowledge of things and much skill in making judgements? Since it would not be safe to acquire that kind of prudence from our own experience alone, we must surely have recourse to history '*as in a mirror, to beautify our life and make it like the virtues of others.*'[44] We are never allowed, I say, to recover our good reputation once it

[43]   Psalm 92:5; quoted in Hebrew.
[44]   Plutarch, *Lives: Timoleon*, LCL 98, 1.1 (p. 261).

begins to be tarnished by blemishes that cling to us from unwelcome suspicions. Thus it is surely incumbent on girls not only to avoid evils when they encounter them but to anticipate them even before that happens.

Finally, I cannot pass over in silence the arts and (as they are called) the instrumental sciences, which necessarily follow the principal sciences as ladies-in-waiting follow their queen, without adding something about the delight we should experience in *being able to speak many languages*, especially if one studies them in order to use them rather than boast; for languages are trusty custodians or, rather, interpreters of those things that a wise antiquity bequeaths to us. When it speaks to us in its own idiom, it presents to our mind a genuine image of itself and affects our senses with a certain wonderful grace and charm, which understandably we fail to find in all translations, even the best of them. If at some time I wished to provide a peroration by explaining and proving how pleasant and fruitful it is to extract heaven's doctrine from those very sources, it would amount to nothing more than what is expressed in the proverb: '*to lend light to the Sun.*'

However, to bring this discussion to a conclusion, I introduce one exemplar who is always before my mind—the exemplar, I say, of the incomparable princess Jane Grey, who (as is universally agreed) will never be equalled in any other age or in any other nation. Michelangelo of Florence, who describes the history of her life and violent death fully and sympathetically following a discussion he had with Feckenham (who had reported her death to her relatives), noted the following among other things.[45] In comparison with other gifts that were less valued—such as the nobility of her ancestry, her physical beauty, being in the youthful prime of her life, and other remarkable gifts that she had received from God and by which she could otherwise have achieved glory and favour in this world—she announced magnanimously that nothing pleased her more in her whole life than knowledge of the three languages that are called the languages of the learned. If the desire or delight that such

---

[45] John of Feckenham (1515–1584/5), a Roman Catholic priest, visited Lady Jane Grey (1537–1554) in prison days before her execution and invited her to renounce her Protestant religious beliefs, which she refused to do. She had been queen for only nine days before her internment. 'A Conference between the Lady Jane Gray, and Mr Feckenham, four days before her Death, touching her faith and religion' appears in *The Phenix* (London: Morphew, 1708), vol. II, 37–39, and in various editions of John Foxe, *The Book of Martyrs* (Manchester: Whalley, n.d.), Bk VI, 389–95. Van Schurman refers to Michelangelo Florio (1515–1572), who was chaplain to Jane Grey and reported the conversation with Feckenham in his *Historia de la vita e de la morte de l'Ill.striss. Signora Giovanna Graia* (Venice: Richardo Pittore, 1607). He refers to learning the languages of scholars on p. 71.

knowledge can bring us in this life were to be described as true happiness, she confessed that she had realized it herself in the study of good literature and especially of the holy Scriptures. Although many people may greatly censure this kind of study in a woman, she judged that their opinion was unreasonable because it brought her so much spiritual consolation, which she continued to experience inwardly. Behold the words of a swan, which were expressed in the final act of a glorious martyr rather than in the shadows of a scholastic disputation. Who, I ask, would not venerate them as an oracle?[46]

I have not hesitated to write here at length about important issues, by relying undoubtedly on the indulgence of your paternal love for me. But I stop at this point, lest I appear to have decided not to leave anything unsaid or to have forgotten completely your responsibilities. Farewell, dear father to me in many ways, and do not fail to extend my greetings to your most beloved wife.

Anna Maria Schurman, who remains completely at your command
Utrecht [6 November 1637]

Rivet to van Schurman

To the most noble young woman, who excels in every kind of virtue, Anna Maria van Schurman:

Your most elegant dissertation on behalf of your sex, concerning the capacity of women, in virtue of their natural ability, to undertake all the liberal arts and sciences, by equalling or possibly surpassing the native ability of men, left me undecided for some time.

. . .

The opportunity [to reply to me] arose from what I wrote in a certain letter in which, while I praised your thesis and admired your success, I did not concede that one may apply to all women in general what I thought was appropriate for you in particular and for a few others.

. . .

My hypothesis, which you cite, was the following: 'It may not be appropriate for many to choose this kind of life; it may be enough that

---

[46] According to a popular Greek legend, mute swans were said to sing for the first time as they were dying; hence the term 'swan-song'. It was used in Aeschylus' *Agamemnon* (458 BC) and by many subsequent authors, including Plato in the *Phaedo* (85B).

some people, who are called to it by a special inspiration, become out-standing now and again.' Outstanding in what? I refer to studies in phi-lology, philosophy, and the like, which involve expertise in languages, and to the whole collection of those disciplines that are known collec-tively as the '*encyclopaedia*'. I therefore maintain my own opinion, that such study is neither appropriate nor necessary. There is already much that, as you say, you concede immediately, if I understand that married women or any others who cannot avoid family-related duties are occu-pied by household cares. That certainly applies to those who comprise most members of your sex; the remaining members who are free for these studies are few. Likewise, I do not think that you want to claim that all women who are exempt from household duties are fit for the study of letters.

Thus, if you look only at what I wrote, either we do not disagree at all or, if we do, we disagree only slightly. That is true even if we dis-cuss the question that you subsequently identify as the principal one—whether the study of letters and fine arts is appropriate especially for a young woman in these times—unless you understand the term 'young woman' indefinitely, as applying universally or (in other words) as apply-ing to all women. Otherwise, I have readily accepted this kind of study in the case of some 'who are called to it by a special inspiration'. What if I add that I also concede that it applies to as many young women as pos-sible or that I even desire that outcome? But I would want that study to be qualified, in advance, in relation to the direction it should take, what arts and sciences should be included, and by what curriculum it should be established and developed, so that even here the maxim 'nothing in excess' would be observed.[47] I would also want the objective of women's study to be determined so that, once it is agreed, [only] those studies that are suitable or necessary for that objective would be selected.

Now since it is undisputed that the female sex is not suited for political or ecclesiastical offices and especially for teaching publicly, why would young women labour to acquire learning that is designed for those objec-tives from which they are excluded, unless perhaps you make an excep-tion for a few who, in some nations, are allowed to succeed to the throne when male heirs are unavailable? 'But I suffer not a woman to teach' (says

---

[47] 'Nothing in excess' was one of the phrases carved into the temple of Apollo at Delphi.

the Apostle), 'nor to usurp authority over the man, but to be in silence.'[48] If women are bound by this, then it is particularly appropriate that young women not be involved in it. It follows that they do not need the specific learning that is concerned with speaking well, if you consider how that learning is used—unless perhaps you object, which you already do, that they could benefit from the art of speaking well so as to judge the skill of others who practise that art. But who will be the judges? Such a judgement should be subject to an honourable modesty.

I shall say the same thing about the art of discussing topics, for you will readily grant that it is not sufficiently in keeping with a young woman's conduct to acquire the skills used in arguments and to assume the leading role in a scholarly disputation. Let women be satisfied if they acquire this skill by using their natural cleverness and from their experience of ordinary conversation and public teaching in church, in which they are not prevented from *hearing the Word* [of God].[49]

What you infer from this, however—namely, that women are very suited to studies or, at least, that they enjoy abundantly those supports for learning that are provided for men, because they are engaged in honest leisure and are excused from public duties—does not seem to me to prove what you intended.

First, if we consider the age that is most suitable for beginning one's studies, the development of males coincides with that of women until they reach *adulthood* (before which men are not appointed to public offices). Secondly, young women should not be reared with so much leisure that they are always able to devote time to cultivating their natural ability, because they have to take care of their household duties as long as they are under parental control and may not therefore be able to enjoy the leisure about which Seneca wrote: 'Leisure without letters is death and the grave of a living human being.'[50] But I would not want to condemn all young women to the distaff and the spindle, so that they are never admitted to more serious occupations, although women who were princesses in former times—among the Greeks, Romans, pagans or Christians—did not think that such work was unworthy of them. I think that you have read the

---

[48]   I Tim. 2: 11–15.

[49]   The last phrase is quoted in Greek from Matt. 13: 23.

[50]   'Leisure without study is death; it is a tomb for the living man;' *The Epistles of Seneca*, vol. II, LCL 76; Letter 82.4.

elegant book by Juan Luis Vives on the Christian woman. Consider only the whole of Book I, Chapter 3, concerning the early instruction of girls.[51] You will see there that it was always considered praiseworthy even in the judgement of the Holy Spirit that, not only married women but especially young women, including those who belong to a royal family, would occupy themselves in duties that involve manual work. But we do not, for that reason, go to the other extreme. Nor did Vives do so, when he added a fourth chapter about teaching girls, in which he elegantly and sensibly discussed the question: what kind of learning is appropriate for the inferior sex?[52] For you will not be angry with me, no matter how much Gournay disagrees, if I hold with the Apostle that '*the woman is a weaker vessel*;'[53] and if you accept the opinion of Vives, we will easily agree.

. . .

Before you persuade me [of your thesis] I would wish that you establish for me colleges of learned women, in the academies of which those young women whom you would commit to such studies would be educated. You yourself would readily admit that they could not all be self-taught, or that they would all have parents who would arrange for them in their homes the kind of education that you happened to enjoy. Nor would it be appropriate for them to attend schools for males, integrated with the boys. You will agree with me as follows: however much the study of good literature and languages, especially those languages in which God recorded his word for us, would be a great aid for those who ought to decipher the true meaning of the Spirit, it would not be possible for everyone to drink from those fonts. Nor does everyone have the judgement required to clarify ambiguous words or sentences, and to choose their most appropriate meaning. It is

---

[51] Juan Luis Vives (1493–1540), *De Institutione feminae Christianae* (1st edn. 1524); Eng. trans. note 7 above. Bk. I, Ch. 3 emphasizes the household duties of women: 'But I should not wish any woman to be ignorant of the skills of working with the hands, not even a princess or a queen ... the working of wool was always the occupation and skill of a good woman' (p. 59). 'In addition, she will learn the art of cooking...' (p. 60).

[52] Vives discusses the education of young women in Bk. I, Ch. 4: 'On the instruction of young Girls.' In §29 he suggests that 'it is not fitting that a woman be in charge of schools or have dealings with or speak to men ... it is best that she stay at home and be unknown to others ... since woman is a weak creature and of uncertain judgement and is easily deceived ... she should not teach, lest when she has convinced herself of some false opinion, she transmit it to her listeners in her role as teacher and easily drag others into her error, since pupils willingly follow their teacher' (p. 72).

[53] I Peter 3:7; 'Likewise, ye husbands, dwell with [them] according to knowledge, giving honour unto the wife, as unto the weaker vessel...'

healthier for some people to be content with the small streams, in which it often happens that, by reading attentively what others have translated and made available to them in their own vernacular, in humility and peace, and while invoking God's name, they may discover and elicit meanings that are hidden from experts in those languages. I say this, not to minimize the praise of those women who, like you, have made so much progress that they can understand the sacred books in their original languages. My aim rather is to prevent the arguments that you offer from causing scruples in the minds of those women who have no hope of matching your achievements.

The magnificent works of God, about which the Psalmist writes, may be celebrated by everyone, although only a few people know in detail about the rotation of the heavens, the relative positions of the planets, the influence of the stars, and similar phenomena. Thus it often happens that those who are considered most knowledgeable about such things are seen to turn away from God and to attribute everything to nature rather than to God. In contrast, those who rely on simple observation are over-awed and celebrate the wonderful works of God. They are completely satisfied with their author, while the very learned tire their brains vainly in such things and, after lengthy disquisitions, are left to dine on fresh air.

. . .

The Hague, 18 March, 1638

Van Schurman to Rivet

Reverend Sir and venerable father in Christ: I am indebted especially to your kindness for having deigned to reply so comprehensively to my trifles, at a time when you are busy with so many important duties. Indeed, your opinion struck me initially as significant, because it seemed to constitute a non-trivial objection to my thesis. However, when it was thoroughly examined in detail, I understood that—in your principal claim—your opinion agrees fully with what I wish to propose.

Nonetheless, I was quite concerned initially that I seem to have communicated to your mind a meaning that is very far from what I intended, either because of the misleading obscurity with which I expressed myself or, perhaps, because of my inability to make distinctions. In other words, I seem to have supported uncritically an invidious and empty claim about the superiority of our sex in comparison with yours to such an extent that

I would dare to propose it casually to you (whose time is so precious that it would be almost morally wrong to waste even a small fraction of it). For I see now that this is how you have understood everything that I proposed against the current state of the controversy about custom—'whether in these times above all the study of good literature and the arts is appropriate for young women'. You interpret the phrase 'above all' as if I used it, not in comparison with occupations or duties that are acceptable according to the customs of our own day, but rather in comparison with your own sex, and that I claimed that women are more suited to study than men. If that were proposed as a hypothesis, the arguments that I would deploy in support of my thesis would seem to be not only weak and insulting, but they could also rightly be accused of a novel and arrogant vanity.

That interpretation is so far removed from what I consider to be consistent with the modesty that becomes a young woman or, at least, my own innate shyness that it annoys me to read the otherwise outstanding treatise of Lucrezia Marinella: *The Nobility and Excellence of Women, and the Defects and Deficiencies of Men*.[54] Likewise, I can by no means disapprove of the elegant and charming little dissertation of the most noble Gournay: *The Equality of Men and Women*, though I would not dare, nor do I wish, to approve fully of everything that she wrote there. I may appeal, however, in the interests of brevity to the testimonies of the wise people that she included in her treatise.

Evidently, if the virtues that are appropriate for young women are to be preached correctly, I wish very much that the responsibility for doing so be handed over to you [i.e. men], as outstanding heralds of the virtues, since we would be fully satisfied if we were restricted to the theatre of a solitary conscience. My aim here was absolutely nothing more than to know precisely and accurately your judgement about how we [young women] might best use our leisure time. To realize that aim more easily, I took advantage of your own words in which you propose 'that it may not be appropriate that many women would be such'.[55] It is not that I wish to challenge any of those words; but I wish to understand accurately what precisely you meant to say.

---

[54] Lucrezia Marinella (1571–1653), *Nobiltà et l'eccellenza delle donne, co' diffetti et mancamenti degli uomoni* (1601); Eng. trans. *The Nobility and Excellence of Women, and the Defects and Vices of Men*, trans. A. Dunhill (Chicago: University of Chicago Press, 1999).

[55] Van Schurman does not quote exactly the words used earlier by Rivet.

Besides, I submitted my opinion, which I thought was in keeping with equity or rather with my own affections. I then introduced various arguments to explain my position with no other aim than that you might discern, with the acuity of your judgement, if they seemed to contain anything that was valid against the usual voices of ignorance and the tyrannical laws of custom. I thought that these few words should be pursued at greater length, so that you might have a clear idea of my thinking, since I know that you can cope with any argument once it is clearly expressed.

I re-read with great pleasure the two chapters from Juan Luis Vives that you suggested I should read, together with the previous chapters, in which the author prescribes guidelines for instructing Christian women that are so polished and clear that I would think they deserve to be applied as much as possible to the studies of young women today. For that reason I am very pleased that you suggested him as an interpreter of your opinion, the authority of which I embrace most freely about this question as I do about many others.

Farewell, dearest father, and I pray to the supreme power that you may continue to enjoy the good health that you have recently recovered. From one who loves and cherishes you with the deepest affection,

Anna Maria van Schurman, Utrecht, 14 March 1638[56]

Van Schurman to Princess Elizabeth of Bohemia[57]

Madame:

It would amount to ignoring the grandeur of Your Highness and the lowliness of my condition if I attributed to my merit, rather than to your absolute discretion, the fact that you were pleased recently to honour me with a letter from your hand and that you graciously inquired about my health and the things that occupy me at the moment. As regards my health, it is—thank God!—sufficiently good and fit to accept the honour of your

---

[56] The date must be wrong, because this letter replies to the preceding one from Rivet, which was dated 18 March 1638. They may have used Old Style and New Style calendars.

[57] While all the other texts by van Schurman included in this edition were written in Latin, this letter and the letter to Gournay were written in French.

commands. My studies, however, have not progressed sufficiently to justify a favourable report on them; at least, I do not think that they are worthy of the public's expectations, as you wish to persuade me.

It is true that I have great respect for the scholastic doctors, and that they could undoubtedly provide me with helpful opportunities to exercise my mind, if I were not distracted so often by other responsibilities. I do not wish to deny that they sometimes go astray with vain, dangerous, and even blasphemous speculations, and that this has provoked the censure of several learned men of our time. Nonetheless, that should not prejudice the soundness or excellence of the ideas that are usually admired in their works, when there is a question either of clarifying the secrets of philosophy or of defending the deepest mysteries of the Christian faith against profane sceptics and atheists. It would be difficult to decide if they were more ingenious in creating doubts or more skilled in resolving them, more rash in investigating deep and difficult questions or more competent and successful in unravelling them. Therefore, in my opinion, they have combined very well two qualities, subtlety and realism, which are rarely compatible. In fact, it is not surprising that they have reached such a high degree of perfection because they have not scorned the legacy of their predecessors or the riches of all previous centuries and it is easy, according to the philosophers' rule, 'to add something to what others have discovered.'[58] It provided enough glory for them to have allowed themselves to be guided by those two great stars of divine and human sciences, Saint Augustine and Aristotle, whom people have never been able to obscure despite the clouds and confusions of errors that they have tried to oppose to their brilliant light.

To avoid distracting Your Highness too long, I shall conclude once you have allowed me to say that I remain, as I have been and shall be for the rest of my life, Madame,

Your very humble, very obedient, and very faithful servant,
Anna Maria van Schurman
26 January 1644

---

[58] Quoted in Latin, and most likely borrowed from Francis Bacon, *De Augmentis Scientiarum*, Bk. IX, *The Works of Lord Bacon* (London: Henry Bohn, 1853), II, 430; *The Works of Francis Bacon*, trans. J. Spedding *et al.* (London, 1875), V, 118: 'For I could not be true and constant to myself or the argument I handle, if I had not determined to add as much as I could to the inventions of others.'

Van Schurman to Marie de Gournay

Mademoiselle:

If I have revealed what I feel about the benefits that your heroic virtues have procured for our sex, it was only to fulfil a duty that justice would have required of me. Indeed, the letter with which you have honoured me by writing to me demonstrates well that the extent of your courtesy is not proportionate to the merits of those to whom it is directed, and that it acknowledges no limits apart from those that it sets itself.

As a result, it would seem a small matter for you to thank me for something that was legitimately due to you, if you had not given me hope that my name would achieve immortality some day by the favour of your Muse. I certainly would wish to be as worthy of that felicity as you are prompt and generous in promising it to me, and that you might be able to find harmony and symmetry between the excellence of your style and the lowliness of the subject matter. But, whatever may happen in that context, I imagine—as in a sweet dream—that the signs of your affection that will undoubtedly be read in it will not be less glorious than the honour of a commendation that I would have deserved.

As regards your opinion that I devote too much time to the study of languages, I can assure you that I devote only my leisure hours to such study, and sometimes after fairly long intervals, with the single exception (with your permission) of the sacred language [i.e. Hebrew]. For, apart from the fact that its subject matter is the word of God, which should be the first object of our thoughts, and that there is no translation that communicates to us as successfully [as the original text] the simplicity and grandeur of those mysteries, it has various properties and features that cannot be equalled by all the elegance of either Greek or Latin. What Saint Jerome says: 'Let us learn those things on earth, the knowledge of which will persevere with us in heaven',[59] may be applied very well to Hebrew, which (according to the opinion of the most learned) will continue to be used in the next life. It is an infallible proof of your good grace that you think that my mind was born for higher things. For my part, if I cannot satisfy

---

[59] St Jerome, Letter 53: 'Let us learn upon earth that knowledge which will continue with us in heaven;' *Corpus Scriptorum Ecclesiasticorum Latinorum*, vol. LIV, ed. I. Hilberg (Leipzig: Freytag, 1910), 464.

your great expectations of my ability, I shall at least try to follow your good advice, as someone who is, Mademoiselle,

Your very humble, very obedient, and very faithful,

Anna Maria van Schurman

Utrecht, 26 January 1640.[60]

---

[60] The date printed in the *Opuscula* is 1647, which is probably a misprint for 1640, since Marie de Gournay had died in July 1645, and this letter replies to one from Gourney dated 20 October 1639.

Excerpts from *Eukleria*[61]

Chapter 1

§VI... Following the example of Augustine, the most candid of the Church Fathers, I hereby retract openly all my writings which reflect such a shameful frailty of the mind or a worldly and vain mentality. Nor do I recognize them any longer as mine. At the same time, I reject all those writings of other people and especially those eulogistic verses [about me] that are characterized by vainglory and the spirit of impiety, as foreign to my condition and profession, and I distance myself far from them. I also wish to ask their authors, if any of them are still alive, to consider weighing them in the scales of the Sanctuary itself[62] and then decide if they will be held accountable before the Supreme Judge for such words, not only those that are superfluous but also those that sometimes corrupt and harm others by example, unless they condemn them as I do or even recant and correct them.

§VII. Someone may object at this point that this was an abuse rather than a proper use of learning and of the glory of fame, and that—as in the case of other things, including the very best—one should remove the abuse but retain the underlying reality. I find it difficult to summon up what is required to reply fully and accurately to that objection. The principle just quoted should be limited to things that are genuinely good and whose use is necessary, and to those that pertain to God purely and truly, but not to creatures like us who are outside God. I am not willing to undertake an examination of those vain sciences, or to retrace my steps in the labyrinth

---

[61] *Eukleria seu Melioris Partis Electio* (Altona: C. van der Meulen, 1673). This autobiography was published in 1673, towards the end of Van Schurman's life. I have excerpted some retrospective comments in which Van Schurman qualifies the views about study that she defended in her earlier work.

[62] An allusion to Prov. 16: 11, where God is said to hold the ultimate scales by which justice is measured: 'A just weight and balance are the Lord's: all the weights of the bag are his work.'

that scholarly and prudent men[63] have already portrayed with sufficient intelligence and wisdom in their published writings. But the best of them was the holy Ecclesiastes, in this most wise of sayings: 'Of making many books there is no end; and much study is a weariness of the flesh. The conclusion of the whole matter is to worship God and to observe his commandments, because that is the whole [duty] of man.'[64]

Therefore, lest I waste my own time and that of others (for it is very just to be parsimonious in our use of time) or distract my mind too much with the vain image of past events when combined with those in the present, let my mind be guided by that simplicity that I think will protect it so that it is open to better things. I think it is enough for me to indicate here, in a few words, what necessarily occurs to all those who are held captive by a desire for knowledge, because of the common darkness of human minds and their deviation from what is right and good: I was not either sufficiently cautious or lucky always to have distinguished between use and abuse in the course of all my studies, and I have not observed a proper balance in all of them. Thus, I have not devoted the best days of my life consistently to the most necessary things. Indeed, on the contrary, if I were to consider carefully all the stages of my life, together with the studies in which I was occupied at various times, and if I combined that whole pattern of studies into a single image that would be made public to everyone, I think it would resemble a monster. But there are enough monsters in the world already.

Chapter 2

§XI. I wish that I had guarded against the vainglory of people as faithfully as against the special comfort of worldly things. Many factors obstructed me, and it would be long and superfluous to list them here. I will therefore outline only briefly how I was introduced to the world stage. It occurred initially when I was invited by some devotees of learning to celebrate with my verses the inauguration of Utrecht University, especially by Dr Gisbertus Voetius, the first professor of theology there.[65] Subsequently, if I believed

---

[63] Here and in subsequent cases, the word 'men' translates van Schurman's exclusively male '*viri*'.

[64] Ecclesiastes 12: 12. Van Schurman omits the word 'duty' in the final sentence, thereby obscuring the meaning of the final phrase. The King James translation uses 'man' here to include men and women.

[65] Utrecht had a Higher School prior to March 1636, when it was promoted officially to the status of a university. Voetius (1589–1676) was its first professor of theology and subsequently served a number of one-year appointments as its rector.

that I should defer for some time to the vanity of the sciences, which should be respected as distinguished handmaidens of Theology as their queen, I did so willingly. Indeed, from then on I believed that it was my duty to protect carefully the little lustre of my fame as a good that was common to the republic of learning and, insofar as modesty allowed, that I should even add to it so that, among other greater lights, I would also contribute, as a star of the sixth magnitude,[66] some clarity to that vast sphere of learning or what is called the encyclopaedia. I confess, however, that before that time I was not open to being carried away by these thoughts. For although the celebrated doctor and professor of theology, André Rivet, among some other famous friends, contributed studiously to the notoriety of my name, nevertheless, as a result of my innate modesty and a sincere wish to remain in obscurity, I tried to avoid celebrity as if it were a great burden. Such obscurity and quiet would have continued happily if I had not been diverted from my plan, not so much by popular applause as by the outstanding goodwill of some of the most famous men of that period. I understood very much later the extent to which that was contrary to Christian humility and the renunciation of all creatures.

It would have been futile to moderate that fame, as it expanded far and wide and gathered momentum in the process, if (something that is worth noting here) the hatred of worldly theologians had not taken care of it effectively first. Their hatred resulted from the fact that I consistently fled from their company and their sermons, in the composition of which they expended a considerable amount of labour and (in the familiar expression) midnight oil. Not only did they lack even an ounce of sound learning and genuine eloquence, but they especially failed to provide a taste of one drop of the oil that the spirit of Christ pours into the hearts of his own people, and by which all the tedium of a dutiful listener is alleviated. That was the reason why, by a certain law of retaliation, they thought that I should be condemned together with my studies and should be denigrated by slandering me among their colleagues.

§XII. I shall make explicit here just two or three things that indicate how I initially deviated from what is right into worldly servitude, which seemed

---

[66] When stars were observed prior to the invention of telescopes, there was an ancient ranking of stars from the first magnitude (the brightest) to the sixth magnitude (i.e. the faintest visible to the naked eye). Van Schurman's metaphor suggests that she aspired to be one of the least stellar contributors to learning.

to quite a number of people at the time to make me happy and wise. First, since fame itself preceded and guided me (for it seemed to me that I had an obligation to prevent the favourable things that were said about me from lapsing into the infamy of a lie), I applied my mind to things that were too numerous, too varied, and were even vain. Secondly, I did not observe a proper balance either in my use of time or in relation to the sciences themselves. Nor did I always give primacy to those things that were most capable of glorifying God, edifying my neighbour, and making my soul more pleasing to God. Thirdly, and principally by following human instinct, which attracted me more to human than to purely divine things, I clung with too much affection to various sciences and arts and at least sought, even if I failed to find, some pleasure and peace in them. All these things will be easily apparent to anyone who examines the course of my life.

§XIII. I was certainly surprised, recently, at the intemperance of the early studies that I undertook when—not without blushing—I reviewed the *Dissertation* that I sent to Dr André Rivet about the studies of a Christian woman, where one may read the following words: 'I consider that all genuine disciplines or, as it is called, the whole *encyclopaedia*, would be [completely] appropriate for a Christian woman (as a proper and universally applicable good or adornment of a human being).'[67] I believed at that time that I ought to learn everything that I could possibly know in order to flee from ignorance and, indeed, I invoked there the words of the Philosopher: '*in order to escape from ignorance*'.[68] However, I did not wish to recommend to others anything of which I was not convinced myself. Nonetheless, it is clear from what I wrote how far my thoughts had strayed from the warning of our Saviour, that 'one thing is necessary'.[69]

§XIV. Besides, even if I had striven towards the order and proper balance that should be observed in one's studies, the following words in the same *Dissertation* show that I failed to realize it.

The sciences or arts that are most closely related to sacred Scripture and the moral virtues, and that are most helpful to them, should be considered most

---

[67] Van Schurman does not quote the original text exactly; among other minor changes, she omits the word 'completely'.

[68] Van Schurman quotes Aristotle's *Metaphysics* ($982^{b}20$) in Greek and then provides a Latin translation.

[69] Lk. 10: 41.

important. We think that grammar, [and indeed general] logic and rhetoric fall into that category, although logic should be included among the first on our list, since many people have rightly thought of it as the key to all sciences. Next in order are physics, metaphysics, and history, etc., and knowledge of languages, especially of Hebrew and Greek, all of which can help us achieve a more complete and better understanding of sacred Scripture (to say nothing of other [books]).[70]

It is clear from this that I did indeed subordinate everything to the study of theology, as if it were supreme. This subordination was extended almost to infinity, however, before reaching it limits in pure theology, since it would have required so many and such varied aids for understanding sacred Scripture that those scriptural studies would easily exceed the limits of the very brief lives of mortals. And, in truth, unless God's generosity decided otherwise, I would have died before completing the full course of such preparations.

§XV. Let us look for example at the 'study of languages', which the learned describe as the carriers of the sciences, to which indeed I devoted very many hours even though I often found that they were obstacles for me. But, I ask, for what purpose? Was it so that, with Cato (who learned Greek when he was sixty years old), I would be able to reply to anyone who inquired about it, 'that I would be so much more learned when I die' or, since I was younger, that I might live as a much more learned woman? At any rate, I did not suggest that such study would be my primary distinction, but that I depended on the Greek and Hebrew languages and thought of them as the original languages of the sacred Scriptures. I had also become convinced that the other eastern languages were like the daughters or branches of Hebrew and, to that extent, were worthy of love and the commendation of learned men, and that I should learn them with unwavering labour. These included especially Syriac, Arabic, and Ethiopic, because they have the most root words from which merely derivative terms appear in sacred Scripture, and therefore they shed some light in discerning the inner meaning of the latter. But if we love the truth, since there are very few words whose meaning remains hidden in learned translations today or are unknown to experts in the Hebrew language, was this not a case of lighting

---

[70] Van Schurman quotes the original text with minor changes; the phrase 'and indeed general' was added, and the original term 'authors' was substituted by 'books'.

torches in daylight, or turning a fly into an elephant,[71] or at least playing games about a serious issue? Besides, a certain spiritual gift is much more necessary here, to which those linguistic studies contribute little or nothing. Either the sacred Scripture is read in the light of the Holy Spirit, or it is not. If not, it is futile to adopt a grammatical explanation of one word or another in order to decipher its innermost spiritual meaning. If one is taught by that Master [i.e. the Holy Spirit], then the true and life-giving meaning of sacred Scripture or its universal sense, which is made accessible to us by a habit of praying in that universal light, will not depend on knowing some word or some extremely rare root. God alone and his Spirit is the unique, infallible, and true interpreter of the sacred Scriptures.

§XVI. Nonetheless, I rejoice in the fact that I acquired some knowledge of various languages, so that at least I did not think that one should erect a temple to them, as if to an unknown God (as the Athenians once did).[72] I thought instead that this great apparatus—like some kind of choral training for vainglory, with it splendid signs of very esoteric learning, or like the decoration of a magnificent palace and excessively large furniture—by which Christians (evidently in private) burden themselves, should be left to learned people, unless perhaps some child of God (who has been divinely inspired and granted spiritual skill and cleverness) provided the Christian world with some kind of universal grammar that has been desired for such a long time by prudent men, or some kind of spiritual lexicon that could be used for the conversion of gentiles or Jews. My own conviction now, however, is that the slightest experience of God's love can give us a truer and deeper knowledge of sacred Scripture than the most comprehensive science of that sacred language itself. I also think the same judgement should be made about all the other sciences.

§XIX. I do not conclude, however, that we should reject completely and indiscriminately all true sciences and useful or necessary arts. Nor do I deny that those who are pure of heart may be able to use some of them in a pure and useful way. What I am saying, rather, is that most of them are vain or superfluous; they occupy people's foolish minds so fully that they are prevented from

---

[71] Alludes to a proverb quoted above in a letter to Rivet, p. 101. The metaphors are also found in Erasmus, *Collected Works of Erasmus: Adages* (Toronto and London: University of Toronto Press, 1989–91), trans. R. A. B. Mynors, I, ix, 69 (vol. 32), and II, v, 6 and 7 (vol. 33).

[72] In the Acts 17: 22, 23, Paul records his experience of preaching to the Athenians: 'Ye men of Athens, I perceive that in all things ye are too superstitious. For as I passed by ... I found an altar with this inscription, To The Unknown God.'

seeking more significant realities. Things that are good in themselves are not good for everyone. For just as all things work together for good for those who love God,[73] so likewise all things work together for evil for those who do not love God. Thus all those who are worldly—since they lack the perspective of faith, fail to see God in his own light, are not instructed by God's love (which Augustine rightly calls the great teacher[74]) and are deprived of the spirit of God—change all doctrines, including that of sacred Scripture, into the odour of death (in the words used by the Apostle), both for themselves and for their followers.[75] Therefore, they ought to use as few doctrines as possible lest they abuse many of them and thus aggravate their own damnation.

[73] Rom. 8: 28.
[74] This is developed extensively by Augustine in *De doctrina christiana* (*On Christian Doctrine*), especially in Bk. I, Ch. 39, and is summarized in Sermon 43.7 as: 'Believe that you may understand.'
[75] 2 Cor. 2: 16, where Paul reflects on the impact of preaching the gospel on those who are saved or damned. In relation to the latter he wrote: 'To the one we are the savour of death unto death.'

François Poulain de la Barre

A Physical and Moral Discourse concerning the Equality of Both Sexes[1]

Preface: The Plan and Purpose of this Discourse

There is no topic more sensitive than explaining one's views about women. When a man speaks in their favour, he is immediately assumed to be motivated by gallantry or love. It is very likely that most people, if they judge this book by its title, will conclude immediately that it results from either gallantry or love, and will be pleased to know its true purpose and objective, which are as follows.

The best idea that may occur to those who try to acquire genuine knowledge, if they were educated according to traditional methods, is to doubt if they were taught well and to wish to discover the truth themselves. As they make progress in this search for truth, they cannot avoid noticing that we are full of prejudices,[a] and that it is necessary to get rid of them completely in order to acquire clear and distinct knowledge.

With the objective of introducing such an important maxim, I thought it was best to choose a specific, clear-cut example that is interesting to everyone. Thus, once I have shown that an opinion as old as the world, as widespread as the earth, and as universal as the human race is a prejudice or an error, those who are learned may eventually be convinced that they must make their own judgements about things when they have examined them and, if they wish to avoid being deceived, that they should not trust the opinions or sincerity of others.

---

[a] That is, judgements that are made about things without examining them.

[1] *Discours physique et moral de l'égalité des deux sexes, où l'on voit l'importance de se défaire des préjugez* (Paris: Jean Du Puis, 1673).

Among all the prejudices, no one has found a more appropriate one with which to illustrate my thesis than that which is commonly accepted about the inequality of the sexes.

Criterion   If one considers the current situation of men and women, one
of Truth   sees that they differ more in their civil functions and those that depend on the mind than in those that depend on the body. If one looks for an explanation of this situation in popular discussions, one finds that all parties—both those who have studied and those who have not done so, and even women themselves—agree in saying that women are excluded from the sciences[2] and public life because they lack the ability to participate in them, that they are less intelligent than men, and that their current inferior status in everything is just as it ought to be.

When I examined this opinion by applying the criterion of truth—which is not to accept anything as true unless it is based on clear and distinct ideas—I came to two conclusions. One was that this opinion is false, and is based on prejudice and popular belief; the other was that the two sexes are equal, that is, that women are as noble, as perfect, and as capable as men. That can be shown only by refuting two kinds of opponent: the common people, and almost all scholars.

Since the former opponents have no basis for their beliefs apart from custom and superficial appearances, it seems as if the best way to combat them is to get them to see how women have been dominated and excluded from the sciences and from public life. By guiding them through the various stages and principal interactions of everyday life, they will have an opportunity to acknowledge that women possess advantages that make them equal to men. This will constitute the first part of this treatise.

The second part is used to show that the arguments of scholars are all useless. Once the thesis of equality is established by reference to positive reasons, women are defended against the faults of which they are usually accused by showing that such alleged deficiencies are imagined or insignificant, that they result exclusively from the education they receive and that, in fact, they point to significant ways in which women are superior.

This question about equality may be addressed in two ways. One is to use a gallant approach, that is, to employ flowery language and a playful style. Alternatively, it may be addressed philosophically and by reference to principles, to achieve a fundamental understanding of it.

---

[2] See the comment on the translation of this term in the Note on the Texts and Translations.

Those who have an accurate idea of true eloquence realize that these two approaches are almost incompatible and that it is nearly impossible to enlighten the mind and entertain it at the same time. It is not that it is impossible to combine flowery speech with reason; however, this combination often hinders the realization of the objective that one should have in a discourse, which is to convince and persuade. When something pleasant entertains the mind, it distracts it from focusing on fundamental issues.

People look at women from different perspectives. Thus, if one adds an element of gallantry to a book about women, those who read it will allow their thoughts to stray too far and will lose sight of what should concern them. For that reason, since there is nothing more important for women than this question—in the discussion of which one must say what is most convincing and true in their defence, insofar as a frivolous world tolerates it—I thought it was necessary to speak seriously and to advise readers of this. Otherwise, I was afraid that any hint of gallantry would encourage readers to skim over it lightly or would turn away serious readers.

I realize that many people will be displeased by this discourse, and that those whose interests and principles are opposed to what is defended here will not miss an opportunity to criticize it. To answer their objections I advise intelligent readers, especially women who are not duped by those who exercise authority over them, that if they take the trouble to read this treatise with the care that is required at least by the variety of questions that are discussed here, they will notice that the essential criterion of truth is clarity and evidence. That will enable women to decide if the objections they face are worth considering or otherwise. They will be able to notice that the most specious objections will be made by people whose current profession seems to commit them to rejecting experience, sound judgement, and even themselves in order to embrace blindly everything that agrees with their prejudices and their self-interest, and to fighting against every truth that appears to challenge them.

I hope that the ill-effects that an irrational fear might make people dread from this project will not affect a single woman, and that those effects would be counterbalanced by the great benefits that women may gain from it. There is perhaps no more natural or more sure way of rescuing women from the idleness to which they have been reduced and from its harmful effects than to encourage them to study—almost the only thing that women are allowed to do nowadays—by informing them that they are as competent to do so as men.

Just as only those who are unreasonable abuse the advantages that they enjoy from custom to the detriment of women, so likewise only women of poor judgement would use this work to rebel against those men who would treat them as their equals or their companions. Finally, if anyone is shocked by this discourse for whatever reason, let them blame the truth rather than the author. To alleviate their chagrin, they could pretend that this is only an intellectual game. It is certain that this trick of the imagination, or something similar, which prevents the truth from taking hold of us, will make it much less unpalatable for those who have difficulty in accepting it.

Part I

Which shows that the commonly accepted belief is a prejudice and, if one compares impartially what is observed in the conduct of men and women, one must recognize that the two sexes are completely equal.

People are full   People are convinced of innumerable things that they cannot
of prejudices   justify, because their convictions are based only on superfi-
cial appearances, by which they have allowed themselves to be persuaded. They would have believed the opposite if the impressions they receive from the senses or from custom had been otherwise and had affected them in a similar way.

Apart from a few scholars, everyone thinks that it is indubitable that the Sun moves around the Earth, despite the fact that what we observe in the revolutions of the days and the years leads those who examine it to believe that it is the Earth that moves around the Sun.[3] People imagine that animals have some kind of knowledge that guides them, when they reason like primitive people who suppose that there are little souls inside the clocks

---

[3] Galileo defended the heliocentric theory in his famous *Dialogue concerning the Two Chief World Systems* (1632), and Descartes had endorsed heliocentrism at about the same time in a treatise of natural philosophy entitled *The World* that was published posthumously in 1664. Poulain uses this controversy to illustrate his claim that the observed astronomical facts were consistent with two different theories, and that almost all scholars joined the uneducated by accepting appearances at face value. Galileo was notoriously condemned for publishing his theory, and Poulain anticipates a similar degree of incredulity and scholarly opposition to his theory of equality.

and machines that they are shown though they know nothing about their construction or their inner springs.[4]

If we had been reared in the middle of the ocean without ever getting close to land, we would surely have believed—as children do when they depart on a boat—that it is the shoreline that moves relative to us when we move along in a boat. Everyone believes that their own country is the best because it is more familiar to them than others, and that the religion in which they were reared is the true religion that must be followed, even if they may never have thought of examining it or comparing it with other religious traditions. We always feel more supportive of compatriots than of foreigners, even when the law favours the latter. We are more comfortable with members of our own profession, even if they are less intelligent or virtuous, and the unequal distribution of goods and offices causes many people to conclude that human beings are not equal to each other.

If one examines the foundations of all these various beliefs, one finds that they are based only on self-interest or custom. One also finds that, if someone's opinion is based only on prejudice, it is incomparably more difficult to change their minds than if they had been convinced by reasons that seem strong and persuasive to them.

One may include among such beliefs the commonly held opinion about the difference between the sexes and, especially, everything that follows from that belief. There is no belief more ancient or widespread. The learned and the ignorant are so biased in believing that women are inferior to men, both in their capacities and their merit, and that they deserve the dependent status that they currently occupy, that they would certainly consider the contrary view as an extraordinary paradox.[b]

What one needs to do to make correct judgements   Nevertheless, it would not be necessary to invoke any positive reasons in order to establish this opinion [about equality] if people were more impartial and less self-interested in their judgements. It would be enough to show them that, up to now, the discussion of this topic has been superficial and biased against women. To judge soundly whether our sex has some natural superiority over women, one would have to consider the question seriously

---

[b] An opinion that is the opposite of what is commonly believed.

[4] Descartes had argued that it would be ridiculous to believe that clocks or similar machines operate because they have a 'form' that is similar to the human soul, and he proposed adopting a mechanical explanation of animal motion. See Descartes to Plempius (3 October 1637), to Buitendijk (1643), to the Marquess of Newcastle (23 November 1646), to More (5 February 1649), AT I, 414; IV, 65; IV, 573–6; V, 277–8.

and without self-interest, and to reject anything that we had believed merely on the basis of someone else's report without having examined the matter ourselves.

It is certain that any man who assumes this attitude of impartiality and disinterest will realize that, on the one hand, it is a lack of understanding and undue haste that makes him believe that women are less noble and less excellent than us, and that some natural indispositions make them subject to the faults and imperfections that are attributed to them and to being despised by so many people. On the other hand, he will realize that the very appearances that deceive people about this issue, when they consider them superficially, would succeed in correcting them if they examined them in greater depth. Finally, if this man were a philosopher,[5] he would find that there are physical explanations that prove incontrovertibly that the two sexes are equal both in body and mind.

However, since there are not many people who are capable of implementing this advice on their own, it would remain useless unless we worked with them and helped them to apply it. Since the opinion of those who have not studied is most common, we must begin by examining that.

What men believe about women
If one asks each man individually what he thinks about women in general, and if he agrees to tell us honestly, he will surely say that women were created only for us and that they are hardly suited to anything more than raising children in their infancy and taking care of the home. The more perceptive among them would add that there are many women who are intelligent and morally good. They would say, however, that if one looks more closely at those who best exemplify these traits, one always finds something that betrays their sex: they lack the steadfastness, control, and the depth of understanding that people imagined they had, and that it is divine providence and men's wisdom that exclude them from the sciences, from government and from civil offices; that it would be amusing to see a woman appointed to a university chair and teaching rhetoric or medicine as a professor; to see them marching

---

[5] The term 'philosopher' is used here to mean someone who is familiar with the physical theory or natural philosophy of the period. For Poulain, that meant a proponent of the new Cartesian natural philosophy, rather than someone who taught traditional scholastic philosophy in French colleges. Louis de Lesclache distinguishes various meanings of the term that were then in use in *Les advantages que les femmes peuvent recevoir de la Philosophie, et principalement de la Morale* (Paris: 1667).

in the street followed by police commissioners and sergeants to enforce the law; pleading before a judge as a lawyer; sitting in court to deliver a judgement as head of a parliament;[6] leading an army into battle, or addressing commonwealths or princes as head of a diplomatic mission.

I admit that all that would surprise us, but only because it would be novel. However, if women had been admitted when the various states of the kingdom and the functions they exercise were established, we would be as used to seeing them in those offices now as they are to seeing us in them, and we would not find it any more unusual to see them as judges in the courts than as customers in shops.

If we press people a little, we will find that their strongest reasons come down to saying that, as far as women are concerned, things have always been the way they are at present; that this is a sign that things should be as they are; and if women had been capable of studying the sciences and holding offices, men would have admitted them alongside themselves.

The false idea of custom   These arguments result from the belief that men are impartial and from a widespread false concept of custom: if some practice is well established, then we think that it must be right. Since it is believed that men should never act contrary to reason, most people cannot imagine that reason was ignored when the practices that they see established so universally were first introduced. They assume that reason and prudence initiated such practices because both reason and prudence force us to respect them as long as one cannot avoid doing so without great inconvenience.

Why women are believed to be inferior to men   Everyone sees in their own country women who are so dominated that they depend on men for everything. They have no access to the sciences or to any position that provides an opportunity to display their intellectual gifts. No one reports ever seeing women otherwise. It is known that they have always been like that, and there is no place on earth where women are not treated as they are here. There are even some places where women are treated like slaves. In China, their feet are bound up tightly from infancy to prevent them from leaving their houses, where they almost never see anyone apart from their husbands and their children. Ladies are controlled just as rigidly in Turkey. They are not much better off in Italy.

---

[6] The French *parléments* exercised both judicial and subsidiary legislative functions by implementing royal decisions at a local level in different regions.

Almost all the people of Asia, Africa, and America use their women as they use servants here. Everywhere they are assigned only what are considered menial tasks; and since they alone take care of the trivial concerns of the household and the children, it is generally believed that they are in this world for that reason alone and that they are incapable of doing anything else. People find it very difficult to imagine that things could easily have been different, and it even seems as if we could never change the current situation no matter how hard we tried.

When the wisest legislators founded their republics, they put in place nothing that was favourable to women in this respect. All laws seem to have been passed simply to maintain men's possession of what they currently have. Almost all those who were considered learned and who addressed questions about women said nothing favourable about them. Indeed, one finds that men's conduct in this respect is so uniform, in every century and throughout the whole world, that it seems as if they conspired or, as some imagine, that they were driven by some hidden instinct—that is, by a general command of the author of nature—to act in this way.

How to judge ancient customs
That seems all the more convincing when one considers how women themselves tolerate their condition. They accept it as if it were natural for them, either because they do not think at all about what they are or because, having been born and reared in dependency, they think about it in the same way as men. Both men and women tend to believe, about all these issues, that their minds are as different as their bodies and that there should be as great a distinction between the sexes in everything as there is between those functions that are specific to each sex. This conviction, however, just like most of our convictions about customs and practices, is nothing but a pure prejudice. It is based on how things appear to us when we fail to examine them more closely, and we would correct our misperception if we took the trouble to trace it back to its origin. That would involve evaluating what was done in earlier times by reference to current practices, and judging ancient customs by comparison with those that we see developing in our own day. If we had followed that rule, we would not have fallen into so many mistakes in innumerable judgements. And, in respect of the current condition of women, we would have recognized that they were dominated only by the law of the strongest, and that it was not because of a lack of natural capacity or merit on their part that they failed to share the advantages that give men a superior position in society.

How people   Indeed, when we think honestly about human affairs, both
have always   past and present, we find that they are all similar in one
been governed respect: that reason has always been the weakest factor. It
seems as if all histories were written simply to show—what everyone sees in their own day—that force has always prevailed since the first appearance of human beings. The greatest Asian empires were created from the beginning by usurpers and thieves, and the remnants of the Greek and Roman monarchies were inherited by those who thought they were strong enough to resist their masters and dominate their peers. This kind of conduct is equally apparent in every society. If men act that way in relation to their peers, it is most likely that each of them did the same thing initially, and with more reason, in relation to their wives. It happened more or less as follows.

Historical con-   When men realized that they were stronger and that they
jecture: how were physically superior to women, they imagined that they
men assumed were superior in every respect. This had a relatively insignifi-
mastery   cant effect at the beginning of the world. Things were very
different then to how they are now: there was not yet any government, learning, civil offices, or any established religion, and the ideas of dependence that prevailed then were not at all harmful. I imagine that people lived like children and that every advantage was treated like a game; men and women were simple and innocent then, and they were equally involved in cultivating the earth and in hunting, just as savages are today.[7] Men went about their own business and women about theirs; whoever made the greatest contribution was most respected.

Since the interruptions of pregnancy and its after-effects reduced the strength of women for periods of time and hindered them from working as they had done before, their husbands' assistance became absolutely necessary, even more so when they had children. This resulted in nothing more significant than a few signs of esteem and favour as long as the families consisted of just a mother, a father, and a few small children. However, when families expanded and the father, his mother, the children's children and brothers and sisters, young and old, all lived

[7] This picture of a golden age is repeated less hypothetically in *De l'excellence des hommes contre l'égalité des sexes*, PO, 392: 'In the first epoch of the world—some shadow of which survives in the innocent love of shepherds and shepherdesses and in the pleasures of a rustic life, as long as it is not disturbed by fear of armies or enemies—all people were equal, just, and honest, and they had no regulations or laws apart from common sense.'

in the same house, this dependence also extended further and became more noticeable. One then saw the mistress of the house submit to her husband, the son honouring his father, and the father in turn being in charge of the children. Since it is very difficult for brothers always to live together harmoniously, one could conclude that it did not take a long time before they squabbled with each other. The strongest among the older brothers was unwilling to concede anything to the others; sheer force obliged the younger ones to submit to their seniors, and the girls followed their mother's example.

It is easy to imagine that the various household chores then became specialized. The women were required to remain at home to take care of the children and to assume responsibility for indoor duties; since the men were freer and stronger, they took control of duties outside the home. When the mother and father died, the oldest son wanted to dominate. Since the girls were used to staying indoors, they did not consider leaving home. A few of the younger boys who were dissatisfied and more fearless than the others refused to submit, and were forced to leave and to form a new clan. They met others who were in a similar situation, discussed their common lot, and easily made friends; and since none of them had any property, they looked for ways of acquiring some. Because goods could not be acquired without stealing them from others, they took advantage of the most convenient victims and, to protect their new acquisitions, they also seized the owners to whom the goods belonged.

The voluntary dependence that had obtained within families ceased as a result of this invasion. Fathers and mothers, together with their children, were forced to obey an unjust usurper. The condition of women became even more intolerable than before; for, rather than marry members of their own family who would treat them like sisters, as they had done previously, they were forced to accept as husbands unknown strangers who considered them merely as the most beautiful part of their booty.

Why women were excluded initially from occupations   It is customary for victors to despise those among the conquered who are weakest. Since women appeared to be such because their duties required less strength, they were regarded as inferior to men.

Some men were content with this first level of usurpation; but other more ambitious ones, encouraged by the success of their victory, decided to extend their conquests. Since women were too humane to participate in such plans, they were left at home, while men were chosen as suitable for enterprises that required more strength. At this stage, people valued things only insofar as they were thought suitable for whatever objectives they had in mind; and when the desire to dominate others became one of the strongest passions and people were satisfied only by violence and injustice, it is not surprising that men—the sole instruments of domination—were preferred to women. Men were used to consolidate the conquests that had been made; they alone were consulted to establish tyranny because they alone were capable of imposing it. In this way, women's gentleness and humanity were the reasons why they were excluded from governing states.

The example of princes was soon followed by their subjects. They all tried to take advantage of their neighbours, and individuals began to dominate their own families in a more absolute way. As soon as some lord found that he was master of a people and of a reasonably large region, he turned it into a kingdom. He made laws to govern it, chose officers from among the men, and appointed those who had served him best in his campaigns to positions of authority. There was such a remarkable preference for one sex rather than the other that women were even less respected than before. Since their temperament and duties made them far removed from carnage and war, they were deemed capable of contributing to the protection of kingdoms only by helping to populate them.

It was impossible to establish states without making distinctions among those who composed them. Decorations were introduced to identify those who were honoured, and marks of respect were instituted as evidence of the distinctions that were drawn between different people. In that way the public deference that one shows to those in authority was linked with the idea of power.

How women were excluded from the ministry of pagan religions It is not necessary here to say how God became known to mankind; however, he has been worshiped continuously since the beginning of history. The worship of God was institutionalized only when people assembled to form public societies. Since it had been customary to honour those in power with marks of respect, it was thought necessary to honour God also with ceremonies that expressed what people felt about his greatness. Temples were built, sacrifices were instituted, and the men who were already in charge of governing did not miss the opportunity to take control of everything pertaining to religion. Since custom had already forewarned women that everything belonged to men, they did not ask to participate in the ministry. The idea of God was very corrupted by fables and poetic fictions, and consequently people constructed male and female divinities and established priestesses for religious services for women; all this, however, was controlled by priests at their discretion.

Women have also been observed occasionally governing large states. One should not conclude, however, that they were invited to do so out of a spirit of reparation; rather, they had become so skilled in management that it was impossible to deprive them of their authority. There are hereditary states today in which women succeed men and become queens or princesses. Nonetheless, there is reason to believe that when women were allowed initially to rule these kingdoms, the only reason for doing so was to avoid civil war. Likewise, if regencies were tolerated, it was only because they believed that mothers, who always had such extraordinary love for their children, would take special care of their states during their children's minority.

Why women were excluded from the sciences   Since women were restricted to housework and had enough to keep them busy at home, it is not surprising that they discovered no sciences, most of which initially were only the work and occupation of those who were lazy and idle.

The Egyptian priests, who had little to do, enjoyed talking together about those natural phenomena that affected them the most. By applying their reasoning, they made observations the fame of which excited the curiosity of some men who came to consult them. Since the sciences were merely in their infancy at that stage, they did not attract women from their homes. Besides, the jealousy that already clouded their husbands' judgement would have convinced them that their wives were visiting the priests because they loved them rather than for the knowledge they possessed.

As soon as a number of men acquired some knowledge, they assembled in certain places to discuss it at their leisure. As each one expressed his ideas, the sciences developed. They founded academies to which women were not invited and they were thus excluded from the sciences as from everything else.[8]

---

[8] In early modern Europe, there were official academies such as the *Académie française* (1635), the *Académie royale des sciences* (1666) and, in England, the Royal Society (1660), to which women were not admitted. See Frances A. Yates, *The French Academies of the Sixteenth Century* (London and New York: Routledge, 1988), Chap. xii. There were also informal meetings or *salons*, many of which were organized by women as an alternative venue for intellectual and literary discussion. See Steven Kale, *French Salons: High Society and Political Sociability from the Old Regime to the Revolution of 1848* (Baltimore and London: Johns Hopkins University Press, 2004).

The restrictions within which women were kept did not prevent a few of them from having access to the conversations or writings of scholars. Within a short time they rivalled the most accomplished scholars; however, since the demands of etiquette did not allow men or other women to visit them for fear of causing offence, they failed to acquire any disciples or followers, and everything they learned died with them in vain.

If one considers how fashions are introduced and how they develop from day to day, it is easy to see why people were not much concerned about them at the beginning of the world. Everything was simple and crude then, and people were concerned only with basic necessities. Men skinned animals and made clothes from them by joining the skins together. Style came later; when everyone was dressing as they wished, the most attractive styles prevailed. Those who were subject to the same prince took care to follow his example.

Why women became involved in frivolity
Fashion differed from government and the sciences, insofar as women were involved in it equally with men. When the men noticed that women were more beautiful, they made sure not to deprive them of this. Once men and women realized that they looked better and appeared more graceful with various stylistic improvements, they competed with each other for them. However, since men's occupations were more important and demanding, they were prevented from giving much attention to such things.

Women displayed their prudence and skill in this context. Once they noticed that external adornments made men treat them more gently and that their own condition became thereby more tolerable, they exploited everything that they believed would make them more amiable. For that purpose they used gold, silver, and precious stones as soon as they were in vogue. Since men had prevented them from displaying their intellectual gifts, they applied their energies exclusively to whatever could make them look more attractive. They succeeded admirably, and their clothes and beauty won them more esteem than all the books and knowledge in the world. This tradition became too well established to allow any possible change subsequently; the same practice has been passed on to us, and it now seems to be a tradition that is too old to criticize.

It seems clear from this historical conjecture, and is consistent with the usual behaviour of all men, that men retained the public benefits from which they excluded women only by their power. For, if they were to

How men should justify their treatment of women claim that it was based on reason, they would have to share their privileges only with the most capable men; they would make their choices among men with great discernment; they would admit to study only those in whom they notice a greater disposition for scientific research and would appoint only the most competent to civil offices and exclude all others; finally, they would appoint every man only to the things for which he is most suitable.

How men are appointed We see that, in practice, the very opposite happens and that men are appointed to various civil offices only by chance, or out of necessity or self-interest. Children learn their father's profession because that is the one that they had always heard about. One child is forced to be a lawyer although he would have much preferred to be a soldier if he had been allowed to choose; and the most gifted man in the world would not be appointed to an office if he did not have the money to pay for it.[9]

How many people remain impoverished who would have become distinguished had they been given a little encouragement, and how many peasants would have become great teachers if they had been sent to school? It would be a serious mistake to pretend that the most skilled people today are those who, in their generation, showed most aptitude for the things in which they now excel and that, among such a large number of people enslaved in ignorance, there is none who would have become more qualified if they had enjoyed the same opportunities as them.

On what basis, then, could one be certain that women are less gifted than us and that it is not luck, but some insurmountable necessity, that prevents them from participating as equals in society? I do not claim that they are all suited to the sciences and to public office, or that each woman is capable of doing everything. No one claims that about men either. I ask only that, considering the two sexes in general, we recognize that there is as much aptitude in one as in the other.

---

[9] The purchase of offices was so common that Montaigne remarked in the *Essais*, I: 23, 117–8A; *Essays* ('On Habit'), 132: 'What is more uncouth than a nation where, by legal custom, the office of judge is openly venal and where verdicts are simply bought for cash? where, quite legally, justice is denied to anyone who cannot pay for it, yet where this trade is held in such high esteem that there is formed a fourth estate in the commonwealth, composed of men who deal in lawsuits, thus joining the three ancient estates, the Church, the Nobility, and the People?' See Roland Mousnier, *La vénalité des offices sous Henri iv et Louis xiii* (Paris: Presses universitaires de France, 1971).

Comparison of young children of both sexes   Consider only what occurs in children's games. Girls display more gentleness in them, more character and more skill; as long as fear or shame does not smother their thoughts, they speak in a more vivacious and pleasing manner. Their conversations are livelier, freer, and more humorous. They learn more quickly whatever they are taught, on condition that they get the same instruction as boys. They are more assiduous and patient at work, more obedient, more modest, and have more self-discipline. In a word, one notices that they possess to a greater extent all the excellent qualities which, when found in young men, persuade us that they are more suited to great things than their peers.

Nonetheless, although what is observed about the two sexes when they are still in their cradles is already enough to conclude that the more beautiful of the two shows the greatest promise, that evidence is completely ignored. Teachers and lessons are reserved for boys. Great care is taken to teach them everything that is deemed most appropriate to train their minds, while women are allowed to languish in idleness, indolence, and ignorance and to remain in the most lowly and vile work.

Besides, one only needs eyes to recognize that the two sexes are like two brothers in the same family, in which the youngest often shows that, despite the neglect with which he was reared, the only way in which the older son is superior to him is by having had the benefit of being born first.

Study is useless for most men   What use is the education that men usually receive? For most of them, it is useless for the purpose for which it is given. It does not prevent many of them from falling into dissoluteness and vice and others from remaining permanently ignorant or even from becoming more ignorant than they had been previously. If they already possess any inkling of decency, cheerfulness or civility, they lose it by studying. They are at odds with everything and vice versa. They display so much rudeness and boorishness in their manners at home that one would imagine that they had spent their youth travelling in a country where they met only savages. What they have learned is like contraband goods that they would not dare or could not offer for sale. If they wish to re-enter society and behave properly there, they have to attend a ladies' school to learn politeness, kindness, and all the etiquette that is essential today in polite society.[10]

---

[10] The '*école des dames*' mentioned here does not refer to a girls' school—since none such existed at the time—but to the *salons* that were established and run by women and were widely accepted as cultivating the social characteristics that defined *honnêtes gens.* See for

If one thought further about this, one would consider women lucky rather than despise them because they are not involved in the sciences. For if, on the one hand, they are thereby deprived of the opportunity to develop their talents and their characteristic advantages, on the other hand they have no opportunity to ruin or lose them. Despite this privation, they develop intellectually, in virtue and in grace, as they get older.[11] If, impartially, one were to compare young men when they finish their studies with women of the same age and of comparable intelligence, without knowing how each group had been reared, one would conclude that the men's education was the exact opposite of what they received.[12]

The difference in manners between the two sexes Even women's appearance—their facial expression, their looks, the way they walk, their demeanour and gestures—has a certain sobriety, wisdom, and respectability that distinguishes them from men. They observe good manners carefully in everything; no one could be more discreet than them. One never hears a double-meaning word from their lips; the least offensive expression hurts their ears, and they cannot bear the sight of anything that offends modesty.

Most men behave in exactly the opposite way. They walk too hurriedly, their gestures are bizarre, their eyes wander, and they are never happier than when they discuss and dispute things that should remain unspoken or hidden.

Comparison of women with the learned If one engages in conversation with women, individually or in a group, and with those whom society calls learned, the difference between them is immediately obvious. One would conclude that whatever men put into their heads during study serves only to disturb and confuse their minds. Few are able to express themselves clearly, and their efforts to think of appropriate words makes one lose interest in anything worthwhile that they have to say; unless they are very intelligent and in the company of others like that, they cannot sustain an hour's conversation.

---

example J. du Bosc, *L'honnête femme* (Paris: Pierre Billaine, 1632) and François Du Soucy, *Le triomphe des dames* (Paris: chez l'autheur, 1646), and Molière's *L'école des femmes* (1662).

[11] There is a similar argument to the effect that women develop intellectually despite the obstructions they encounter in Gournay, p. 59 above.

[12] The argument that women benefit from a lack of formal schooling was familiar in Descartes, who argued that scholastic education corrupted the natural intelligence of human beings (men or women). See *The Principles of Philosophy* (AT IX, 9), where Descartes writes to Princess Elizabeth: 'one must conclude that those who have learned least from what has been called philosophy up to now are most capable of grasping the true philosophy.'

Women, by contrast, express what they know clearly and in an orderly fashion. Words come easily to them. They begin speaking and continue as they wish, and their imagination is inexhaustible when they feel free. They have a knack of expressing their feelings with a sweetness and charm that impresses their listeners as effectively as reason, whereas men usually express their feelings in a dry and harsh way.

If one broaches a subject with moderately intelligent women, they grasp what is at issue much more quickly; they consider it from more points of view and their minds are more receptive to any truth that is uttered in their presence. When they get to know the speaker a little and are not suspicious of them, one notices that their prejudices are not as deep-seated as those of men and are less obstructive to any truth they hear. They are far removed from the spirit of contradiction and dispute to which the learned are so subject. They do not quibble vainly about words nor use those mysterious technical terms that are so useful for camouflaging one's ignorance.[13] Everything they say is intelligible and sensible.

I have enjoyed speaking with women of every social class, whom I was able to meet in towns or in the country, in order to discover their strengths and weaknesses, and I found more common sense in those who were not stultified by necessity and work than in most of the writings that are highly regarded among ordinary scholars.[14]

The opinion of a great philosopher When speaking about God, it never occurred to any woman to tell me that she imagined God was like a venerable old man.[15] On the contrary, they said that they could not imagine God, that is, that they could not represent him by using the idea of a man. They concluded that God exists, because they did not understand themselves and everything in their environment as effects of chance

[13] Cartesians argued that the technical Latin terms used by scholastic philosophers served merely to camouflage their lack of understanding; see Louis de la Forge, *L'Homme de René Descartes* (Paris: Jacques le Gras, 1664), 183–4; Malebranche, ST, 642–3.

[14] 'Common sense' (*le bon sens*) refers to an innate capacity to make sound judgements rather than the acceptance of what is commonly accepted as true. Descartes begins the *Discourse on Method* as follows: 'Common sense is the best distributed thing in the whole world...the ability to judge well—which, strictly speaking, is what is meant by "common sense" or "reason"—is naturally equal in all human beings' (ATVI, 1–2).

[15] Poulain rejected the scholastic principle, derived from Aristotle, that we acquire ideas exclusively from sensory perceptions. Arnauld and Nicole argued that, if one followed that principle, one would have to imagine God as a venerable old man. *La Logique ou l'art de penser* (Paris: Vrin, 1981), 44. Cartesians drew a sharp distinction between imagining something and having a concept of it, and they argued that it is impossible to have a picture of God in one's imagination that resembles anything physical.

or of some mere creature. They also concluded that the outcome of their day-to-day decisions did not depend only on their prudence because they were often successful in ways that they had not anticipated, and that such unforeseen success must be due to divine providence.

The opinions of philosophers   When I asked them what they thought about their own soul, they did not reply that it was a very subtle flame, or the disposition of their bodily organs, or that it was capable of extending or contracting.[16] On the contrary, they replied that they understood well that it was distinct from their bodies. The only other thing they could say about it with certainty was that they did not believe that it was similar to anything they could perceive by the senses and that, if they had studied, they would know exactly what it was.

There is no nurse who would say, as physicians do, that their patients are getting better because the digestive faculty is performing its functions well.[17] And when they see a large quantity of blood spurting from a vein, they laugh at people who deny that blood circulates through veins that are interconnected.[18]

When I asked why they believed that rocks exposed to the Sun and the rains are more quickly eroded in the south than in the north, none was so foolish as to reply that it results from the fact that the moon chews them up, as some philosophers are happy to claim. Women claim instead that the heat of the Sun dries the rocks and that subsequent rain softens them more easily.

A scholastic question   I deliberately asked more than twenty women if they did not believe that God could raise a stone to the beatific vision by means of some obediential or extraordinary power.[19] I could

---

[16] Descartes mentions these views briefly in the Second Meditation, AT VII 26; they were associated with Heraclitus, Aristotle, and the Stoics.

[17] This mocks the pseudo-explanations of scholastic natural philosophers in the seventeenth century who invented specific faculties with corresponding special names (usually in Latin) to explain every natural phenomenon. For example, digestion was explained by the *faculté coctrice*, which amounts to explaining digestion by reference to a capacity to digest food. In the notorious example used by Molière in *Le malade imaginaire* (III, xiv, interlude), sleeping powder was said to make people fall asleep because it has a *virtus dormitiva*; *Oeuvres complètes*, ed. G. Couton (Paris: Gallimard, 1971), II, 1173.

[18] The theory that the blood circulates throughout the body was first proposed by William Harvey (1578–1657) in *De motu cordis et sanguinis in animalibus* (1628). Descartes subsequently endorsed Harvey's discovery in the *Discourse on Method*, Part V (AT VI, 46–55), though he disputed the explanation offered by Harvey. Nonetheless, most physicians still refused to accept blood circulation at the time when Poulain was writing.

[19] Scholastic philosophers distinguished between a thing's natural capacities and other extraordinary capacities it might acquire as a direct result of God's miraculous intervention. The latter were said to result from obedience to divine commands; hence the name 'obediential'.

get no response from them, however, except that I was mocking them by asking such a question.

The benefits of learning The most beneficial results of learning are the discernment and precision required to distinguish what is true and evident from what is false and obscure, and thereby to avoid falling into error and deception. People are inclined to believe that men, or at least those among them who are regarded as learned, are better in this respect than women. Nonetheless, if one had a little of this precision that I speak about, one would discover that it is one of the features that men lack most of all. They are not only confused and obscure in their discourses; it is precisely this feature that enables them to dominate and to win the trust of simple and credulous people. They even reject what is evident and clear, however, and they despise those who speak in a clear and intelligible manner as too simple and common. They are the first to believe anything obscure that is presented to them, as if it were more mysterious. To be convinced of this, one only has to listen to them with minimal attention and then demand that they explain themselves.

Women have intellectual precision Women's disposition is completely different from that. One notices that women who are a little worldly-wise cannot bear to hear even their children speaking Latin in their presence. They are suspicious of others who do so, and they often say they fear that this foreign language conceals some impertinence. Not only do they avoid using the technical terms of the sciences, which are said to be sacrosanct; despite the fact that they have good memories, they cannot remember them even when they have heard them repeated often. When one speaks obscurely to women, they admit honestly that they are not bright or intelligent enough to understand what one says, or else they realize that those who speak in that way are not adequately educated.

Finally, if one considers how men and women communicate what they know, one will conclude that the former are like workers who labour in quarries and who extract very rough and shapeless rocks from them, while women are like architects or skilled stonecutters who know how to polish whatever stones they have and make the best use of them.

Not only are there many women who judge things as if they had been given a better education, without the prejudices or confused ideas that are characteristic of scholars; one also sees a great number of women with such sound judgement that they speak about the subject matter of the most advanced sciences as if they had studied them all their lives.

Women have   Women express themselves gracefully. They have the art of
the art of   finding the most appropriate terms available and commu-
speaking   nicating more in one word than men manage with many
words. In a general discussion of language, they propose ideas
that are found only among the most accomplished grammarians. Finally,
one finds that they learn more about language simply by using it than most
men achieve by combining use with study.

Women are   Eloquence is a talent that is so natural to women and so
eloquent   characteristic of them that no one could dispute it. They
convince people of anything they wish. They know how to
prosecute and defend without having studied law, and there is scarcely a
judge who has not discovered that they are as good as professional lawyers.
Is there anything more powerful or convincing than the letters of many
ladies about all the concerns of daily life, and especially about the passions,
the impact of which displays all the beauty and skill of eloquence? They
treat the passions so sensitively and describe them so simply that one has
to admit having experienced them just like that, and that all the rhetorical
treatises in the world could not teach men something that women can do
without any difficulty. Works of eloquence or poetry, exhortations, sermons
and discourses, are not too sophisticated for their taste and their critiques
lack nothing except the special words and rules that are used in the schools.

I certainly hope that this treatise will not escape their scrutiny either.
Some will find something to criticize in it, because it is not adequate to the
importance and dignity of the subject matter, because the style is not sufficiently complimentary, or that it is not expressed in a sufficiently noble,
forceful, or formal manner. Others will say that it fails to address some questions or that important discussions are omitted. Nonetheless, I also hope
that my good will, and my intention to say only what is true and to avoid
excessively strong claims that would make it sound like a novel, will excuse
me in their eyes.

They possess   Women have another advantage insofar as the eloquence
eloquence   of their behaviour is much more animated than in men. We
in their   need only notice in their expression that they wish to influ-
behaviour   ence us in order to surrender to whatever they wish. They
have an air of nobility and grandeur, a free and majestic bearing, a proper deportment, natural gestures and engaging manners, a facility
with speech, and a gentle and flexible voice. The beauty and graciousness
that accompanies their speaking opens our hearts and penetrates our minds.

When they speak of good and evil, their faces display an honesty that makes them more persuasive. When they are enamoured of virtue, their heart is on their lips, and the idea of virtue that they express, enhanced by figures of speech and their characteristic charms, appears a hundred times more beautiful.

It is a pleasure to hear a woman pleading a legal case. No matter how complicated a case may be, she unravels it and explains it clearly. She outlines exactly her claims and those of the party she represents. She explains how the case arose, how she presents it, the various authorities on which she relies, and all the preliminary procedures she has initiated. One finds throughout women's conduct of legal cases a certain competence that men lack.

They understand the law and how to practise it

That is why I think that, if women studied law, they would be at least as successful as men in that profession. One sees that they prefer peace and justice more than us; they find quarrels unpleasant and intervene spontaneously to resolve them amicably. Their application helps them to find a special slant or expedient to reconcile opinions, and they naturally implement the principal rules of equity, on which all law is based, in managing their own households and those of others.

They have an aptitude for history

The writings of moderately intelligent women are always well structured, and they include a certain felicity that makes them more effective than ours. They know how to discern what is relevant or irrelevant to a subject, to disentangle the interests involved, to identify the character of the personalities, to uncover their plots and follow those that are more or less important once they have identified them. All of that is more evident in the stories and novels of contemporary learned ladies.[20]

They know theology

How many women have learned as much from sermons, conversations, and small books of piety as the doctors of theology learn from Saint Thomas in lecture rooms and in their studies? The soundness and depth with which they speak of the greatest mysteries and the whole of Christian morality is such that they would often be taken as great theologians if they wore a theologian's hat and could quote a few passages in Latin.

---

[20] Probably refers to the work of Madeleine de Scudéry (1607–1701), who wrote many novels and other works in support of women's education, such as *Les femmes illustres* (Paris: Sommaville & Courbé, 1642), which was published under the name of her brother George.

They
understand
medicine

It seems as if women were born to practise medicine and to restore health to the sick. Their cleanliness and kindness go half way towards relieving pain. They are not only skilled in applying therapies but also in discovering them. They find innumerable remedies that are considered insignificant because they are much less expensive than those used by physicians and are not officially prescribed. Nonetheless, they are much more reliable and easy because they are natural. Finally, women make observations in the course of their practice so carefully, and apply their reason to them so well, that they often make all the school textbooks redundant.

They know
the opposite
of astrological
fantasies

Country women, who are used to working in the fields, know the vagaries of the seasons very well, and their almanacs are much more reliable than those published by astrologers. They explain the fertility and infertility of different years so simply by reference to the winds, rains, and everything that affects the weather, that it is impossible to hear them without feeling sorry for the learned who explain such phenomena by reference to the aspects, conjunctions, and ascendants of planets. That makes me think that, if they had been taught that the changes that occur in a human body may result from its particular constitution, and from exercise, the climate, nourishment, education and the contingencies of human interaction, they would never have dared to attribute the body's dispositions and changes to the influence of the stars, which are bodies that are several million leagues away.[21]

Why do
women not
speak about
some sciences?

It is true that there are sciences that women do not speak about, because they are not practical or concerned with society. Algebra, geometry, and optics rarely emerge from laboratories or scientific academies into the world of everyday living. Since their primary function is to give precision to our thinking, they should appear only secretly in ordinary life, like the hidden springs that facilitate the operation of great machines. In other words, one should implement those sciences in one's daily conversations,

---

[21] The possible influence of the stars or planets on human health was the subject of much discussion, not only among astrologers, but even among proponents of the new mechanical natural philosophy. See, for example, Claude Gadroys, *Discours sur les influences des astres, selon les principes de M. Descartes* (Paris: Jean-Baptiste Coignaret, 1671).

and think and speak precisely and geometrically without revealing that one is a geometrician.

All this is more evident among ladies   One can easily make all these observations about mental qualities in the case of women of relatively modest social status, but if one goes as high as the royal court and has access to the conversations of ladies, one could notice something entirely different there. It seems as if their intelligence is naturally commensurate with their social status. With their precision, discernment, and decency, they have an intellectual ability that is keen, refined, and relaxed, and there is something lofty and noble that is characteristic of them. One might say that both things and people approach them only with respect. They always view things in the best light and, when speaking about them, they give a very different impression than is usually the case. In a word, if one shows someone with the least sensitivity two letters from ladies of different social status, they will immediately recognize which of their authors is more noble.

Learned women, who are very numerous, are more worthy of esteem than learned men   How many ladies have there been, and how many are still alive today, who should be numbered among the learned, unless one wished to rank them even higher?[22] The age in which we live includes more learned women than all previous centuries together, and since they have equalled men they are more worthy of esteem for reasons that apply only to them. They had to overcome the indolence in which women were reared, renounce the pleasures and laziness to which they had been reduced, overcome many public obstacles that prevented them from studying, and surmount the unfavourable ideas that are commonly held about learned women, in addition to similar ideas that people hold about women in general. They achieved all that; and whether the challenge involved made their minds more lively and penetrating or whether such qualities are natural to them, they have become proportionately more clever than men.

Nonetheless, one could say—without diminishing the favourable opinion that these illustrious ladies deserve—that it was chance or external conditions that made them successful, just like the most learned men, and that

---

[22] The practice of listing learned women became a commonplace in the seventeenth century. See, for example, Marguerite Buffet, *Nouvelles observations sur la langue françoise avec Les Éloges des illustres sçavantes, tant anciennes que Modernes* (Paris: J. Cusson, 1668).

One must   there are innumerable others who would have succeeded
acknowledge   just as well had they had access to similar opportunities. Just
that, in gen-   as it is rather unfair to believe that all women are indiscreet
eral, women   simply because one knows five or six who are such, one
are capable of   should be equally fair and conclude that women are capable
scientific study   of scientific study because one sees that a number of them
have been able to raise themselves to such heights.

It is commonly assumed that the Turks, barbarians, and savages are not
as capable of study as Europeans. Nonetheless, it is certain that if one saw
five or six of them here in France who were capable or who had the title of
doctor—which is not impossible—one would correct one's judgement and
concede that, since such people are human like us, they are capable of the
same things, and if they were taught they would be equal to us in everything.
The women with whom we live are surely as important to us as barbarians
and savages and we should think about them no less favourably or reasonably.

If, despite these observations, common folk refuse to accept that women
are as capable of scientific study as we are, they should at least acknowledge that such study is less necessary for women. One applies oneself to
science for two reasons: one is to know the subject matter being studied,
and the other is to become virtuous by means of this knowledge. Since this
life is so short, science should be directed exclusively towards virtue; and
since women are already virtuous, one could say that—by a unique good
fortune—they already possess the principal benefits of a formal education
without having studied.

Women are   What we observe daily should convince us that women are
as virtuous   no less Christian than men. They accept the Gospel with
as men   humility and simplicity. They implement its maxims in an
exemplary way. Their respect for everything that pertains to
religion has always been so great that they are accepted without challenge as more pious and devout than us. Admittedly, their religious
worship becomes excessive; but I do not find such excess very blameworthy. It is adequately explained by the ignorance in which they are reared. If
their zeal lacks discretion, their conviction is at least genuine; and one could
say that, since they cling to virtue so strongly even in the darkness of ignorance, they would embrace it very differently if they understood it fully.

It seems as if compassion, which is the virtue of the Gospel, was destined
for their sex. News of their neighbour's misfortune hardly reaches their
ears when it touches their hearts and brings tears to their eyes. Is it not the

Women are
charitable
case that they distribute most generously to the needy during public calamities? Is it not ladies who still take special care of the poor and sick in parishes today, or who go to visit them in prisons and look after them in hospitals? Is it not the dutiful young women, scattered throughout various parts of the city, who have assumed responsibility for bringing them food and necessary medicines and to whom the title 'charity'—which they practise with such dignity—has been given?[23]

Women of the
Hôtel-Dieu
Finally, even if there were no women in the world who exercised this virtue towards their neighbours apart from those who look after the sick at the *Hôtel-Dieu*, I still do not believe that men could claim justly, for that reason, that they are superior to women.[24] Those are the women who deserve to be included in any gallery of heroic women.[25] It is their lives that should be celebrated with the greatest praise, and their deaths should be honoured with the most excellent panegyrics, because that is where one can see the Christian religion, i.e. truly heroic virtue, being practised in strict compliance with its commandments and counsels. One sees young women renounce the world and themselves, committed to permanent chastity and poverty, taking up their cross (the most difficult cross in the world) to place themselves for the rest of their lives under the yoke of Jesus Christ. They dedicate themselves to a hospital in which all kinds of sick people are admitted without discrimination (irrespective of what country or region they come from), and are all cared for equally. Following the example of their Spouse [Jesus Christ],

[23] Saint Vincent de Paul and Saint Louise de Marillac founded a religious order of women called the Daughters of Charity in 1633, with a special mission of visiting the poor and sick and taking care of them in their own homes. This foundation represented a significant departure from the tradition, within Catholicism, of religious women being confined to permanent residence in a convent.

[24] The *Hôtel Dieu* was a hospital in central Paris which cared especially for indigent sick patients. In 1634 Saint Vincent de Paul introduced the Ladies of Charity to assist the religious sisters of the Hôtel Dieu. The ladies in question were lay people, including many of noble rank, who devoted their time to works of charity in the parishes. Poulain adapts one of the phrases, *femme forte*, that was reserved for heroic women, and applies it to ordinary women who did extraordinary charitable work.

[25] The phrase 'gallery of heroic women' reflects one of the standard genres of writing in favour of women in the period, which combined illustrations of women renowned for virtue (such as Judith in the Old Testament) and a discussion of the virtues for which they were famous. See for example P. le Moyne, *La Galerie des femmes fortes* (Paris: 1647), and M. de Scudéry, *Les femmes illustres … avec les veritables portraits des ces Heroines, tirez des Medailles Antiques* (Paris: 1642).

they assume the care of all kinds of human illness without being disgusted by seeing constantly the most atrocious sights, listening to abuse and the cries of the sick, and smelling all the infections of the human body. It is characteristic of the spirit that inspires them that they carry the sick from one bed to another in their arms and that they encourage the unfortunate patients, not with empty words, but with an effective and personal example of patience and indomitable charity.

Could one imagine anything greater among Christians? Other women are no less inclined to comfort their neighbours. They merely lack the opportunity or they are distracted by other tasks. I also think that it is equally unacceptable to conclude from this, as is commonly done, that women are naturally the servants of men, and to claim that those who have received special gifts from God are the servants or slaves of those for whose benefit they exercise those gifts.

How women live as celibates No matter what lifestyle they adopt, women's conduct always involves some remarkable features. It seems as if those who are unmarried while still living in society remain there only to provide others with a good example. Their faces and behaviour display Christian modesty. Virtue is their principal adornment. They avoid worldly companionships and distractions, and their dedication to works of piety shows clearly that they are not involved in the cares and demands of marriage, so that they can enjoy a much greater freedom of mind and not be bound to anything apart from pleasing God.[26]

How they live in convents There are as many monasteries managed by women as by men, and their lives there are no less exemplary. Their retreat from the world is greater than in the case of men, their penitence is just as austere, and abbesses are just as good as abbots. Women make rules with admirable wisdom and govern their spiritual daughters with such prudence that no disorder ever arises. Indeed, the fame of religious houses, the great wealth that they possess, and their solid buildings are the result of the good order with which their superiors manage them.

---

[26] Voluntary celibacy was an unusual lifestyle for women in this period, although chosen by some intellectual women such as Marie de Gournay or Gabrielle Suchon, the latter of whom wrote *Du Célibat volontaire ou la vie sans engagement*, ed. S. Auffret (Paris: Indigo, 1994; 1st edn. 1700); some sections are translated as *On the Celibate Life Freely Chosen, or Life without Commitments*, in *A Woman who Defends all the Persons of her Sex: Selected Philosophical and Moral Writings*, trans. D. C. Stanton and R. M. Wilkin (Chicago and London: University of Chicago Press, 2010), 237–93.

How they live Marriage is the most natural state and the most usual one
in marriage for human beings. Once married, people are committed to
it for life. The married state coincides with those periods of
one's life in which one ought to act only rationally, and the various contingencies of nature or chance to which marriage is subject, which apply to
a greater extent to those in that state, provide an opportunity for married
people to display more intelligence than usual. One does not require much
experience to realize that women are more suited to marriage than men.
Daughters are able to manage a home at an age when men still need a tutor,
and the most common way of rearing a young man well is to put him in
the care of a woman who will restrain him by example, moderate his fits of
passion, and rescue him from debauchery.

What forbearance is required of women to live at peace with their husbands! They submit to their commands, do nothing without consulting
them, restrain themselves in many things to avoid displeasing them, and
often deprive themselves of the most innocent enjoyments to avoid suspicion. It is well known which of the two sexes is more faithful to the other,
which one accepts more patiently the difficulties that occur in marriage
and displays more wisdom when they occur.

How women   Nearly all homes are ruled only by women, to whom their
rear their   husbands have handed over their management. The care
children   they take in their children's education is much more significant for the families and more important for the state
than what they devote to their property. They apply themselves totally to
the protection of their children. They have such great fear of any evil that
might befall their children that they often lose sleep over it. They deprive
themselves willingly of the most necessary things so that their children
lack nothing. They cannot bear to see them suffer the slightest without the
deepest suffering themselves. One could say that their greatest suffering is
being unable to console their children while attending to their pains.

Their solici-   Who is unaware of the dedication with which women work
tude for their   to instruct children in virtue, insofar as their age allows?
children's   They try to make them know and love God, and they teach
education   them to adore God in a way that is appropriate to their age.
They take care to place them under the guidance of a tutor
as soon as they are ready for it, and they choose the tutor with the greatest
care to improve their education. It is even more praiseworthy that they supplement their instruction with good example.

A more   If one wished to go into great detail about all life's contingencies
detailed anal- and all the virtues that women display in them, and to examine
ysis would   the most significant features of them, one would discover the
favour women material for a more comprehensive eulogy. One could show
how far their sobriety extends in the use of food and drink, their
patience in coping with difficulties, and their strength and courage in bearing
with suffering, tiredness, sleeplessness and children; their moderation in respect
of pleasures and passions; their tendency to do good; their prudence in business
affairs, and their honesty in everything. In a word, one could show that there
is no virtue that they do not share with us and, on the contrary, that there are
many significant faults that are characteristic of men.

These are my general and common observations about women as regards
their qualities of mind, the use of which is the only thing that should be
invoked to differentiate between people.

Since there are hardly any situations in life in which one cannot find
examples of people's disposition, genius, vice or virtue, and ability, those
who would wish to correct their views about women have ample opportunities for doing so in public or private, at the royal court or the convent
grill, at entertainments or in religious exercises, with the poor or the rich,
in whatever state or condition women may be. If one examines impartially and honestly what can be observed about women one finds, even if
there are a few things that are less favourable to them, that there are many
more that are very much in their favour; that it is not because they are less
deserving but rather because of misfortune or a lack of strength that their
condition is not equal to ours and, eventually, one will conclude that the
common view about women is a popular and ill-founded prejudice.

Part II

*Which shows that the testimonies that may be invoked against the view that the
sexes are equal, which are borrowed from poets, orators, historians, jurists, and philosophers, are completely unfounded and useless.*

The fact that learned people hold the same view confirms common folk
in their opinion about women. Thus, since the dominant public opinion of
those whose views are trusted agrees with certain general appearances to
the detriment of women, it is not surprising that unsophisticated and uneducated people hold such a low opinion of women. The result, as in many
other things, is that people are confirmed in one prejudice by another.

Since the concept of truth is linked naturally with that of scientific knowledge, whatever is proposed by those who have a reputation for learning is accepted as true. However, there are many more people who are wise in name only than those who are genuinely wise; consequently, most people who rely merely on what the majority thinks agree with the former, and they endorse their views even more readily to the extent that they coincide with what they already believed themselves.

The popular view adopted by the sciences
For that reason, when common folk see that poets, orators, historians, and philosophers also claim publicly that women are inferior to men and that they are less noble and perfect, they become more convinced of their own opinion because they fail to realize that the science of such people is the same prejudice as their own, except that it is more long-winded and specious, and that they merely add to what we know from custom the opinions of the ancients, on whose authority all their certainty depends. I find that, in relation to the sexes, those who have studied and those who have not done so fall into the same mistake, which is to judge that what is said about the sexes by those whom they respect is true because they had decided in advance to believe them. What they should do, instead, is not to accept what they say before knowing that they state only what is true.

Against the authority of poets and orators
Since the objective of poets and orators is merely to please and persuade, the way things appear to us is enough to convince most people about something. Thus, since exaggeration and hyperbole are very appropriate to this objective, they arbitrarily present things as good or evil, great or small, by magnifying ideas in accordance with their needs and, using a common ploy, they attribute to all women in general what they observe in only a few individuals. If they saw a few women who are hypocrites, they feel justified in claiming that all women are subject to the same fault. The embellishments with which they decorate their discourses are very effective in exploiting the credulity of those who are carelessly uncritical. They speak with great facility and elegance, and exploit various stylistic devices that are attractive, pleasant, and unusual, and dazzle the mind and hinder it from discerning the truth. There are some poems or plays that seem to be very convincing; people believe them because they fail to realize that their truth and persuasiveness results from rhetorical devices, metaphors, proverbs, descriptions, similes, and emblems. Since such writings display much skill and wit, people imagine that they also contain a corresponding amount of truth.

One person believes that women like to be deceived because they have read Sarasin's sonnet about the fall of the first woman, which implies that she would not have fallen had she not listened to the devil's wooing.[27] It is true that this image is humorous and the story is well told; Sarasin uses it appropriately in the context of his sonnet and the Fall is pleasant. However, if the poem is examined in some depth and translated into prose, there is nothing more false or insipid than it.

There are people who are simple-minded enough to imagine that women are more inclined to anger than men, because they have read how poets represented the Furies in the form of women, without realizing that this is merely a poetic image and that painters who depict shrews with a woman's face also depict the devil in the guise of a man.

I have seen attempts to show that women are fickle because a famous Latin poet said that they were always changing, and a Frenchman compared them humorously to a weathervane that moves with the wind.[28] Such a conclusion fails to appreciate that all these ways of speaking about things are suitable only for misleading the mind rather than instructing it.

Common eloquence is a verbal optics that makes objects appear with any shape or colour one likes, and there is no virtue that could not be represented as a vice by exploiting the strategies that it provides.

There is nothing more common than to find authors writing that women are less perfect and noble than men, although they give no reasons at all for their views. It seems very likely that they were convinced of this in the same way as common folk: women do not share with us in observable advantages, such as the sciences or positions of authority, which are the commonly accepted indications of perfection; therefore, they conclude, they are not as perfect as us. To take this conclusion seriously, however, one would have to show that they are excluded from these preferential positions because they are not suited to them. But it is not as easy to show that as one might imagine, and it will not be difficult to demonstrate the contrary in what follows and to illustrate how this error results from having only confused ideas of perfection and nobility.

[27] Jean-François Sarasin (1615–54), *Sonnet à Monsieur de Charleval*, in *Les oeuvres de Monsieur Sarasin* (Paris: Augustin Courbé, 1656), 72: '*Elle aima mieux pour s'en faire conter, / Prester l'oreille aux fleurettes du Diable, / Que d'estre femme & ne pas coquetter.*' ('She [Eve] preferred to be courted and to listen to the wooing of the devil rather than to be a woman and not to flirt.')

[28] Juvenal, Satire VI in *Juvenal and Perseus*, LCL 91, pp. 235–95, and Molière, *Le Dépit amoureux*, IV, ii, v. 266–7.

All the arguments of those who hold that the fair sex is not as noble or excellent as ours are based on believing that, since men exercise all the authority, everything must be arranged for their benefit. I am convinced that one would believe the exact opposite, and with even greater conviction—namely that men are there for the sake of women—if women held all authority, as they did in the amazons' empire.[29]

It is true that women are employed here only in positions that are regarded as the lowest. It is equally true that, as far as reason or religion are concerned, they are not therefore less worthy of esteem. There is nothing low apart from vice and nothing great apart from virtue, and since women display more virtue than men in their lowly occupations they deserve to be more highly esteemed. I am not even sure that, if one considers only their normal occupation of nourishing and educating human beings in their infancy, they do not deserve the highest rank in civil society.

Women are more worthy of esteem than men in respect of their occupation If we were free and living without a commonwealth, the only reason we would have to unite together would be to protect our lives and to enjoy peaceably those things that are necessary for that purpose,[30] and we would have more esteem for those who contributed more to our objective. That is why we got used to regarding princes as foremost in the state, because their care and foresight is the most general and most extensive, and we esteem those who are below them proportionately. Most people rate soldiers higher than judges, because soldiers directly confront those who threaten life in the most frightening

---

[29] The amazons were frequently quoted in the literature of the period both in support of women and, on the contrary, to prove how badly women behave when they exercise power. For example, Rolet argued in *Tableau historique des ruses et subtilitez des femmes* (Paris: 1623), 12–13: 'There is no one who has not heard of the tyrannical domination of the Amazons, who expelled all the men from their country and were so barbaric even towards their own children that, when they gave birth to a male child, they immediately killed him, thereby showing their desire to expand their tyrannical empire and to prevent any man from becoming king.'

[30] Refers to the contract theory of political authority that is particularly associated with Hobbes and Locke. According to that theory, individuals in a state of nature (a hypothetical condition prior to the political organization of people in commonwealths in which they are still free individuals) would voluntarily associate in a binding contract to achieve basic objectives, such as self-preservation and security. They would rationally establish some person or group of people with authority to enforce the terms of the contract on participating individuals. The political authority of their ruler(s) thus derives exclusively from the freely assumed contract of the individuals involved rather than, for example, from God. Poulain outlines this theory under 'Law and Politics', p. 164.

ways, and everyone values people in proportion to their usefulness. Thus women seem to be the most worthy of esteem because the service they provide is incomparably greater than that provided by all others.

What women deserve One could do without princes, soldiers, and merchants completely, as people did at the beginning of the world and as savages still do today. But it would be impossible to do without women in one's infancy. As soon as states are pacified adequately, most of the people in authority might as well be dead or useless, whereas women never cease to be necessary for us. Justice officials are useful only for protecting the property of those who possess it, whereas women are there to protect our lives. Soldiers are at the service of mature people who are capable of protecting themselves, while women are at the service of people at a time when they still do not know who they are or whether they have enemies or friends, and when their only defence against those who attack them is to cry. Those in authority, magistrates, and princes often act only for their own glory and self-interest, whereas women act only for the good of the children that they rear. Finally, there is nothing comparable in any condition of civil society to the care and pains, the fatigue and duties, to which women subject themselves.

It is pure fantasy, therefore, to claim that women are less worthy of esteem. If a man tamed a tiger, he would be generously rewarded; those who are able to train horses, monkeys, or elephants are greatly esteemed. A man is praised if he writes a small book that requires only a little time or effort, whereas women are neglected although they devote many years to nourishing and educating children. The only explanation one can find for this situation, if one looks carefully, is that one task is more common or familiar than the other.

Against evidence gleaned from history What historians say unfavourably about women has a greater impact on minds than orators' speeches. Their testimony is trusted more because they appear not to propose anything on their own authority; it also coincides with what people already believe, because they report that women in previous ages were the same as they are believed to be today. Nonetheless, all the authority that historians exercise over people's minds is merely the result of a fairly common prejudice about the past, which is pictured as a venerable old man who, since he is very wise and experienced, is incapable of being mistaken or of saying anything other than the truth.

The ancients, however, were no less human than we are, nor any less subject to error. Therefore, one should not accept their opinions today any more than one would have done in their own day.[31] In former times the general opinion of women was much as it is today, and with as little justification. Thus one should be suspicious of everything that men have said about women because they are both judges and litigants.[32] When someone quotes the opinions of a thousand authors against women, that history should be considered as nothing more than a tradition of prejudices and errors. There is also as little accuracy and truth in ancient histories as there is in popular stories, and it is well known that there is almost none in the latter. The ancients added their own passions and interests to their histories, and since most of those authors had only confused conceptions of vice or virtue, they often mistook one for the other. People who read them today and share the popular bias against women make the same mistake. Given their prejudices, the ancients took care to exaggerate the virtues and merits of their own sex and, motivated by the opposite interest, to weaken and undervalue the merits of women. This is so easily recognizable that it is unnecessary to provide examples.

Historical evidence in favour of women   Nonetheless, if one knows a little about interpreting the past, one will find enough evidence to show that women were not surpassed by men, and that the virtue they displayed is more excellent when it is examined truthfully in all its circumstances. One will notice that women showed equally convincing signs of intelligence and ability in every kind of situation. There were women who governed large states and empires with a degree of wisdom and moderation that is unparalleled; others dispensed justice with an integrity that matches that of the Areopagus.[33] Many restored their kingdoms to peace by their prudence and wise counsel, and restored their husbands to their thrones. Women have been seen leading armies or defending themselves on the city ramparts with a degree of courage that is beyond heroic. How

[31] This is a characteristically Cartesian comment on the authority of ancient authors, to the effect that the mere age of an opinion is no indication of its truth or otherwise. See, for example, Nicolas Malebranche, 'Reasons why we prefer to follow authority rather than to use our minds' (ST, 138–39).

[32] This argument about the lack of impartiality in men's judgements about women appears in other contemporary literature, for example in Vigoureux's *La défence des femmes, contre l'Alphabet de leur prétendue malice et imperfection* (Paris: Pierre Chevalier, 1617), 154

[33] The Areopagite Council of Athens exercised various judicial functions from the sixth century BC. Poulain accepts it in this text as a symbol of ideal justice.

many women have there been whose chastity could not be compromised either by appalling threats or by wonderful promises, and who endured the most horrible torments in the name of religion with amazing magnanimity? How many women have made themselves as competent as men in all the sciences, have delved into what is most obscure in nature, most subtle in politics, or most fundamental in morality, and have mastered the most obscure parts of Christian theology? Thus the history that is abused by those who are biased against women in order to vilify them can be used by those who examine it impartially to show that the female sex is no less noble than ours.

Against   Lawyers' opinions about women carry a lot of weight for many *lawyers*   people because they profess specifically to give everyone their due.

Nonetheless, they subject women to the power of their husbands like children under the control of their fathers, while claiming instead that it is nature that assigns women to the lowest functions in society and removes them from public offices.

People think that they are on firm ground when they repeat this, but one can reject the opinion of lawyers without challenging the respect that they deserve. They would be hard pressed if they were required to explain intelligibly what they mean by 'nature' in this context, and to explain how nature distinguished the two sexes, as they claim.

One must assume that those who enacted or compiled the laws—being men—discriminated in favour of their own sex, as women might have done had they been in a similar situation. Since laws were enacted from the beginning of civil society in the same way as they are today in relation to women, lawyers who were also prejudiced attributed to nature a distinction that results only from custom. Besides, they felt no need to change the social arrangements that they found already in place in order to achieve their objective, which was to govern a state well by dispensing justice. Finally, if they obstinately claim that women are naturally dependent on men, one could confront them with their own principles, because they themselves acknowledge that dependence and servitude are contrary to the order of nature, which makes all human beings equal.[34]

---

[34] Poulain seems to appeal here to a natural law that makes all human beings equal. However, the versions of natural law that were most likely available to him, such as those of Grotius or Hobbes, did not defend the equality of the sexes.

Since dependence is a purely physical or civil relation, it should be con-sidered only as an effect of change, violence, or custom, apart from chil-dren's dependence on those who give them life. Besides, does it not expire at a certain age when human beings are assumed to have enough reason and experience to govern themselves and are emancipated by law from the authority of others?

Between people of more or less the same age there should be only a reasonable dependence, by which those who are less enlightened submit voluntarily to those who are more so. Thus if one were to remove the legal privileges that make men the heads of families, one would find that wives' submission to their husbands is based on nothing other than experience and knowledge. Both sexes commit to each other freely at a time when women are as reasonable and, in some cases, more reasonable than their husbands. The promises and agreements of marriage are reciprocal and their marital rights are equal. If the law gives the husband more authority over their property, nature gives women more power and right over the children.[35] Since the will of one spouse is not binding on the other, if a wife is obliged to do what her husband requests, the latter is no less obliged to do what his wife indicates as his duty. Apart from what is reasonable, the only way that a wife may be constrained to submit to her husband is by the latter's superior strength. That is what is called acting like a Turk to a Moor, and not like an intelligent human being.[36]

Against Philosophers   There would be little difficulty in rejecting the views of the learned people that we have just discussed, because it is easy to recognize that their profession does not require them to become well informed about the real nature of things. Poets and orators are satisfied with how things appear and what is probable, just as historians are satisfied with the testimony of antiquity and lawyers need only custom to fulfil their professional duties. However, one cannot dismiss the opinions of philosophers as easily, because it appears as if they are exempt from all the

---

[35] Hobbes argued that, in a state of nature, the paternity of any child is uncertain while it is relatively easy to determine the mother of a child; and since the mother nourishes the child and preserves their life, she acquires a natural domination over that child. See *Leviathan*, ed. R. Tuck (Cambridge: Cambridge University Press, 1991), II, xx, 140. The civil laws of mar-riage change such a natural domination.

[36] The Moors were natives of parts of North Africa that correspond to modern Algeria and Morocco. Both Turks and Moors were considered to be barbarian, and the expression above is equivalent to 'acting like a barbarian'.

previous objections, as indeed they ought to be, and that they may be assumed to examine matters much more closely. This supports the credulity of common folk and makes philosophers' views seem indubitable, especially when they coincide with what one already believes.

Scholastic philosophers   Thus common folk become more convinced of the inequality of the sexes when they see those whose judgements they regard as a guide holding the same view as themselves, because they fail to realize that almost all philosophers have no other guide apart from common opinion and that they do not make up their minds scientifically, especially in relation to this question. They imported their prejudices into the schools and learned nothing there that would help them escape from them. On the contrary, all their knowledge is based on judgements that they made since their infancy, and they think that it is a crime or a mistake to raise doubts about anything that one believed before the age of reason.[37] They are not taught to understand human nature by reference to the body and mind, and what they are generally taught could easily serve to prove that there is only a difference of degree between us and brute animals. They are taught nothing at all about the sexes; they are assumed to know enough about them. They are far from examining the ability of the sexes and the natural and genuine differences between them, which is very interesting and is possibly among the most important questions in natural philosophy[38] and morals. They spend whole years and, in some cases, their whole lives discussing trifles and entities that are constructed by reason,[39] or wondering if there are imaginary spaces outside the world and if atoms or the small particles of dust that appear in sunlight are infinitely divisible. How can one trust what such scholars say in relation to important and serious questions?

Nonetheless, one could imagine that the principles of scholastic philosophy, despite being so poorly taught, would be adequate to discover which of the two sexes is naturally superior to the other. However, only those who

[37] Descartes often compared the principles of scholastic philosophy to the uncritical beliefs of children, and argued that such assumptions must be challenged and corrected when necessary. See for example *The Principles of Philosophy*, I: 71: 'the principal cause of error results from the prejudices of childhood', and art. 76, where he recommends reliance on reason rather than 'the uncritical judgements of ... childhood' (AT VIII-1, 36, 39).

[38] I have translated Poulain's term '*la physique*' as 'natural philosophy' because it includes disciplines such as anatomy and physiology and is wider in scope than physics today.

[39] 'Beings of reason' are realities that exist only in someone's thought, in contrast with realities that exist outside the mind.

do not know them or those who are biased in their favour would come to that conclusion. Self-knowledge is absolutely necessary in order to address this issue properly, especially knowledge of the body, which is the organ of the sciences, just as one must understand how telescopes are made in order to understand how they enlarge distant objects. Scholastic philosophers speak about the body only in passing, no more than they speak about truth and scientific knowledge, i.e. about the method for acquiring true and certain knowledge, without which it is impossible to consider properly whether women are as capable as we are of acquiring such knowledge. Without distracting myself by reporting their opinion on this issue, I shall set out here in general what I think about it.

What is science? Since all human beings are created alike, they all have the same sensations and the same ideas of natural objects—for example, of light, heat, and hardness. All the scientific knowledge that one tries to acquire about such things is reducible to knowing truly what particular internal or external disposition of each object produces the thoughts or sensations that we have of it. The only thing that teachers can do to help us acquire such knowledge is to apply our minds to what we perceive, so as to examine its appearances and its effects, without hurry or prejudice, and to show us the order that we must follow in arranging our thoughts in order to find what we are looking for.[40]

What is liquidity? For example, if an uneducated person asked me to explain the liquidity of water, I would not make any claims about it initially. Instead, I would ask them what they had observed about it, for instance: that water spreads out if it is not enclosed in a vessel, that is, all its parts separate and dissociate from each other without anyone introducing a foreign body; that one can stick one's fingers into it without any difficulty and without experiencing the kind of resistance found in hard bodies; if salt or sugar is put into water, one perceives that these two kinds of body gradually get smaller and are dissipated throughout the liquid.

Up to this point, I would not have taught them anything. If I got them to understand, in a similar way, what is involved in being at rest or in motion, I would show them that the nature of liquids consists in the fact that their

---

[40] This reflects one of the fundamental principles of Cartesian natural philosophy, which had been developed in the first paragraphs of Descartes' treatise *Le Monde* (AT XI, 3–6), to the effect that the sensations we experience of external stimuli, such as light, heat, and so on, may not correspond to the realities that cause those sensations, and that knowledge of the external sources of our sensations is gleaned only by hypothesizing their probable causes.

unobservable parts are in perpetual motion, which requires them to be contained within a vessel and easily allows hard objects to enter them. Since the parts of water are small, smooth, and sharp, they insinuate themselves on impact into the pores of sugar by shaking and dividing its parts and, as they move about in every direction, they carry with them into every part of a vessel the parts of sugar that they have separated.

This understanding of liquids, which is separated from the main body of natural philosophy, would be much clearer if it were seen in context. It contains nothing that ordinary women could not understand. If all the rest of our knowledge is introduced in a methodical way it presents no greater difficulty; the attentive student finds that every rational science requires less intelligence and less time that one needs to learn embroidery or tapestry well.

Learning embroidery and tapestry requires as much intelli- gence as learn- ing natu- ral philosophy In fact, we acquire ideas of natural phenomena involuntarily and they always occur in us in the same way.[41] Adam had those ideas just as we do; children have them in the same way as the elderly, and women have them in the same way as men. These ideas are repeated, strengthened, and linked together by the continuous use of the senses. The mind is always active, and anyone who understands well how it operates in one context discovers without difficulty how it operates in all others. There is only a difference of degree between a sensation of the Sun and a sensation of a spark; it requires no special skill or physical training to think about it properly.

The crafts that I mentioned above are very different. They require a much greater mental application. Since our ideas of them are arbitrary, they are more difficult to learn and to retain. That is why it takes so much time to learn a craft well, because it presupposes a lot of practice. One needs skill to keep things in proportion on a canvas, to distribute the silk and wool evenly, to mix the colours appropriately, not to bunch the points together nor separate them too much, not to put more in one row than another, and to make the variations imperceptible. In a word, one has to know how to make and vary art works in a thousand different ways to become proficient whereas, in the sciences, one only has to look in an orderly way at things

---

[41] Refers to the Cartesian account of the origin of ideas, according to which ideas of natural phenomena occur in each perceiver passively and in a similar way, without any effort or training on their part. In contrast, one requires training to acquire ideas of artificially made things.

that are already completely finished and always uniform. The only difficulty that prevents us from succeeding results less from the objects being studied or the ways in which the human body works than from the relative incompetence of teachers.[42]

Accordingly, one should not be very surprised any longer to find both uneducated men and women discussing issues that pertain to the sciences, because the method used for learning them involves nothing more than improving common sense, which is compromised by haste, custom, and usage.[43]

This general understanding of scientific knowledge may be enough to convince unbiased people that men and women are equally capable of acquiring it. Since the opposite view, however, is more entrenched, one has to rely on principles in order to disprove it completely. Thus by adding the physical explanations that are about to be introduced to the favourable features of women that were expounded in Part I, readers may be completely convinced of women's equality.

Women, when considered from the perspective of the principles of sound philosophy, are as capable as men of every kind of knowledge.

The mind
has no sex

It is easy to see that sexual differences apply only to the body. Since, strictly speaking, the body alone is involved in the reproduction of human beings and the mind merely gives its assent and does so in the same manner in everyone, it follows that the mind has no sex.[44]

---

[42] Descartes argued that acquiring knowledge is not similar to learning a craft; all one needs to acquire knowledge is the natural light of the intellect, which is shone by the inquiring subject onto different objects of inquiry; *Rules for Guiding one's Intelligence in Searching for the Truth* (AT X, 359–60).

[43] See note 14, concerning common sense.

[44] This was a commonplace among defenders of women's equality. It is found in Augustine *On the Trinity: Books 8–15*, ed. G. B. Matthews (Cambridge: Cambridge University Press, 2002), 89–92, and in Cornelius Agrippa, *Declamation of the Nobility and Preeminence of the Female Sex*, trans. Albert Rabil Jr. (Chicago: University of Chicago Press, 1996), 43. In the seventeenth century it was proposed among others by Marie de Gournay (this volume, p. 65); P. Le Moyne, *La Galerie des femmes fortes* (Paris, 1647), 250: 'one must say boldly and without fear of damaging it that philosophy has no sex, no more than intellects; that the true philosophy came for women as much as for men and, being the crowning perfection of the mind and the completion of reason, all reasonable souls are equally capable of its discipline;' Queen Christina of Sweden, *Ouvrage de Loisir ou maximes et sentences de Christine reine de Suède*, in *Mémoires pour servir à l'histoire de Christine reine de Suède*, 2 vols. (Amsterdam and Leipzig: Mortier, 1751), vol. I, 26: 'It is true that the soul has no sex;' Marguerite Buffet, *Traitté sur les Eloges des Illustres Sçaventes, Anciennes & Modernes* (note 22), 200.

The mind is   If the mind is considered in itself, it is found to be equal and
equal in all   to have the same nature in all human beings, and to be capa-
human beings ble of every kind of thought. The least significant thoughts
                engage it in the same way as the greatest ideas; the mind is
just as necessary if we think about a mite or an elephant. Whoever knows
what is involved in the light and fire of a spark also knows what the light of
the Sun is. When one becomes used to thinking about things that pertain
only to the mind, one sees them all as clearly as those things that are more
material, which are known by means of the senses. I fail to see any greater
difference between the mind of an ignorant and uncultured man and that
of an enlightened and sophisticated man than between the mind of the
same man at the age of ten and the age of forty.

The source   Since there appears to be no greater difference between the
of differences minds of men and women, it follows that the differences
between people between them do not result from their minds. The constitu-
                  tion of the body, but especially education, training, and the
perception of everything in our environment, are the natural and observable causes of so many differences that can be seen everywhere between
the sexes.

The mind acts   It is God who unites the mind with the body of a woman
in women in   as with that of a man, and who unites them by means of
the same way   the same laws. This union is established and maintained by
as in men   sensations, passions, and acts of the will;[45] and since the mind
                  acts in the same way in both sexes, it is equally capable of the
                  same things in both of them.

It perceives   That is even clearer if one considers only the head, which is
things in the   the unique organ of scientific knowledge and in which the
same way in   mind exercises all its functions. Even with the most detailed
both sexes   anatomical investigations, we cannot observe any difference
                  in this organ between men and women. The brains of the
latter are completely similar to ours; they receive and combine sensory
impressions there in the same way as we do, and they store them for the
imagination and memory in exactly the same way. Women hear as we do

[45] This account of mind–body union was proposed by Descartes in *The Passions of the Soul* (AT XI), and developed in greater detail in Louis de la Forge, *Traité de l'Esprit de l'Homme* (Paris: Girard, 1666): Engl. trans. *Treatise on the Human Mind*, trans. D. M. Clarke (Dordrecht: Kluwer, 1997), especially Chapters 13–15.

with their ears, they see with their eyes, and they taste with their tongues; there is nothing special in the disposition of these organs apart from the fact that those of women are usually more delicate, which is to their advantage. Thus external objects affect them in the same way as they affect us, by means of light to their eyes and sound to their ears.

Women are capable of metaphysics What would prevent them, therefore, from reflecting on their own selves to examine the nature of the mind, how many kinds of thought there are, and how thoughts are stimulated on the occasion of certain bodily movements? What would prevent them subsequently from examining the natural ideas that they have of God and from organizing their thoughts in an orderly fashion, having begun with spiritual things, and engaging in the science called metaphysics?[46]

Women are capable of studying natural philosophy and medicine Since women also have eyes and hands, could they not dissect the human body themselves or see a dissection being done by others; could they not consider the body's symmetry and structure, notice the diversity, differences, and relations of its parts, their shapes, movements, and functions, and the changes to which they are subject, and conclude from all that how to maintain them in good condition and to restore them to that condition if they ever lose it?

For that purpose, they would need only to understand the nature of external bodies that have some relation to their own by discovering their properties and everything that enables them to affect their body favourably or otherwise. They could do that simply by using their senses and by various experiments that are performed on such bodies; since women are equally capable of both kinds of experience, they can learn natural philosophy or medicine as well as us.

Does one need so much intelligence to know that breathing is absolutely necessary for the preservation of life, that it functions by taking air through the nasal passage and the mouth into the lungs, where it refreshes the blood that circulates through them and modifies it in various ways by mixing with the blood vapours and exhalations that are sometimes observable, depending on whether it contains more or fewer gross particles?

[46] This summarizes Descartes' approach to metaphysics in the *Meditations*, in which he advised readers to reflect on their own minds and thereby acquire an idea of what is meant by a spiritual reality; by extrapolating that idea one generates an idea of God. See AT VII, 188.

What is taste?   Is it so difficult to discover that, insofar as the body is
                        concerned, the taste of different foods is determined by
various ways in which they are dissolved by saliva on the tongue? No one
fails to notice that, following a meal, any food that one puts in one's mouth
is divided in a completely different way and causes a less pleasant sensation
than the food that had been eaten previously. It is no greater challenge to
discover anything else that needs to be known about other functions of the
human body, once they are examined methodically.

Women can   The passions are surely what are most interesting in this
know the   context. There are two things that may be noticed about
passions   them: (a) bodily motions, and (b) the thoughts and emo-
                   tions of the soul that are joined to them.[47] Women are capa-
ble of knowing this fact just as easily as we are. The causes that stimulate
the passions can also be known once one understands, by studying natural
philosophy, how things in our environment enter our bodies and affect us
and how, by experience and practice, we accept or reject them voluntarily.

They can   By regular reflection on the objects of the three sciences
learn logic   that we have just mentioned, a woman can notice that the
                   order of her thoughts should correspond to that of nature,
that such thoughts are accurate as long as they conform to nature, and that
the only obstacle to such accuracy is hasty judgement. By reflecting on the
method used to arrive at this point, a woman could thereby develop a guide
for subsequent study and thus develop a logic.

If someone claimed, nevertheless, that women could not acquire these
kinds of knowledge on their own—which is a purely gratuitous assumption—it would at least be impossible to deny that they could acquire them
with the help of teachers and books, as the most accomplished people have
done in every age.

Mathematics   One need only invoke the acknowledged sense of what is
                     appropriate, which women possess, to show that they are
capable of understanding mathematical relations. We would contradict ourselves if we doubted that they would also succeed as well as us if they applied
themselves to construct machines, because we attribute more dexterity and
natural intelligence to them.

---

[47] Descartes explained passions (such as love, hate, pride, and so on) as mental events that are
triggered and sustained by corresponding bodily states: *The Passions of the Soul* (AT XI, 349).

They
can study
astronomy
All one needs are eyes and a little attention in order to observe natural phenomena, to notice that the Sun and all the other luminous bodies in the heavens are genuine fires because they affect us and illuminate us in the same way as fires on Earth; that they appear to correspond in sequence to different places on the Earth and thereby make it possible to track their movements and paths. Anyone who can imagine large-scale models in their head and can picture how their mechanisms work can equally well imagine how the whole machine of the world operates, once they have observed carefully the various ways in which it appears to us.

Distinctions
between the
sciences
We have already found that women have all the dispositions that make men capable of learning the sciences that pertain to people as individuals. If we continue to examine this issue carefully, we will also find in them all the dispositions required for sciences that apply to people insofar as they are related to others in civil society.

It is a defect in the common philosophy to make such a big distinction between sciences that it is nearly impossible to recognize how they are interconnected if one follows the method that is characteristic of that philosophy.[48] That limits the scope of the human mind very much by imagining that the same person is almost never capable of studying a number of sciences; it suggests that if one is suited to natural philosophy or medicine one cannot be competent in rhetoric or theology, and that one needs as many distinct kinds of intelligence as there are distinct sciences.[49]

This suggestion results partly from the fact that people often confuse nature and custom by considering the aptitude of some individuals for one science rather than another as an effect of their natural make-up, whereas it is often simply a contingent inclination that results from necessity, education, or habit. It also results partly from failing to notice that, strictly speaking, there is only one science in the world, namely, the science of ourselves, of which all other sciences are mere applications.

[48] Descartes argued, in the *Discourse on Method* (AT VI, 17), that there is a single method for acquiring all scientific knowledge.
[49] In his dedication of *The Principles of Philosophy* to Princess Elizabeth, Descartes praised her ability to master disparate disciplines, in contrast with those who could study geometry but not metaphysics or vice versa: 'I recognize that your intelligence is the only one to which all these disciplines are equally clear, and for that reason I describe it as incomparable' (AT VIII-1, 4).

In fact, the difficulty one experiences today in learning languages, morals, and everything else results from not knowing how to relate them to this general science. Thus it may happen that those who believe that women are capable of studying natural philosophy or medicine would deny that they are therefore also capable of the sciences just mentioned. The difficulty, however, is similar in both kinds of science; what is at issue in all cases is clear thinking. Clear thinking involves applying one's mind seriously to the objects that are presented to us. In that way we form clear and distinct ideas of them, we look at them from every angle and in all their different relations, and we make judgements about them only in respect of what is manifestly true. To accomplish a perfect science, all one needs is to arrange one's thoughts in a natural order.[50] That involves nothing that is beyond the capacity of women, and those who are taught natural philosophy and medicine according to this method would be capable of advancing in all the other sciences too.

Women are capable of learning Grammar   Why would it be impossible for women to recognize that our need to live together in society requires us to communicate our thoughts by external signs, and that the most appropriate way of doing so is by speaking, which consists in using words that have been agreed among speakers? Why could they not recognize that there must be as many kinds of word are there are kinds of idea, and there must be some connection between the sound and the meaning of words to make it possible to learn and remember them more easily, so that we do not have to multiply them to infinity; that words must be arranged in the most natural order—one that matches as much as possible the order of our ideas—and that we should not use more words in a discourse than are necessary to make ourselves understood?[51]

These reflections would make any woman capable of working, as an academician, towards the improvement of her native language, by reforming or deleting inappropriate words, introducing new ones, adjusting word-usage in accordance with reason and with what is known about languages.[52] The method by which she learned her native language would serve a woman marvellously in learning foreign languages, to decipher their finer details

[50] Descartes suggests, in the *Principles of Philosophy*, I. 24, that a perfect science (*scientia perfectissima*) is constructed by deducing our ideas of natural phenomena from first principles (AT VIII-1, 14).

[51] Cf. *La Logique ou l'Art de Penser*, 42ff.

[52] The *Académie française*, which excluded women members, was officially responsible for the kinds of linguistic study mentioned here.

and to read foreign authors, and thus to become very competent in grammar and what are called the humanities.

Rhetoric   Women, just as much as men, speak only to communicate what they know about things and to encourage others to act as they would wish—which is called persuading. They succeed in that naturally much better than us. To do so in an artful manner they only need to study how to present things as they appear to them or how they would appear if they were in the position of those whom they wish to persuade. Since all human beings were created in the same way, they are nearly always affected emotionally by objects in similar ways; if they are affected differently, that results from their natural inclinations, their habits, or their social status. That is something that a woman would recognize with little reflection and practice. And since women know how to arrange their thoughts in the most appropriate way, to express them politely and graciously and to adjust their gestures, facial expression, and voice accordingly, they would possess genuine eloquence.

Morality   It is not credible that women could practise virtue to such a high degree without being capable of understanding its fundamental principles. Indeed, a woman who has already been instructed in the way proposed above would discover the rules of conduct herself by discovering the three kinds of duty that comprise the whole of morality, the first of which refers to God, the second to ourselves, and the third to our neighbours. The clear and distinct ideas that she would form from her mind, and from the union of the mind and body, would lead her infallibly to acknowledge that there exists another spirit, who is infinite and is the author of the whole of nature, and to experience towards God the feelings on which religion is based. When she learns in natural philosophy what constitutes the pleasure of the senses, and how external things contribute to the perfection of the mind and the preservation of the body, she would not fail to conclude that it is self-defeating if one does not use sensual pleasures in moderation. If she subsequently came to consider herself as participating in civil society with other similar people, subject to the same passions as them and having needs that cannot be satisfied without mutual assistance, she would acquire effortlessly the thought on which our whole system of justice depends, namely, that one must treat others as one would wish to be treated oneself and, for that reason, that one should control one's desires, which when not regulated (what is called cupidity) cause all life's troubles and evils.

Law and   She would become more convinced of the last of these duties if
Politics   she pressed on further and discovered the foundation of politics
and jurisprudence. Since both of these disciplines are concerned only with the obligations of human beings to each other she could conclude that, in order to understand people's obligations in civil society, one must understand what led them to form a society in the first place. She would therefore imagine human beings as if they were outside that society, and she would find them all completely free and equal, with only a desire for self-preservation and an equal right to everything that would be necessary to achieve it. But she would also notice that this equality would involve them in war or a permanent state of mutual distrust, which would be inconsistent with their objective, and that the natural light of reason would dictate that they could not live in peace unless everyone surrendered their rights and made contracts or conventions. She would also see that, in order to validate these decisions and to protect people from anxiety, it would be necessary to have recourse to a third party who would have authority to force everyone to observe what they had promised to others. Since this person is chosen only for the benefit of their subjects, that should be their exclusive objective; and to realize that end (for which they were established), they would have to have authority over property and people, war and peace.

By examining this issue in depth, what would prevent a woman from discovering what is meant by natural justice, a contract, authority, and obedience? Why would she not understand the natural law, the legal penalties that should be used, what is meant by civil law and the law of peoples, and what are the obligations of princes and subjects? In a word, she would learn from her own reflections and from books whatever is required to be a lawyer and a politician.

Geography   When a woman has acquired a perfect knowledge of
herself and a sound understanding of the general rules of human conduct, she may perhaps wish to know how people live in foreign countries. Since she will have noticed that variations in weather, seasons, place, age, diet, company, and exercise had caused various changes and different passions in herself, she would have no difficulty in recognizing that such changes produce the same effects in whole populations.

Different peoples have varying inclinations, customs, lifestyles, and laws depending on whether they live more or less near the sea, in the north or the south, whether there are plains, mountains, rivers, or forests in their

The source of   territory, and whether the lands are more or less fertile and
the diversity   produce characteristic types of food. They also vary in rela-
of morals   tion to the trade and business dealings they have with other
between   peoples, near and far. A woman could study all these things
nations   and thereby learn about the lifestyles, riches, religions, government, and interests of twenty or thirty different nations,
as easily as those of an equivalent number of families. Indeed, it is no more
difficult to understand from a map the location of kingdoms, or the relation
between seas and lands, islands and continents, than to know the districts
and streets in a town and the roadways in the province where one lives.

Secular   By knowing the present she may become interested in knowing
History   the past also, and what she would learn from geography would
assist her greatly in this project by providing a better understanding of matters such as wars, travels, and negotiations, by identifying
the places where they occurred, and the routes, paths, and the boundaries
between states. Her general knowledge of the way in which human beings
behave, which is gleaned from her reflections on herself, would enable her
to understand politics, passions, and interests and would help her to discover
the motivation and driving force of enterprises, the origin of revolutions,
and to supplement large-scale plans with the tiny details that made them
successful and escaped the notice of historians. According to the accurate
ideas of vice and virtue that she would have, she would notice the flattery,
passion, and ignorance of authors and would thereby protect herself from
the corruption that results from reading histories, in which these faults are
usually found. Since ancient politics was not as subtle as its contemporary
equivalent and the interests of princes were less interconnected and com-
merce was less widespread in former times than today, it requires more
intelligence to understand and decipher the gazettes than the works of Livy
or Quintus Curtius.[53]

Church   There are many people who find church history more inter-
History and   esting and more reliable than secular or civil history because
Theology   they find that it presents a greater challenge to reason and
virtue, and that the passions and prejudices camouflaged in

---

[53] Gazettes were periodical publications that became popular in the seventeenth century.
Théophraste Renaudot founded the first gazette in 1631, a weekly paper of eight to twelve
pages that provided local and foreign news of political, religious, and scientific developments.
Livy (59 BC–17 AD) was a celebrated author of a multi-volume history of Rome, *Ab urbe
condita*, and Quintus Curtius (*d*.53 AD) was author of *The History of Alexander* (LCL 368, 369).

the name of religion give a very characteristic twist to the mind's conduct. A woman would apply herself to this with greater dedication to the extent that she thought it was more important. She would be convinced that the books of Scripture are no less authentic than all the other books that we have;[54] that they contain the true religion and all the maxims on which it is based; that the New Testament, in which the history of Christianity begins properly, is no more difficult to understand than the Greek and Latin authors; that those who read it with a childlike simplicity, seeking only God's kingdom, will find its truth and meaning more easily and pleasantly than that of enigmas, emblems, and fables. When she has regulated her mind by the morality of Jesus Christ, she will find herself in a position to direct others, to unburden them of scruples, and to resolve their moral dilemmas with greater authority than if they had filled their heads with all the casuists in the world.

I cannot see how, in subsequent studies, anything could prevent her from observing as easily as a man how the Gospel was passed from hand to hand, from one kingdom to another, from century to century, up to our own day. Nor can I see why she would not acquire the concept of a true theology by reading the Church Fathers or find that it consists only in knowing the history of Christians and the specific thoughts of those who write about it. In that way she would make herself sufficiently competent to write works about religion, and to preach the truth and combat novelties by showing what has always been believed about disputed questions in the whole church.

Civil Law   If a woman is capable of learning from history what all public societies are, how they were formed, and how they preserve themselves by means of a defined, stable authority that is exercised by magistrates and various officers who are subordinated to each other, she is no less capable of understanding the application of this authority, in laws, ordinances, and regulations, to the conduct of those who are subject to it both in respect of relations between people according to their various conditions and in respect of the possession and use of property. Is it so difficult to know

---

[54] This anticipates Poulain's thesis that books of Scripture must be authenticated in the same way as other ancient books, and that this issue must be resolved before accepting their content as divine revelation: *La doctrine des protestans sur la liberté de lire l'Écriture Sainte* (Geneva: Fabri & Barrillot, 1720).

the relation between a husband and his wife, a father and his children, a head of a house and his domestic servants, a lord and his vassals, between those who are allies, or a tutor and a pupil? Is it so mysterious to understand what is meant by possessing something as a result of buying it, or to understand an exchange, a donation, a bequest, a will, a prescription or a usufruct, and what are the conditions required to validate these practices?

Canon Law   It does not seem as if greater intelligence would be required to understand the spirit of Christian society than that of civil society and to form an accurate idea of the authority that is characteristic of the former and the foundation of all its conduct, in order to distinguish precisely between the authority that Jesus Christ gave his church and the domination that belongs only to temporal powers. Having made this distinction, which is absolutely necessary to understand canon law properly, a woman could study canon law and could notice how the church modelled itself on civil law and how secular and spiritual jurisdiction became entangled. She could understand what the church hierarchy is, what are the functions of prelates, what are the relative jurisdictions of church councils, popes, bishops, and pastors. She could understand church discipline, its rules and its modifications, and what are canons, privileges, and exemptions, how benefices are established, and what is meant by using or possessing them. In a word, she could understand the customs and rules of the church and the duties of all those who compose it.[55] There is nothing in all this that a woman is not well capable of understanding, and in that way she could become very expert in canon law.

Those are a few general ideas about the most specialized kinds of knowledge that men have used both to display their intelligence and to get rich, and which they have possessed for such a long time to the detriment of women. Despite the fact that women have no less right to them, men have thought about women and treated them with such injustice that there is nothing comparable in the use of material goods.

In that context, people concluded that the prescription of material goods was practised to defend the peace and security of families. In other words, if someone enjoyed someone else's property without objection and in good faith for a certain period of time, they were allowed to retain possession of it, without anyone being able subsequently to claim otherwise. But it was

---

[55] Poulain writes about '*l'Église*' as if there were only one church, although there were many Christian churches that claimed to follow the teachings of the New Testament.

never decided that those who were dispossessed, by negligence or otherwise, were incapable of recovering their possessions in some other way and no one ever regarded their inability to do so as anything other than a provision of civil law.

In contrast, people were not satisfied simply to not invite women to participate in the sciences and various offices following a lengthy prescription; they went much further and argued that their exclusion was based on some natural incapacity on their part.

Women are not excluded from the sciences because of some natural indisposition
Nonetheless, there is nothing more illusory than this assumption. Whether one considers the sciences themselves or the bodily organ that is used to acquire them, one finds that both men and women are equally well disposed to them. There is only one method and one way of introducing the truth as its appropriate nourishment into the human mind, just as there is only one way of introducing food into stomachs of every kind to nourish the body. As regards the various dispositions of the head, which make it more or less suitable for scientific knowledge, if one considers the evidence in good faith, one must admit that it favours women.

Who are most suited to the sciences?
One cannot deny that, among human beings, those who are very coarse and materialistic are usually stupid and that, in contrast, the more refined are always the most spiritual. I find that this experience is too general and invariable to require the support of reasons. Since the fair sex is endowed with a more refined temperament than us, if they applied themselves to study they would certainly be at least as successful as us.

I anticipate that many people will reject this opinion because they will think it goes too far. I can see no alternative, however; people imagine that the honour of our sex requires us to claim primacy in everything, whereas I believe that it is a question of justice to render to everyone what belongs to them.

Both sexes have an equal claim to the sciences
All of us, both men and women, have the same right to the truth, because everyone's mind is equally capable of knowing the truth and we are all affected, in the same way, by the objects that make impressions on our bodies. This natural right to the same knowledge results from the fact that we all have the same need for it. There is no one who does not search for happiness, which is the objective towards which all our actions are directed.

However, no one can pursue this objective successfully without clear and distinct knowledge. Even Jesus Christ and Saint Paul invited us to hope for such knowledge, in which the blessedness of the afterlife consists.[56] Misers consider themselves happy when they know that they possess great riches, while ambitious people are happy when they perceive themselves as superior to their counterparts. In brief, the whole of human happiness, genuine or imaginary, consists only in knowledge, that is, in people thinking that they possess whatever good they desire.

That is why I believe that the only source of true happiness in this life is true ideas that are acquired by study, that are unchanging, and are independent of the possession or lack of property. Thus what makes misers incapable of being happy, as long as they know only that they possess riches, is that this knowledge would have to be accompanied by the desire or imagination of possessing them only in the immediate present if they were to be happy. Once they imagine themselves losing their riches or losing control of them, they can no longer think about them without being miserable.[57] It is completely different with self-knowledge, and with all the sciences that result from it, especially those that affect how one lives one's life. Since the two sexes are capable of the same happiness, they have the same right to everything that may be used to acquire it.

Virtue consists in knowledge   When it is said that happiness consists principally in knowledge of the truth, one does not exclude virtue; on the contrary, virtue is considered its most essential feature. However, virtue does not make people happy except to the extent that they know either that they possess it or are trying to acquire it. In other words, although seeing someone practising virtue is enough to consider them happy, even if they do not know clearly that they are virtuous and even if their practice (while accompanied by a confused or imperfect knowledge) may contribute to the acquisition of happiness in the next life, it is certain that those involved

---

[56] I Cor. 13: 12: 'Now we see through a glass, darkly; but then face to face: now I know in part; but then shall I know even as also I am known.'

[57] This argument cannot show that knowledge alone makes one happy, since one's happiness also depends on one's desires. As Poulain argues, misers are unhappy because they desire to possess their riches indefinitely into the future and, since they cannot know that this will happen, the possibility of future loss compromises the happiness of knowing what they currently possess. Cf. Boethius, *The Consolation of Philosophy*, trans. P. G. Walsh (Oxford World's Classics, 1999), 27: a rich man 'must inevitably fear the loss of what he is in no doubt can be lost, and therefore his enduring anxiety does not permit him to be happy.'

cannot consider themselves really happy without being aware of the fact that they behave as they ought, just as they could not believe they were rich if they did not know that they possessed riches.

Why so few people love virtue

The reason why so few people have a desire and love for genuine virtue is that they do not know it and, without being aware of it when they practise virtue, they do not experience the satisfaction that it produces and the happiness that we are talking about. That results from the fact that virtue is not a simple speculation about the good that we are obliged to seek but an effective desire that results from one's convictions about it, and one cannot enjoy practising it without an emotional feeling. It is similar to some of the most excellent drinks that sometimes taste bitter or lacking any sweetness if, as one is drinking them, one's mind is distracted by something else and is not applied to their effect on the palate.

One has to be learned in order to be genuinely virtuous

The two sexes need education, not only to find their happiness in the practice of virtue, but even more so in order to practise virtue well. Our actions are determined by our convictions, and one is more convinced of one's obligations to the extent that one knows them more perfectly. These brief comments about morality are enough to show that self-knowledge is very important to convince people of the duties to which they are obliged. It would not be difficult to show how all the other sciences contribute to the same objective or to show that the reason why so many people practise virtue so poorly or become dissolute is simply a lack of self-knowledge.

Why are some learned people not virtuous?

Because we observe the vices of many people who otherwise pass for well-educated, it is commonly believed that being learned is not a precondition for being virtuous. That suggests, not only that science is useless for virtue, but that it is often detrimental to it. This mistake causes weaker and less educated minds to be suspicious of most of those who are reputed to be more enlightened than others and, at the same time, it makes them distrust and reject the most noble sciences.

People fail to realize that it is only false learning that allows or forces people to embark on a dissolute life, because the confused ideas of ourselves and of what determines our conduct that result from false philosophy cloud the mind so much that, without knowing itself or the things in its environment, or the relations between them, and being incapable of supporting the weight of the difficulties that arise in this obscurity, it is forced to surrender and to abandon itself to its passions because reason is too weak to resist them.

Study would not make women proud   The strange opinion among common folk that study would make women more evil and proud is based only on an unreasonable fear. Only a false science could produce such a bad effect. It is impossible to learn genuine science without becoming more humble and virtuous, and nothing is more conducive to humbling one's pride and being convinced of one's weakness than considering all the detailed parts of the human body, the subtlety of its organs, the almost infinite number of changes it undergoes, and the painful irregularities to which it is subject. No meditation is more likely to inspire humility, moderation, and gentleness in any human being than realizing (by studying natural philosophy) that their mind is linked to their body and noticing that it has so many needs. Since the functioning of the mind depends on the most minute parts of the body, it is constantly exposed to a thousand kinds of disturbance and unpleasant experiences. Whatever knowledge it has acquired, the slightest thing is enough to confound it completely; a small amount of bile or blood that is hotter or colder than usual may throw it into a fit, into madness or anger, and cause it to experience terrible convulsions.[58]

Very important advice for all learned people   If these considerations were entertained in a woman's mind, as in that of a man, they would be much more likely to banish pride than to introduce it into their minds. If a woman had filled her mind with the best knowledge available, and if she recalled all her previous conduct to see how she had reached the fortunate condition that she would then enjoy, she would discover a reason for being even more humble rather than the opposite. She would be bound to realize, in such a review, that she was previously subject to innumerable prejudices from which she was able to liberate herself only by fighting strenuously against the effects of custom, example, and the passions that controlled her despite her efforts; that all her efforts to discover the truth were almost completely useless and that it was only by chance that she discovered the truth when she thought least about it, in

---

[58] Henricus Regius, in *Fundamenta physices* (Amsterdam: Elsevier, 1646) and in subsequent expanded editions of this text, developed the Cartesian theory into what he called an 'organic' link between the mind and body and the extent to which mental experiences are affected significantly by bodily conditions.

circumstances that occur hardly once in a lifetime and to very few people. She would conclude infallibly that it is unjust and ridiculous to despise or scorn those who are not as enlightened as we are or who hold different opinions, and that one should rather have more compassion and sympathy for them. It is not their fault if they do not see the truth as we do. Rather, the truth eluded them when they searched for it, and there remains a veil of some kind on their part or on ours that prevents the truth from appearing to their minds as clearly as possible. If one considers that she would then hold true what she previously believed was false, she would undoubtedly conclude that she might subsequently make further discoveries as a result of which she would consider false or mistaken what had earlier appeared to be very true.

If any women have become arrogant as a result of studying, there are plenty of men who fall into the same vice daily; that should not be regarded as an effect of the sciences they learned but of the fact that they had been presented to them as mysteries. Since, on the one hand, this kind of knowledge is often very confused and, on the other, those who possess it think that they are in some way better than others, one should not be surprised if women adopted it as a reason for feeling superior. It is almost inevitable that the same thing occurs to them in this situation as those who are born poor, with few resources, and who subsequently acquire a great fortune by their own efforts. When they see themselves achieving a status to which similar people were unaccustomed, they are overtaken by a fit of dizziness and begin to see things completely differently to how they really are. It is at least very likely that the alleged pride of educated women is insignificant in comparison with that of men who assume the title of masters and sages. Women would be less subject to pride if they had an equal opportunity as men to share in the privileges that produce it.

The sciences are neces- sary for other things apart from employment

It is therefore a popular mistake to imagine that study is useless for women because, it is said, they have no access to the positions for the sake of which one undertakes study.[59] Study is just as necessary for women as happiness and virtue because, without it, it is impossible to have either of the latter perfectly. Study is necessary in order to acquire precise thoughts and just conduct. It is necessary to know ourselves well and the things that surround us, to use them properly,

[59] This was one of the objections made to van Schurman; see above, pp. 103–4.

and to regulate the passions by moderating our desires. One of the uses of the sciences is to make ourselves competent to assume various offices or responsibilities, and one has to acquire as much science as possible to become a judge or a bishop because otherwise it would be impossible to discharge the duties of those offices. However, it would be sordid and base to use the sciences for the sole purpose of acquiring those offices and enjoying the happiness that results from the benefits and advantages of their exercise.

There is no prescription in scientific matters   It is therefore a lack of understanding or a secret and blind self-interest that causes people to say that women should remain excluded from the sciences because they have never participated in them publicly. Physical goods are not like mental goods; prescription does not apply to the latter, and one retains a right to recover them no matter how long one has been deprived of them. Since the same physical goods cannot be possessed simultaneously by several people without reducing each one's share, it was thought to be in the best interests of families to give legal protection to those who possessed them in good faith rather than to their previous owners.

It is completely different, however, in the case of mental goods. Everyone has a right to everything that results from sound judgement; the province of reason is boundless, and it exercises an equal jurisdiction over everyone. We are all born as judges of what affects us and, even if we do not all enjoy an equal power to control them, we can at least all know them equally. Since all people enjoy the use of the light and the air without thereby harming anyone else, they can all likewise possess the truth without injuring each other. The more the truth is known, the more beautiful and luminous it appears. The more people who search for it, the sooner it is discovered, and if both sexes had pursued it equally it would have been discovered much sooner. Thus truth and the sciences are imprescriptible goods, and those who have been deprived of them can acquire them without injury to those who are already masters of them. Therefore, only those who wish to dominate other people's minds by credulity have any reason to fear this development; they fear that, if the sciences became so common, the distinction that accompanies them would also become common and the glory that they crave would be diminished by sharing it.

That is why there is no reason why women should not apply themselves to study as we do. They are capable of making good use of study

Women are
no less capable
of civil offices
than men

and of deriving the two benefits that one might expect from it: (1) to have the clear and distinct knowledge that we naturally seek, the desire for which is sometimes smothered and overwhelmed by confused thoughts and by the needs and distractions of daily life; (2) to use this knowledge to guide their own conduct and that of others in various social states in which they participate. This is not the commonly held view. There are many who would readily believe that women could learn the physical or natural sciences, but refuse to accept that they are as suitable as men for what are called social sciences, such as morality, jurisprudence, and politics, and that if they are capable of regulating their own conduct by applying the principles of these sciences they cannot thereby do the same for others.

People are convinced of this because they fail to notice that the mind needs only discernment and accuracy in all its actions, and that anyone who displays these qualities in one context is capable of applying them as easily and in the same way to everything else. Morality and social science do not change the nature of our actions; the latter always remain physical, because morality involves merely knowing how people evaluate the actions of others in relation to their ideas of good and evil, of vice and virtue, of justice and injustice. Once someone understands the laws of motion in natural philosophy, they can apply them to all changes and all variations that occur in nature. Similarly, if someone has once understood the true principles of the social sciences, they do not experience a new challenge when applying them to novel situations that occur.

Those who occupy civil offices are not always more intelligent than others just because they were more fortunate, and it is not even necessary that they have more than an average intelligence, even if it is desirable that only those who are most suitable be thus employed. We always act in the same way and by the same laws, whatever office we hold. The only difference is that our care and vision become more extensive as our office is more responsible, because we are required to act more. The whole change that occurs in someone who is placed in charge of others is like someone who, having climbed to the top of a tower, can see further and discover more distinguishable objects than someone who had remained at ground level. For that reason, if women can govern their own behaviour as well as we can, they can also do so for others, and can participate in public offices and positions of authority.

They are able
to teach   The simplest and most natural public use of sciences that have been learned well is to teach them to others, and if women studied in universities with men or in those that were established specifically for them, they could take their degrees and gain the titles of doctor and master in theology and medicine, and in canon or civil law. Their natural intelligence that gives them an advantage in learning would also make them successful as teachers. They would find ways and methods of teaching and would identify strong or weak students skilfully so as to adapt to their abilities. Besides, their facility in expressing themselves, which is one of the most important pedagogical talents, would make them admirable teachers.

They are
capable of
assuming
ecclesiastical
offices   The profession that comes closest to that of a teacher is being a pastor or minister in the church, and nothing other than custom can be shown to exclude women from this. They have a mind just like ours, which is capable of knowing and loving God, and thus of leading others to know and love Him. They share the same faith as us; the gospel and its promises are addressed equally to them. The obligations of charity apply to them also, and if they know how to practise charity in their actions, could they not also teach its principles publicly? Anyone who can preach by example can do so even more readily by word of mouth, and a woman who would add her natural eloquence to the morality of Jesus Christ would be as able as another to exhort, direct, and correct, to admit those who are worthy into the society of Christians and to expel those who, having been admitted as members, refuse to observe its rules. If men got used to seeing women presiding in church, they would be no more disturbed by it than women are when they see men in the same office.

They are able
to exercise
authority   We have assembled in society only to live in peace and to find everything necessary for body and mind in mutual assistance. It would be impossible to enjoy those benefits undisturbed without some authority. In other words, it is necessary to have some people who have the power to make laws and to impose penalties on those who break them. Those who use that authority properly must know its scope, and must be convinced that they should use it only for procuring the safety and benefit of those who are its subjects. Since women are as capable of this conviction as men, why could men not submit to them and agree, not only not to resist their orders, but also to contribute as much as possible to enforce obedience on those who would object?

They can   Thus nothing could prevent a woman from occupying a
be queens   throne and, in order to govern her peoples, from studying
their natural dispositions, interests, laws, customs, and practices. Nothing could prevent her from distributing offices on merit alone,
from appointing only those who are suitable to offices in the army and
the judiciary and only enlightened and exemplary people to offices in
the church. Is it so difficult for a woman to learn the strengths and weaknesses of a state and of other states that surround it, to initiate secret intelligence in foreign states to learn their plans and to frustrate their actions, and
to have trustworthy spies and emissaries in every suspicious place to get
precise information about any relevant occurrence there? Does it require
more dedication or vigilance to rule a kingdom than women exercise in
their families or religious women in their convents? They would not lack
subtlety in public negotiations any more than in private discussions, and
since dedication to duty and gentleness are natural to women, their rule
would be less harsh than in the case of many princes. During their reign
one would hope for what one fears in many others, namely, that the subjects follow the example of those who govern them.

It is easy to conclude that if women are capable of exercising all public
authority as sovereigns, they are even more capable of exercising it in del-
egated offices, such as vice-regents, governors, secretaries, state counsellors,
or tax officials.

They can be   From my point of view, I would not be more surprised to
army generals   see a woman with a soldier's helmet rather than a crown on
her head, to see her preside in a council of war as in a council
of state, or to see her training soldiers personally, arraying an army in battle
and dividing it into various divisions than enjoying the fact that someone
else does it. Military art is no different than other arts of which women are
capable, except that it is tougher, makes more noise, and causes more harm.
One needs only eyes to learn from a reasonably good map all the routes
through a country, the passageways that are good or otherwise, and the most
appropriate places for an ambush or an encampment. There are hardly any
soldiers who do not know that one should occupy a narrow pass before
sending their troops through it, that they should plan all their military strategies in accordance with reliable information from trustworthy spies, and that
they should even deceive their own army by ruses and counter-marches to
conceal their plans better. A woman can do all that, and can devise strategies
to take the enemy by surprise—by arranging to have them facing the wind,

the dust, and the Sun; by attacking the enemy from one side and surrounding them from the other; by giving false signals, drawing the enemy into an ambush by a simulated retreat, and by engaging in battle and being first in the breach to encourage her troops. Persuasion and passion are everything, and women display no less ardour and resolution when their honour is at stake than it takes to attack or defend a position.

They are capable of exercising the duties of a judge
What reasonable objection could be made if a sensible and educated woman presided as head of a parliamentary court or any other assembly? There are many able people who would find it easier to learn the laws and customs of a state than the rules of games that women understand very well, while the latter are as easy to remember as an entire novel. Is it not as easy to understand a legal case as the resolution of a theatrical plot, or to report accurately on a trial as to summarize a comedy? All these things are equally easy for those who apply themselves to them equally.

Since there are no other offices or professions in society apart from those that have just been discussed, nor any in which one needs more knowledge or intelligence, one must conclude that women are suitable for all of them.

Apart from natural physical dispositions and people's understanding of the demands and duties of their work, there are some other factors that make someone more or less capable of doing their work satisfactorily. These include their convictions about the obligations involved in a given office or position, religious or self-interested considerations, emulation among peers, a desire to become famous and to make, protect, or increase one's fortune. A man acts differently insofar as he is more or less influenced by these factors and, since women are no less sensitive to them than men, they are equal to men in everything that relates to employment.

Women should apply themselves to study
One may therefore confidently encourage ladies to apply themselves to study while ignoring the trivial objections of those who try to divert them from it. Since they have a mind like ours that is capable of knowing the truth—which is the only thing that is worthy of their attention—they should take care to avoid the reproach of hiding a talent that they could have used beneficially and of stifling the truth by idleness and indolence. There is no other way for women to protect themselves from the error and surprise to which people are so exposed who learn nothing apart from what they read in gazettes, that is, from the simple reports of others, and there is no other way for them to be happy in this life by practising virtue with knowledge.

How study
is useful
for women
Whatever other objectives women may have, they will realize them by studying. If their informal study circles were transformed into academies, their discussions would be more informed, agreeable, and wide-ranging.[60] Every woman can appreciate the satisfaction she would experience in discussing the most interesting topics in contrast with the occasional experience of listening to others speak about them. However superficial their subjects of conversation may be, they would have the pleasure of treating them more intelligently than usual, and the refined manners that are so characteristic of their gender would improve them very much when they are strengthened by sound arguments.

Those who merely wish to please would benefit greatly by study, and the impact of physical beauty would be enhanced a hundredfold when combined with that of the mind. Since less attractive women are always admired more if they are intelligent, the benefits of a mind cultivated by study would provide them with an opportunity to compensate abundantly for what nature or luck had denied them. They would participate in the discussions of the learned and would outshine them in two ways. They would become involved in business, and their husbands could hardly avoid handing over to them the management of the household and taking their advice about everything. If there was any reason why they could not assume a public office, they could at least understand them sufficiently to judge whether they were well exercised by others.

The obstacles to realizing this objective should not dismay us. They are not as great as they are made out to be. What persuades people that great effort is needed to acquire knowledge is that most of those who embark on that enterprise are required to learn a lot of useless things. All science up to now has consisted almost exclusively of knowing the history of our predecessors' opinions and, since people are so committed to custom and to the credibility of their teachers, very few have been lucky enough to discover the natural method. One could practise that method and show that it is possible to educate people in a much shorter time and more enjoyably than is usually imagined.

Women have a disposition that is favourable to the sciences, and the correct concepts of perfection, nobility, and propriety apply to them as much as to men.

We have considered only women's heads up to this point and we have seen that, when considered in general, this part of the body is as appropriate in women as

---

[60] See note 8.

in men for all the sciences of which it is the organ. Nonetheless, since heads are not entirely similar even among men, and some are more appropriate for certain things than others, we must go into more detail to see if there is anything about women that makes them less fit than us for the sciences.

It is noticeable that they have a more joyful and larger countenance than us; they have a high, noble, and broad forehead, which is normally a sign of imagination and intelligence. Indeed, one finds that women are more vivacious and have a better imagination and memory. That means that their brain is so disposed that it receives impressions from objects easily, including the weakest and lightest impressions that escape those with alternative dispositions, and that they store those impressions and present them to the mind when they are needed.[61]

Women are intelligent and imaginative   Since this disposition of the brain is accompanied by heat, it causes external objects to affect the mind more actively, which then responds to them and examines them to a greater extent and creates further images as it wishes. As a result, those who are more imaginative are more ingenious and creative by considering things more quickly from more points of view, and they discover more from a single impression that others do from a long reflection. They are able to represent things in a pleasant and attractive way, and to find suitable ways and strategies to tackle problems; they can express themselves with facility and grace and thereby support a clear presentation of their ideas.

One can observe all these things in women, and I see nothing in such a disposition that may be incompatible with having a good mind. Discernment and accuracy are characteristic of them. One must be somewhat sedentary to acquire those qualities and must stop to consider various objects to avoid the mistakes and errors that occur by flitting about from one thing to another. It is true that the imagination is occasionally carried away by the sheer number of ideas in lively minds but it is also true that this can be avoided by practice. We have seen this in some of the greatest people in this century, who are almost all very imaginative.

This temperament could be said to be most appropriate for society and, since people are not created to live alone forever and remain cooped up in

---

[61] According to this dualist theory, sensory impressions are received in the brain and stored in the memory, and the brain makes these impressions available to a distinct intellectual faculty (the mind), in which it stimulates further ideas. Thus the subtlety and detail of the mind's ideas are partly a function of the brain's sensitivity to sensory impressions. Malebranche makes a similar comment about women's imagination (ST, 130–31).

their study, those who have a greater disposition for communicating their thoughts pleasantly and usefully should be more highly esteemed in some way. Thus women who naturally possess an attractive mind, as a result of their imagination, memory, and brilliance, are able to acquire the qualities of a good mind with little effort.

That is enough to show that, as far as the head alone is concerned, the two sexes are equal. Other parts of the body have interesting features that need only be mentioned in passing. People have always had the common misfortune to spread their passions, as it were, over all natural phenomena. There is hardly an idea of anything that they have not linked with some feeling of love or hate, of praise or scorn. Ideas about the distinction of the sexes are so material and so clouded with feelings of imperfection, vulgarity, indecency and other absurdities, that it is often prudent not to express any opinion about it because it is impossible to do so without stirring up some passion or provoking the flesh against the spirit.

Nonetheless, unfavourable opinions about women are based on this strange mixture of muddled ideas, which is used ridiculously by small-minded people to belittle them. The best balance between the need to explain oneself and the challenge of doing so with impunity is to indicate how we should rationally understand perfection and imperfection, nobility and vulgarity, decency and its opposite.

Ideas of perfection and imperfection Since I understand that there is a God, I easily understand that all things depend on Him. When I consider the natural, internal state of creatures (which, if they are bodies, consists in the way in which their parts are connected with each other) and their external state (which is the way in which their mutual relations involve acting or being acted on by other bodies in their environment), and if I look for an explanation of these two states, I find none other than the will of their creator. I then notice that bodies usually have a certain disposition that makes them capable of producing or being affected by certain effects. For example, human beings are able to hear the thoughts of others with their ears and, reciprocally, can make others hear their own thoughts by using their vocal organs. I also notice that bodies are incapable of such effects if they are disposed differently. I conceive of two ideas as a result of that reflection: one represents the original condition of each thing and all its necessary consequences, which I call its state of perfection. The other idea represents the opposite state, which I call imperfection.

Thus someone is perfect in my opinion when they possess everything required to produce and to be affected by whatever was destined for them by God's creation, and they are imperfect when they have more or fewer parts than are necessary or some indisposition that prevents them from realizing their natural destiny.[62] For that reason, since human beings are creatures who need food for their survival, I do not think of that need as an imperfection, no more than the necessity to excrete the residue that results from the use of food. I thus find that all creatures are equally perfect as long as they are in their normal natural state.

One should not confuse perfection with nobility. They are two completely different things. Two creatures may be equally perfect but unequally noble.

When I reflect on myself, it seems as if my mind, which alone is capable of knowledge, should be preferred to the body and should be regarded as more noble. When I consider bodies, however, without reference to myself—that is, without thinking that they may be useful or harmful to me, pleasant or unpleasant—I cannot conclude that some are more noble than others, since they are all nothing more than matter shaped in various ways. In contrast, when I interact with other bodies and consider that they may benefit or harm me, I begin to think of them differently. Likewise although my head, when considered impartially, does not affect me more than other parts of my body, I still prefer it to all other parts when I consider that it plays a more important role in the interaction of my mind and body.

For the same reason, although all parts of the body are equally perfect, they are regarded differently; even those that are most useful are often regarded with a certain amount of disdain and aversion, because their use is less pleasant or something like that. The same applies to everything in our environment that affects us, because the reason why something pleases one person and displeases another is that it affects them in different ways.

---

[62] There are similar definitions of perfection and imperfection in Marin Cureau de la Chambre, *L'art de connaître les hommes*, 2nd edn. (Paris: Jacques d'Allin, 1663), 15–16; Eng. transl., *The Art how to know Men* (London: Thomas Basset, 1670), 1: 'Everything is perfect to which there is nothing wanting, and which hath whatsoever is necessary for the accomplishment of its nature.'

The idea of   The idea of propriety results from people's involvement in
propriety   society.[63] Thus although there is nothing imperfect or base
in the act of relieving the body and it is even a necessary
and inevitable consequence of its natural disposition, and although all
ways of doing it are equal, some are nonetheless considered less decent
because they are more shocking to those who witness them.

Since all creatures and all their actions when considered in themselves
and without reference to their use or evaluation are all equally perfect and
noble, they are also equally respectable if they are judged in the same way.
For that reason one could say that almost all views about what is respectable or otherwise result from human imagination and arbitrary choices.[64]
That is evident in the fact that something is respectable in one country and
not in another, or is such in a single kingdom at different times; and even
during the same period, among people of different social classes, conditions or sensibility, the same action is sometimes respectable and sometimes the opposite. That is why propriety is merely a way of using natural
things in accordance with people's attitudes, and it is prudent to comply
with those values.

We are all so convinced of this idea, without even reflecting on it, that
our lady friends, whether they are intelligent or discerning, who comply
in public with the demands of propriety just like everyone else, do not feel
obliged to uphold them in private, when they consider them to be importunate and strange burdens.

The same applies to the concept of nobility. In some provinces of the
Indies, labourers hold the same rank as nobles do here; in some countries,
soldiers are preferred to lawyers, while in others it is the exact opposite.
In each country, the choice depends on what they find more attractive or
what they think is more important.

---

[63] The French term *honnêteté* refers to a contested concept of decency, correctness, or respectability; it was an ideal of social conduct that, in the case of women, had connotations of the
virtues that women were expected to cultivate, such as chastity, humility, piety, and so on. Saint
Francis de Sales had a significant influence on this concept in the seventeenth century by combining secular ideas of polite social behaviour with a Christian ideal of married life in his
Introduction to the Devout Life (1609). I have translated the terms *honnêteté* and *honnête* variously
as propriety, decency, respectability (and their adjectival equivalents), depending on the context.

[64] Poulain endorses the thesis that natural phenomena are morally indifferent and that
standards of propriety vary from one country or period to another and reflect the evaluations
made by people. Whether such standards are natural or merely conventional was also discussed
by Moïse Amyraut in the preface to his *Considerations sur les droits par lesquels la nature a reiglé les
marriages* (Saumur, 1648).

If one compares those ideas with the commonly held views about women, it is easy to recognize how the latter are mistaken.

The source of the distinction between the sexes; how extensive it is; that it does not distinguish men and women in relation to virtues and vices; and that temperament in general is neither good nor bad in itself.

The source of the distinction between the sexes Since God wished to produce human beings by making them depend on each other through the intercourse of two people, He made two different human bodies. Each one was perfect in its own way, and they were designed to be as we observe them today. Thus everything that results from their distinctive characteristics should be considered as part of their perfection. There is no reason, therefore, for some people to imagine that women are not as perfect as men, and to consider as a defect in women anything that is an essential feature of their sex and without which it would be incapable of realizing the purpose for which it was created, which is defined in terms of fecundity. Women are destined for the most important function in the world, which is to conceive and nourish us in the womb.

Women contribute more than men to procreation Both sexes are needed if they are to produce their offspring together, and if one knew what ours contributes we would have reason to be very disappointed.[65] It is difficult to understand—as far as children are concerned—how people can claim that men are nobler than women. It is women who conceive us, who form us, give us being, birth, and education. It is true that it is more burdensome for them than for us. This effort, however, is no reason to scorn them or treat them unfavourably, rather than respect them as they deserve. Who would claim that fathers and mothers who work to rear their children, good princes who rule their subjects and magistrates who deliver justice to them, are less admirable than those on whose help and support they depend to fulfil their duties?

On Temperament There are physicians who have discussed at length, to women's disadvantage, the temperament of the two sexes, and who have written endlessly to show that women must have

---

[65] Some Cartesians supported a preformation theory according to which all subsequent generations of any living creature are included in embryo in the first members of the species. According to that theory, the ova contain a woman's children in miniature, and her children's children, and so on indefinitely, while the role of the male is limited to stimulating the development of what is already naturally in place in the ova.

a temperament that is completely different from ours and makes them inferior in everything. The reasons they offer, however, are only feeble conjectures that occur in the minds of those who judge things only on the basis of prejudices and simple appearances.

When they saw that there were greater differences between men and women in their civil roles than in those that are characteristic of each of them, they imagined that that is how things ought to have been. And since they failed to distinguish between what is natural and what results from custom and education, they attributed everything they saw in society to the same cause and imagined that, when God created men and women, He made them in a way that would produce all the distinctions that we currently observe.

That involves exaggerating the difference between the sexes. One should limit that difference to God's plan, which was to have human beings conceived by the intercourse of two people, and one should not extend it beyond what is necessary for that purpose. We also see that men and women are similar in almost everything that pertains to the external and internal constitution of the human body, and that the natural functions on which our survival depends operate in the same way in both of them. Therefore, the only reason why there are some organs in one type of body that are not in the other is to give birth to a third human being. That does not require women to be less strong or vigorous, as some imagine. Since we can decide this issue correctly only by relying on experience, is it not the case that women differ from each other as much as we do? There are strong and weak people of both sexes. Men who were reared in idleness are often worse than women and are the first to give up when they have to work; when they are toughened by necessity or otherwise, however, they are as good as or even better than others.

The same is true of women. Those who are engaged in hard work are stronger than ladies who only ply the needle. That would suggest that if both sexes exercised to the same extent, one could possibly become as strong as the other. That occurred in earlier times in another commonwealth, in which both sexes participated in wrestling and other exercises together, and the same thing is reported about the amazons who are in South America.[66]

[66] An allusion to the *Republic* (452 a–b), where Plato discusses the option of having women engage in wrestling and other competitions in common with men if they are assigned the same roles in society: 'If…we are to use women for the same things as the men, we must also teach them the same things.'

Expressions We should not, therefore, draw any conclusions from certain
that are unfa- common expressions that reflect the current condition of
vourable to the two sexes. For example, if someone wishes to blame a
women should man and mock him for having little courage, resolution or
be ignored toughness, they call him effeminate, as if to say that he is as
cowardly and weak as a woman. On the contrary, if someone
wants to praise a woman who is unusually courageous, strong or intelligent,
they say that she is manly. These expressions that are so flattering to men
contribute significantly to maintaining the high esteem in which they are
held, because people fail to realize that they are only apparently true. Their
assumed truth fails to distinguish between nature and custom, and they are
therefore only contingent or arbitrary opinions. Since virtue, gentleness, and
propriety are so characteristic of women, if their sex had not been so denigrated and if men had been willing to adopt this linguistic usage, those who
wished to praise a man who possessed those qualities to an eminent degree
would have said: 'he is a woman'.

Be that as it may, sheer physical strength should not be used to distinguish between human beings; otherwise, brute animals would be superior to
humans and, among the latter, those who are most robust would be superior.[67]
It is known from experience, however, that very strong men are hardly suitable
for anything other than manual work, whereas in contrast those who have less
physical strength are usually more intelligent. The most accomplished philosophers and the greatest princes were rather delicate, and the greatest generals
might not have wished to wrestle with soldiers of the lowest rank. One need
only visit the courts to see if the greatest judges are as strong as their more jun-
ior ushers. It is therefore useless to rely so much on the make-up of the body
rather than the mind to explain observable differences between the sexes.

Temperament is not an indivisible point; just as there are no two people in
whom it is exactly alike, it is equally impossible to determine precisely how
they differ. There are various kinds of choleric, sanguine, and melancholic temperaments, but these differences do not imply that they are not often equally
capable or that there are not excellent people with every type of temperament.
Even if one assumed that the two sexes have temperaments as different as is
claimed, one can find greater differences still between many men who, despite
that, are believed to be equally capable. Such differences are so negligible that
only those who wish to quibble would think they are significant.

---

[67] This argument became a commonplace; see Marie de Gournay (p. 65).

It is apparent that anyone who claims that this distinction is very important fails to examine carefully everything that we observe in women, and this
mistake makes them fall into the error of those who have a confused mind
and do not distinguish adequately what belongs to each thing. They attribute
to one thing what belongs to another because they find them both present
in a single subject.[68] That is why, when they see so many differences between
women in their behaviour and their roles in society, they fail to notice their
causes and then apply the same differences also to their temperament.

Women can
claim superi-
ority in respect
of the body
Be that as it may, if one wished to examine the relative excellence of the two sexes by comparing their bodies, women
could claim to be superior without even considering the
inner structure of their bodies, in which the most marvellous
thing in the known world takes place, namely, the formation
of a human being, which is the most beautiful and admirable of all creatures. Who could prevent them from claiming that their external appearance
makes them superior, that grace and beauty are their natural and characteristic qualities, and that all this produces effects that are as visible as they are
common, and if what takes place in their heads makes them at least equal to
men, then their external appearance hardly ever fails to make them superior.

Since beauty is just as real an advantage as strength or health, there is no
reason why we should not value it more than those other qualities; and if one
were to judge its value by the feelings and passions that it arouses, which is
how we judge most other things, one would find that there is nothing that
is valued more highly than beauty, since nothing else affects people more. In
other words, nothing affects and arouses the passions more, nothing confuses
them or strengthens them in more ways, than perceptions of beauty.

All tem-
peraments
are more or
less equal
There would be no need to speak any further about wom-
en's temperament if a certain author, who is as famous as he is
respected, had not decided to consider it the source of the faults
that are commonly attributed to women.[69] That very much

---

[68] Descartes proposed an optical theory of how people perceive things distinctly, according
to which the sensitivity of the eye and its adequate functioning is a prerequisite for perceiv-
ing the distinction between one thing or property and another. He applied this by analogy to
mental perception; if ideas fail to reflect distinctions between different things, one acquires
muddled ideas that lead to false judgements about things. See the *Dioptrics* (AT VI, 146) and
The Principles of Philosophy (AT VIII-1, 22).

[69] Marin Cureau de la Chambre, *L'art de connaître les hommes*; Engl. transl., *The Art how to*
know Men, in which the author claimed that 'the Male is hot and dry, and the Female cold and
moist' (French, p. 29; Engl. p. 10) and compared the male to the efficient cause of a couple's
children while the woman was merely the material cause.

supports people's opinion that women are inferior to men. Without reporting his opinion, I will say that if one wished to examine the temperament of both sexes properly in relation to vice and virtue, one would have to look at them in a neutral condition, before there was any vice or virtue in nature. One then finds that what is called a virtue at one time may become a vice at another, depending on how it is used, and therefore all temperaments are equal from that point of view.

What is virtue? To understand this claim better, one must notice that only our soul is capable of virtue, which consists in general in a firm and stable resolve to do what one thinks is best in various circumstances. The body is, strictly speaking, merely the organ or instrument of this resolve, like a sword in one's hands for attack or defence. All the various dispositions that make it more or less suitable for this function should be called good or bad only insofar as their consequences are normally and to a significant extent good or bad. For example, the tendency to flee from threatening evils is indifferent, because some evils cannot be avoided in any other way, and it is prudent to flee from them. However, it is blameworthy timidity if one allows oneself to be rushed into flight when the evil that one encounters can be overcome by a courageous resistance that results in more good than evil.

Women are no more inclined to vice than men Now the mind is no less capable in women than in men of having this firm resolve that defines virtue or of recognizing the situations in which it should be exercised. Women are as capable as we are of controlling their passions, and they are no more inclined to vice than to what is good. One could even tilt the balance in their favour towards the good, because affection for children, which is incomparably stronger in women than in men, is naturally linked with compassion, which could be called the virtue and bond of civil society, because it is inconceivable that society would be established rationally for any other purpose than the mutual satisfaction of the needs and common necessities of its members. If one examines closely how passions arise in us, one finds that the way in which women treat people in distress, almost as if they were their own children, is like a natural extension of the way in which they contribute to the birth and education of human beings.

That the observed difference in the conduct of men and women results from the education that they are given.

It is very important to notice that the characteristics we possess at birth are neither good nor bad, because otherwise it is impossible to avoid the rather common mistake of attributing to nature what belongs only to custom.

The influence of external conditions

We worry needlessly by trying to explain why we are subject to various faults and behave in unusual ways, because we fail to realize how we are influenced by habit, practice, education, and our external circumstances, that is, by the effect of our sex, age, fortune, employment, and our social class. Since all these different perspectives certainly affect our thoughts and passions in innumerable ways, they likewise incline minds to perceive differently the truths that are presented to them. For that reason, if the same principle is proposed simultaneously to ordinary citizens, soldiers, judges, or princes, it affects them and causes them to act in very different ways. Since people hardly bother with anything more than appearances, they use them as the measure and standard of their sensations or feelings. As a result, one person ignores as useless what strikes someone else as very important; soldiers are shocked by something that flatters judges; and people with the same temperament sometimes perceive very differently things that are perceived similarly by those who have very different dispositions but have enjoyed a similar education or degree of wealth.

Women's faults result from their education

We are not claiming that all human beings are born with the same bodily constitution. There would be little evidence to support such a claim. Some such dispositions are quick and some are slow, but this diversity does not seem in any way to impede minds from receiving the same instruction. The only effect of such differences is that some people are instructed more quickly and more easily than others. Thus, no matter what temperament women may have, they are no less capable than us of study and of learning the truth. And if we notice some fault or impediment in some women today, or even that all women do not perceive important things in the same way as men (although our experience shows the contrary), that should be attributed uniquely to the conditions in which they live and the education they are given, which include the ignorance in which they are left, the prejudices and errors they are taught, the example that they get from other women, and all the mannerisms to which etiquette, restraint, reserve, subjection, and timidity reduce them.

The education given to women

In fact, no opportunity is missed to convince women that the great difference they observe between themselves and men results from reason or from divine institution. Their clothing, education, and training could not be more different than ours. A young girl feels secure only at her mother's side or in the care of a governess who never leaves her on her own. She is made fearful of everything and is threatened by ghosts in any part of the house where she might be alone. On public streets and even in churches, there is something to fear if she is not escorted there. She applies her mind exclusively to the great care taken to dress her appropriately. There are so many people looking at her and she hears so many comments about beauty that all her thoughts become narrowly focused accordingly, and the compliments she receives about her appearance cause her to derive all her happiness from them. Since no one speaks to women about anything else, they limit all their ambitions to that and never raise their aspirations any higher. Dancing, writing, and reading are their great occupations, and their whole library is limited to a few small devotional books together with whatever fits into a little portable trunk.

All women's science is reducible to needlework. The mirror is their master and the oracle that they consult. Balls, plays, and fashion are the topics of their conversation, and they think of salons as illustrious academies where they go to get all the news about their sex. If some women happen to stand out from the crowd by reading certain books, which they manage to do with great difficulty in the hope of opening up their minds, they are often obliged to conceal it; most of their friends, out of jealousy or otherwise, never fail to accuse them of affectation.[70]

Intelligence is even more useless for young women from the lower classes who have to work for a living. They are purposely taught a trade that is appropriate to their sex as soon as they are able to learn one, and the necessity to work at their trade without interruption prevents them from thinking about anything else. As soon as they reach an age when they can marry, either they get married or they are confined to a convent where they continue to live in the same way as they did previously.

Is there anything in what women are taught that leads to a solid education? It seems on the contrary that their education was designed to diminish their courage, to cloud their minds, to fill them with only vanity and foolishness, to smother all the seeds of virtue and truth in them, to neutralize any tendency they might have towards great things, and to remove their

[70] I have translated the term 'précieuses' as 'affectation'; the French noun (sometimes translated as 'bluestockings') had negative connotations of upper-class idle women in polite society who pretended to be cultured and educated.

desire to improve themselves, as we do, by depriving them of the means of doing so.

The faults attributed to women are imaginary
When I think about how people regard what are believed to be faults in women, I find that such conduct is unworthy of rational agents. If there are faults that are found equally in both sexes, then the one that accuses the other sins against natural justice. If there are more faults in ours and we fail to see them, then we are rash to speak about women's faults. If we notice our own faults, however, and say nothing about them, we are unjust to blame the other sex that has fewer faults. If women are better than men, then the latter should be accused either of ignorance or envy for failing to recognize that. If someone has more virtue than vice, the former should serve to excuse the latter; and if someone's faults are incorrigible and they lack the means of correcting them or of protecting themselves against them (which indeed women lack), they should be pitied rather than scorned. Finally, if such faults are trivial or only apparent, it amounts to foolishness or malice to pay any attention to them. It is easy to show that this is what happens in the case of women.[71]

Timidity
Women are said to be timid and incapable of defending themselves, of being afraid of their own shadows, frightened by a child's scream, and trembling at the sound of the wind. That is not generally true. There are many women who are as fearless as men, and we know that the most timid among them often make a virtue of necessity. Timidity is almost inseparable from virtue, and all good people are to some extent timid. Since they do not wish to cause harm to anyone and recognize how much evil is found in people, it takes very little to arouse their fear. It is a natural passion from which no one is exempt. Everyone fears death and life's misfortunes; the most powerful princes fear revolt among their subjects and invasion by their enemies, and the most valiant army officers fear being taken by surprise in battle.

People fear inversely in proportion to their belief that they have the power to resist. Fear is therefore blameworthy only in those who are strong

---

[71] It was a commonplace to attribute different versions of the following faults to women. For example, Fénelon discusses curiosity, diffidence, affectation, jealousy, inordinate friendships, loquaciousness, a tendency to cry, false modesty, cunningness, and the 'chief fault' of women, vanity, in *Fénelon on Education*, trans. H. C. Barnard (Cambridge: Cambridge University Press, 1966), 65–74.

enough to overcome whatever evil threatens them. It would be equally unreasonable, in the case of a judge or a scholar who had never thought of anything apart from study, to accuse them of cowardice because they refuse to fight a duel as it would be to accuse a soldier who had spent his whole life in the army of being unwilling to get involved in an argument with a learned philosopher.

Women are reared in such a way that they have reason to fear everything. They lack the education that would prepare them to cope with intellectual challenges. They have never had the training that would provide the skill and strength required for attack or defence. They see that they are exposed to suffer with impunity the outrages of a sex that is very subject to fits of passion; it not only despises women but often treats its own members with more cruelty and anger than wolves display towards each other.

For that reason timidity should not be considered a fault in women but rather a reasonable passion that gives rise to their characteristic modesty and to the two most important benefits in life, namely, an inclination to virtue and an aversion to vice—which most men cannot acquire despite all the education and instruction that they receive.

Avarice   The usual cause of avarice is a fear of lacking goods. Men are no less subject to avarice than women, and if one were to take a count one might find that the former are more numerous and their avarice more blameworthy. Since there is a short distance between any two vices and the virtue that constitutes the mean between them, one is often taken as the other and one confuses avarice with the commendable virtue of thrift.[72]

The same action may be good when done by one person and evil when done by another; it often happens that what is evil in us is not so at all in women. They are deprived of every opportunity to make a living by using their minds because they are excluded from the sciences and professions. Accordingly, since they are less able to protect themselves against life's misfortunes and adversities, they ought to be more affected by them. One should not be surprised, therefore, that when it takes so much effort to acquire even a little property, they take care to protect whatever they have.

---

[72] This refers to the Aristotelian theory of virtues, according to which each virtue is a mean between two vices; *Nicomachean Ethics*, Bk II, Ch. 6 (NE, 29–31).

Credulity   If women believe what they are told so readily, that results from their simplicity, which prevents them from believing that those who are in authority over them are either ignorant or biased. It would also be a sin against justice if we accused them of credulity, because it is even more prevalent among us. Even the most able men allow themselves to be deluded too much by false appearances; their science is often no more than a shallow credulity, though somewhat more extensive than that of women. What I mean is that men are no wiser than others except insofar as they have assented more readily to a greater number of things of which they have retained ideas, such as they are, by recalling them frequently to memory.

Superstition   The same factor from which women's timidity results produces the superstition that even the learned attribute to them. In that respect, however, they are like people who are more wrong about something but convince themselves that they are in the right because they shout louder than others. They imagine that they themselves are exempt from superstition because they notice it in some less educated women, although they are pitifully up to their eyes in the same condition.

Even if all men genuinely adored God in spirit and in truth, and if women offered Him a completely superstitious worship, the women would still be excusable.[73] Women are not taught to know God themselves; they know only what they are told by others. And since most men talk about God in a manner that is unworthy of Him and distinguish Him from creatures only by the quality of being their creator, it is not surprising if women, who know God only from men's reports about Him, offer Him religious worship in terms of the same sentiments that they have towards men, whom they fear and revere.

Chatter   Some people imagine that they can really humiliate women by telling them that they are all chatter-boxes. Women have good reason to feel offended by such an impertinent slur. Their bodies are so happily disposed by their characteristic temperament that they retain the distinct impressions of objects that affect their senses. They subsequently imagine those objects without difficulty and express themselves with admirable facility, as a result of which they initiate and continue their conversations at will since their ideas are activated by the slightest stimulation. Since

---

[73] In John 4:23, Jesus was reported to have discussed with a Samaritan woman the adoration 'in spirit and in truth' that is appropriate to God the Father; meantime, his disciples had gone to town to fetch provisions.

they are able to perceive easily the relations between things because of their mental insight, they move easily from one subject to another and can thus speak at length without letting a conversation lapse.

The benefits of speech are naturally accompanied by a desire to use it whenever the opportunity arises. It is the only bond between people in society, and many find that there is no greater pleasure or anything more worthy of the mind than communicating one's thoughts to others. That is why, since women are able to speak with ease and were reared with other women, there would be something amiss if they did not converse together. They should not therefore be taken as chatter-boxes unless they speak inappropriately about things that they do not understand when they are not trying to have them explained to them.

We should not imagine that the word 'chatter' applies only to talk about clothes or fashions. The chatter of those who gossip is even more ridiculous. That heap of words piled up on each other, which mean nothing in most works, is a much more foolish cackle than that of the lowliest women.[74] One can at least say of the latter's discussions that they are real and intelligible, and that the women involved are not vain enough to imagine, as most learned men do, that they are more competent than their neighbours because they use more meaningless words than them. If men had a similar facility with language as women, it would be impossible to stop them talking. Everyone converses about what they know—merchants talk about their trade, philosophers talk about their studies, and women talk about what they were able to learn. They could claim that they would be able to converse better and more soundly than us if as much effort had been devoted to their education.

Curiosity   What shocks some people concerning the conversations of women is that they show a great desire to know everything. I do not understand the attitude of people who do not like women to be so curious. For my part, I think it is good to be curious, and my only suggestion is that one's curiosity not be importunate. I regard the conversations of women as similar to those of philosophers, in which one is allowed to discuss things that one does not know, and misunderstandings may occur in both of them.

---

[74] Alludes to a well-known misogynistic tract entitled *Recueil général des caquets de l'accouchée* (Paris, 1622).

It is customary for many people to treat those who are curious like beggars: when they are in the humour for giving, they are not bothered by being asked for something, and when they wish to show off what they know they are very willing to be asked questions. Otherwise, they insist that someone is too curious. Because people have convinced themselves that women should not study, they take offence at women's request to be informed about what can be learned from study. I admire women for being curious and I regret that they have no way to satisfy their curiosity, for they are often prevented from doing so only by a well-founded reluctance to inquire of foolish and boorish minds who would mock them rather than instruct them.

Curiosity is a sign of intelligence   It seems to me that curiosity is one of the surest signs of a good mind that is more amenable to being educated. It is the beginning of knowledge that leads us faster and further on the path to the truth. When two people come in contact with the same thing and if one of them looks at it disinterestedly while the other goes closer to get a better view, that shows that the eyes of the latter are more open. The mind in both sexes is equally adapted to the sciences, and its desire for knowledge, which may occur in men and women, is no more blameworthy in one than the other. If the mind is affected by something that it perceives only obscurely, it seems as if it has a natural right to understand it better. Since ignorance is the most distressing slavery that one could experience, it is as unreasonable to condemn someone who tries to escape from it as to blame some unfortunate person who tries to escape from a prison in which they are confined.

Fickleness   Among all the faults that are attributed to women, that of a fickle and unstable temperament is the one that is most objectionable. Men are no less subject to this than women, however; but since they think of themselves as the masters, they imagine that they are allowed to do anything they wish. Thus, once a woman becomes attached to them, they think that the bond should remain indissoluble only on the woman's side, even though they are both equal and each is involved in the relationship for their own benefit.

There would be fewer accusations of fickleness on both sides if one realized that fickleness is natural for human beings, and that the words 'mortal' and 'fickle' are coextensive. Being fickle is an inevitable result of the way we are made. We judge objects—we love or hate them—only on the basis of their appearances, which do not depend on us. The same things appear differently to us, sometimes because they have undergone some change and sometimes because we ourselves have changed. The same food causes us to have completely different sensations when it is more or less seasoned and when it is hot or cold; and even if it remained unchanged we would be affected by it differently if we were sick or healthy. We are indifferent to things in our infancy that we are passionate about ten years later because our bodies have changed in the mean time.

Why we should not accuse others of not loving us If someone loves us, it is because they think we are lovable; and if someone else hates us, that is because we appear loathsome to them. We admire at one time those whom we had previously despised, because they did not always appear to us in the same way—whether it is we or they who have changed. When something is presented to us, we may love it even if we would have hated it fifteen minutes earlier or later.

The contrast that we often find in ourselves when we have opposite reactions to the same object convinces us, despite ourselves, that our passions are not free, and that it is unjust to complain about being treated otherwise than one might wish. Just as love may be evoked by some trivial thing, its loss may be caused by something equally trivial, and this passion does not depend on us any more in its development than its inception. Among ten people who would wish to be loved, it usually happens that the one who is least deserving, who is lowest by birth and least attractive, wins out over the others because they seem to be more cheerful or they have some other feature that is more fashionable or matches our taste at the time.

Artifice If someone realized what they were saying when they accuse women of being more artificial than men, they would be speaking in their favour rather than the opposite, because it amounts to recognizing that they are also more intelligent and prudent than us. Artifice is a secret path to reach one's destination without being diverted. One has to be intelligent to discover this path, and one must be skilful to follow it. It would hardly be objectionable if someone used artifice to avoid being deceived. Deceit is much more common and more harmful in men. That has always been the preferred method of getting appointed to public offices or positions, where there are greater opportunities for doing harm. Whereas men who wish to deceive use their wealth, education, and power, from which people usually lack protection, women may exploit only their caresses and eloquence, which are natural means and more easily resisted if one wishes to guard against them.

Greater Malice   To crown all the accusations and faults, women are said to be more malicious and nasty than men, and all the evil of which they may be accused is included in this claim. I do not believe that those who hold this view claim that there are more women than men who do evil. That would be obviously false. Women are excluded from public offices or positions, the abuse of which causes all public misfortunes, and their virtue is too exemplary and men's misdeeds too well-known to entertain any doubts about this.

Thus, when it is said that women are more malicious, that could mean only that, when they set about doing evil, they do so more skilfully and carry it further than men. So be it. That suggests that women have a great advantage. One cannot be capable of great evil without having great intelligence and, consequently, without being capable of great good. Women should therefore not understand this reproach as more significant than if one objected to the rich or powerful that they are more evil than the poor because they have more resources to cause injury. Women could reply like the rich and powerful that, if they are capable of doing evil, they can also do good, and if the ignorance to which they are condemned is the reason why they are more evil than us, then science would, on the contrary, make them much better.

This brief discussion of the most prominent faults that are believed to be characteristic of and natural to the fair sex shows two things: first, that these faults are not as great as is commonly imagined; secondly, they can be attributed to the minimal education that women are given and that, such as they are, they can be corrected by instruction, for which women have no less aptitude than us.

If philosophers had followed this rule to judge everything that pertains to women, they would have spoken about them more sensibly and would not have fallen into ridiculous absurdities in this context. Most of the ancients and moderns have built their philosophy only on popular prejudices, and since they were already very ignorant about themselves, it is not surprising that they knew others so poorly. Without bothering with the ancients, one may say about the moderns that the way in which they teach the ancients—which makes them believe, though falsely, that they cannot improve on their predecessors—turns them into slaves of antiquity and encourages them to adopt blindly as unchanging truths everything that they find in antiquity. Since everything they say against women is based primarily on what they have read in the ancients, it will be useful to report here some of the strangest thoughts on this subject that have been bequeathed to us by these illustrious dead men, whose ashes and even whose remains are so revered today.

Plato's opinion   Plato, the father of ancient philosophy, used to thank the gods for the three favours that they had given him, but especially for the fact that he had been born a man rather than a woman.[75] If he was thinking of their current condition, I would certainly agree with him. But what makes me think that he had something else in mind is the doubt that he was said to have expressed often about whether women should be classified in the same category as beasts.[76] That would be enough for reasonable people to convict him of either ignorance or stupidity, and to succeed in demoting him from the title 'divine' that he no longer holds except among pedants.

Aristotle's opinion   His disciple Aristotle, for whom the glorious name 'genius of nature' is still preserved in the schools because of the prejudice that he understood nature better than any other philosopher, claimed that women were nothing but monsters.[77] Who would not believe that, on the authority of such a famous author? To call it impertinent would be to shock his supporters too overtly. If a woman, no matter how learned, had written the same about men, she would lose all credibility. People would think that, in order to refute such a stupid claim, it would be enough to reply that it must have been expressed by a woman or a fool. Nonetheless, she would not be any less reasonable than this philosopher. Women have been on earth as long as men; they appear in equally large numbers, and no one is surprised to meet a woman on their travels. To be a monster, even according to the thought of this philosopher, it is necessary to have some extraordinary or surprising feature. But women have nothing of the sort. They have always been made the same, always beautiful and

---

[75] This is not found in Plato's own writings, but was a commonplace based on *Timaeus* (91a–d), and is found explicitly in Lactantius, *Institutiones divinae*, III: 19; Eng. trans. ANF, VII, 90b: 'The saying of Plato is ... that he gave thanks to nature, first that he was born a human being rather than a dumb animal; in the next place, that he was a man rather than a woman.' It was repeated by many misogynists, including Trousset: *Alphabet de l'imperfection et malice des femmes*, 36 (Engl. trans. p. 10).

[76] This is also not found in Plato, though it was commonly attributed to him in misogynistic writings of the period. There are hints of the suggestion in *Theaetetus* 171e or *Timaeus* 41 b–c. Among those who repeated the claim was Erasmus; see Introduction above, p. 2.

[77] Aristotle, *On the Generation of Animals* (728a18–20): 'Now a boy is like a woman in form, and the woman is as it were an impotent male, for it is through a certain incapacity that the female is female, being incapable of concocting the nutriment in its last stage into semen ... owing to the coldness of her nature' (AR I, 1130).

intelligent; and if they are not made like Aristotle, they can say equally that Aristotle was not made like them.

This author's disciples, who lived in the time of Philo, adopted an opinion about women that is no less grotesque than Aristotle's by imagining, based on that historian's report, that women are imperfect men or males.[78] That was probably because women did not have a beard on their chins for, apart from that, I can make no sense of it. The two sexes, in order to be perfect, should be exactly as we see them today. If men are the fathers of women, women are the mothers of men—which makes them at least equal; and one would have as much reason as these philosophers to say that men are imperfect females.

The amusing opinion of Socrates Socrates, the oracle of antiquity for morality, when speaking of the beauty of the fair sex used to compare women with a temple that looks well but is built on a sewer.[79] One could only laugh at that suggestion if it were not so offensive. It seems as if he judged other people's bodies by comparison with his own, or with that of his wife, who was a she-devil who made him loathe her. He spoke about her sex in that way in order to humiliate her, and he was enraged within himself for being as ugly as a baboon.

The opinion of Diogenes Diogenes, nicknamed 'the dog' because he knew only how to bite, when he saw two women passing by one day and conversing together, said to his companions that they were two snakes, an aspic and a viper, who were exchanging venom.[80]

---

[78] Philo of Alexandria (20 BC–54 AD) was a Greek philosopher of Jewish birth. Samples of his negative comments about women are found in *Allegorical Interpretation of Genesis*, LCL 226, II: LIX: 'Pleasure does not venture to bring her wiles and deceptions to bear on the man, but on the woman, and by her means on him ... for in us mind corresponds to man, the senses to woman', and in *Questions and Answers on Genesis*, LCL 380, I: 24–28: 'Inasmuch as the moulding of the male is more perfect than, and double, that of the female, it requires only half the time ... whereas the imperfect woman, who is, so to speak, a half-section of a man, requires twice as many days' (§25); 'woman is not equal in honour with man' (§27).

[79] There are no extant writings by Socrates, and this opinion seems likely to have been borrowed from some gnomologium. There are many misogynistic sayings attributed to Socrates in a collection entitled *The Dictes or Sayings of the Philosophers* (Westminster, 1477), which derived through various intermediate translations from an Arabic text composed by Mubashshir ibn Fatik (eleventh century). *The Dicts and Sayings of the Philosophers*, ed. Curt F. Bühler (London: Oxford University Press, 1941), includes three manuscript sources of this text, but the specific saying attributed to Socrates above is not there, nor does it occur in the French version of the text, by Guillaume de Tignonville, *La Forest et description des grands et sages philosophes du temp passé* (Paris: P. Leber, 1529).

[80] This commonplace was attributed to Diogenes (c.404–c.323 BC), who was a contemporary of Aristotle. It is reported in various collections, such as *Fragmenta Philosophorum Graecorum*, ed. G. A. Mullachius (Paris, 1867), vol. II, 304, frag. 56; Engl. transl. in Robin Hard, *Diogenes*

This apophthegm[c] is worthy of a cultured man, and I am not surprised that it is ranked among the best philosophical sayings. If Tabarin, Verboquet, and Espiègle had lived in his day, we would surely find their stories more witty.[81] This chap had been hurt in some way, and those who know him a little realize that he had nothing else to say.

Democritus   As regards the famous and amusing Democritus, one should not take everything he said literally because he was fond of joking. He was very tall and his wife was very short. When asked one day why they were so mismatched, he replied jokingly in his usual manner that, when one has to choose and there is nothing good to choose from, the smallest is always best.[82] If the same question had been put to his wife, she could have replied just as reasonably that, since a tall husband is no better than a short one, she got hers by drawing lots because she was afraid of getting the worst one had she made the choice herself.

Cato's Thought   Cato, the wise and severe critic, often prayed to the gods to pardon him if he were ever so imprudent as to confide the smallest secret to a woman.[83] The good man had in mind a famous event in Roman history, which antiquarians[d] used as a great argument to show how little discretion women have. A twelve-year old child was encouraged by his mother to inform her about a decision of the Senate at which he had been present and, to avoid her request, he made up a story that the

---

[c] i.e. a saying of an illustrious man.

[d] the lovers of antiquity.

the Cynic: Sayings and Anecdotes (Oxford: Oxford University Press, 2012), 71. Diogenes Laertius attributes the following to him: 'Seeing some women hanged from an olive-tree, he said, "Would that every tree bore similar fruit".' *Lives of Eminent Philosophers: Diogenes*, vol. II, LCL 185, VI.52.

[81] Tabarin is the pseudonym of Antoine Girard or Jean Salomon (1584–1633), a street-theatre performer and prototype buffoon whose stories and farces were published in Paris in 1622. Verboquet is the pseudonymous author of stories and comedies published under the title *Délices ou discours joyeux et récréatifs* (Paris: 1630), which were supposed to cheer up melancholy people. Espiègle is a fictional character renowned for knavish jokes. The stories of Tabarin and Verboquet were also notoriously bawdy. Poulain suggests that the people would think more positively of them if they had written in the time of Diogenes, so that their antiquity would then confer on them a degree of respectability that matches the ridiculous sayings of some philosophers.

[82] Democritus (460–370 BC) was one of the founders of ancient atomism; happiness was a central concern in his ethics, though only fragments of writings attributed to him survive. See *Fragmenta Philosophorum Graecorum* (note 80), I, 351, frag. 180.

[83] See *Plutarch's Lives*, vol. II: *Marcus Cato*, LCL 47, IX, 4–7 (p. 329): 'And as for repentance, he said he had indulged in it himself but thrice in his whole life: once when he entrusted a secret to his wife.'

Senate decided to give every husband a number of wives. She went off immediately to tell her neighbours and to make plans with them, and all the city knew about it within half an hour. I would really like to know what a poor husband would do if, in a city where women were in charge, as in that of the amazons, someone had come to him to report that the city council had decided to give a second husband to each woman. He would surely not have said a word about it.

These are some of the great and sublime thoughts about the fair sex that were entertained by those who are studied by the learned as oracles. What is generally amusing and bizarre about it is that serious people take literally what the ancients often said in a spirit of raillery. Thus it is very true that prejudices and self-interest lead to mistakes even among the very people who are accepted as the most reasonable, judicious, and wise.

Afterword

The strongest objections that can be made against us are drawn from the authority of famous men and from Holy Scripture. As regards the first of these, I think they may be answered adequately by saying that I recognize no authority here apart from that of reason and sound judgement.

As regards Scripture, it is not in any way contrary to the aim of this work, on condition that one understands each of them correctly. It is claimed here that the two sexes are completely equal once they are considered independently of custom, which often makes those who are more intelligent and meritorious subordinate to others. Scripture does not say a single word about inequality; and since its only function is to provide a rule of conduct for people in accordance with the ideas of justice that it advocates, it allows everyone the freedom to judge as they wish about the natural and true state of things. If one keeps that in mind, all the objections that are derived from Scripture are only the sophistries of prejudice, by which passages are understood sometimes as if they applied to all women when they refer only to some specific individuals or, at other times, something is attributed to nature that results only from education or custom or from what the sacred authors say about the customs of their own times.

Conversations concerning the Education of Ladies to Guide their Minds in the Sciences and in Morals[84]

Excerpt from the Second Conversation

[*Editor's note*: Those involved include Sophia, 'a lady who is so wise and accomplished that she could be called wisdom itself'; Eulalia, who is willing to be educated; Timander, who is sympathetic to the Aristotelian tradition; and Stasimachus, who represents Poulain's position.]

Timander: 'If it is true that we fall naturally into error and prejudice, does it not seem that the best way to avoid this is to resort to public opinion; that there is nothing more certain than what is confirmed by general agreement; that, in contrast with each individual being afraid of falling into error by relying on their own judgement, there would be no fear of error if one relied on a large number of people, especially if they are enlightened and clever people who, because they have examined things carefully, would not have allowed their views to be published unless they were the best; that there is little likelihood that so many people would be mistaken or would conspire together in error; that it is not a mistake to choose the main path as the most well-trodden and most certain one; that one should hold onto a tree at its trunk, and that there is less danger of getting lost if one stays with the crowd than if one takes off with only one other person.'

'I tell you', replied Stasimachus, 'that those are the commonplaces that occur in everyone's mind, and especially in women's minds, because they

[84] *De l'éducation des dames pour la conduite de l'esprit dans les sciences and dans les moeurs; Entretiens* (Paris: Jean Du Puis, 1674). I have translated from the Pellegrin edition (Paris: Vrin, 2011), 189–200. These dialogues, which were dedicated to Mademoiselle de Montpensier (1627–1693), a cousin of Louis XIV, are explicitly concerned with the education of ladies although, indirectly, they imply that women of any social class could benefit from education in proportion to their native talents.

were reared in a way that makes them more submissive and timid than men, so that they cling more strongly to custom and popular opinion and therefore find it more difficult to let go of them. But I would like to ask an intelligent lady', he added, 'how she knows that the wider path is the road to truth, that this tree-trunk to which she remains attached is not a phantom that she embraces, that these alleged scholars are genuine, and that they are infallible about any topic they wish to discuss. Since this issue of public authority in scientific knowledge is one of the most important that could be examined in relation to guiding the mind, let us try to examine it properly to the satisfaction of Sophia and Eulalia, and let us defer to another conversation questions about history.'

Popular opinion or public approval provides no certainty

'If we address this question from the point of view of principles, would you not agree that when we compare one person with another, neither is subject to the other? Since they are all naturally equal and are all equally subject to error, it would not be prudent to accept what someone else says simply because they say it. For, if we accept that we are equal, we ought to believe our own opinion as much as that of others; and if we submit to someone else, they ought for the same reason to submit to us, and each one individually ought to submit to all others equally, and thus adopt the opinions and feelings of all their peers because there is no reason to prefer one to another.'

'That is clear', said Timander. 'If we accept as true some opinion or some ideas that we get from others, we would have to have some reason for doing so; however, the most natural and common reason is the title and ability of a scholar!'

'But how can we be sure that someone is clever?' asked Eulalia.

'We can be certain', said Stasimachus, 'either by using our own intelligence or by accepting the testimony of others. We know it by our own powers when, knowing certain things very well, we then judge by the way someone talks about them that they know them as well as we do.'

'In that case', Sophia interrupted, 'our certainty about someone's ability is not based on our favourable opinion of them but on our own ability.'

'Thus if we do not know certain things', added Stasimachus, 'and if someone who is assumed to know them discusses them with us in a way that provides us with clear and distinct ideas, then by paying attention to their ideas we can say that the things in question are as our interlocutor represents them.'

'It is still clear', replied Sophia, 'that the approval that we give that person is based on the truth that they have taught us, and not in any way on some belief that we had that they were well instructed about it.'

'But what should we think of people who fail to make themselves understood?' asked Eulalia.

'When that happens', replied Stasimachus, 'because of a lack of understanding on the part of the listeners, it is up to them to acknowledge their own inadequacy, for it is like talking about colours to the blind.'

'But Eulalia's question is about intelligent people,' said Timander.

'In that case', replied Stasimachus, 'when the topic of their conversation is such that it could be understood by people who are adequately intelligent, and the words they hear fail to provide any understanding, I think they may conclude that those who are speaking to them have nothing more in their minds than words or chimerical images that cannot emerge from the heads in which they were formed. In that case, one can do no more than acquiesce civilly and with apparent interest to such obscure and unintelligible discourses. I cannot understand how a reasonable person could agree deep down with things that are incompatible with their own experience or with meaningless words that the mind cannot understand. Thoughts are for ourselves, and words are for making ourselves understood by others, and it amounts to smothering our desire to know and opposing the nature and perfection of the mind if we stop short at the sounds of words alone. Thus, even if we were convinced that someone was the most intelligent person on earth, that they had examined things without prejudice or error, with as much care and attention as possible, that they had followed the method and all necessary rules for discovering the truth, and that they had anticipated all the objections that might be made against their views; if they still could not make themselves understood about some subject matter, we should pay no more attention to them than if they had never said anything to us about it. All we may conclude from their discourse is that they have told us things that we do not understand, unless we wish to add that they do not understand it themselves.'

'I believe', said Eulalia, 'that the best proof that someone is learned is that they know how to communicate their knowledge to others, and in that respect there are those who are alive and those who are dead. I am satisfied that I cannot be accused of what Stasimachus alleged as such a common occurrence among women, namely, of accepting as true everything that they see in print.'

'Your attitude is the best in the world', replied Stasimachus. 'We are no more obliged to believe someone when they converse with us through their writings than when they do so orally, even if we were convinced that the writings in question were indubitably composed by the author whose name they bear, that they were not altered by copyists, translators, commentators, or objectors, that the books of adversaries are no better and that they were not suppressed or corrupted. If it is permissible to disagree with an author with whom we are speaking, it is much more permissible to examine critically their written works because, in that situation, there is no danger of offending them even if they were written a hundred thousand years ago and if there were as many millions of people who had approved them.'

'That is precisely what bothers me', said Timander. 'For, on the one hand, if someone suggests something to me that I do not understand, I could not accept it blindly as most people do. But, on the other hand, I think I should accept it when I learn that it was accepted by a large number of learned people for many centuries.'

'I am not surprised', replied Stasimachus. 'That is the most common problem that results from confusing what we know with the way in which we came to know it, so that we do not take care about the weight to be assigned to the testimony of many centuries. There are things that we are capable of knowing by ourselves, by using our reason or our natural intelligence, such as those that constitute the subject matter of philosophy, grammar, and other sciences. There are other things that we cannot know without the intervention or report of others, such as those that occur in places where we do not happen to live or at times when we were not alive. It is true that, in the latter case, the testimony of others is absolutely necessary, and when one finds that there is a general and uniform agreement among many people, especially clever people with disparate interests who agree about some fact, I cannot see how one could refuse to accept it. Otherwise, we would have to give up everything that is called history and never again believe anything apart from what we observe.'

'I understand that well', replied Timander. 'But what do you think about things that pertain to reason?'

'You yourself say what we should think about them', said Stasimachus, 'and the difficulty you mention contains its own resolution. For whatever falls within the scope of reason should be known by reason, and in order to know nature well one has to know it oneself. We can use the help that various authors already mentioned have left us, but we should not be more deferential towards them than if we had been their contemporaries, even if their views were adopted for many centuries by many people who were

regarded as learned. The truth or falsity of an opinion is not based on its age
or on the number of people who accepted or rejected it.'

'I had some doubts about that for some time', said Sophia, 'but I have
none any longer. I see clearly that prescription does not apply to opinions,
since there is no prescription in favour of error or against the truth.'[85]

The extent   'To understand better the extent to which we should
to which one   defer to the agreement of the learned about some author',
may trust the continued Stasimachus, 'I must tell you how they usually
agreement of adopt the opinions that they defend. With respect to their
learned people prophets—if I may apply that word here to their great
men—they relate to them, I claim, like sheep that follow
the first sheep they encounter and try to follow it wherever it goes. When
the learned happen to find themselves by chance or otherwise following
the lead of someone else, they think of nothing other than following that
person and imitating them like slaves. Since they merely copy each other,
it is not surprising that for two thousand years there has been such a great
uniformity of opinion among them or, rather, a uniformity of language.'

'The philosopher Aristotle, as the one who has most credit in France, can
provide a better example of this than anyone else. Although he did not say
much that is favourable to women', he added, while looking in the direction
of Sophia and Eulalia, 'and called them monsters, that did not prevent him
from being regarded as one of the most eminent men of his generation.'[86]
His reputation attracted disciples, as happens today to his supporters who
are in fashion. Thus, you will be able to judge how his doctrine and sect was
established and developed by comparison with what occurs today. At the
same time, you can learn something else about this by realizing that, when
we enter public schools to be taught, that is, at a time in our lives when
we accept as true the stories about 'Fearless Richard' and 'the Beautiful
Maguelone' and all the other stories that our grandmothers and nurses told
us, the first thing we learn is the 'Academic Creed', the principal article of
which obliges us to believe that Cicero, Virgil, and Aristotle are inimitable
original minds by reference to which the best works that we possess have

[85] Poulain had argued above, pp. 167–8, 173, that one may acquire or lose legal possession of
material things by prescription; in contrast, the mere length of time during which some opinion was accepted or rejected does not make it true or false.

[86] *Generation of Animals* (737a28): 'For the female is, as it were, a mutilated male, and the
menstrual fluids are semen, only not pure' (AR I, 1144).

been created, and that there is no hope of salvation in the literary world or the sciences unless we accept them as models.[87] Our teachers make sure to engage us in this veneration by the magnificent eulogies that they offer those authors from time to time and, as they get us to learn respectfully the writings they left, they make them even more commendable by the punishments and rewards they use to ensure the success of this training. With these preparatory incentives, we are then promoted (as they say) into philosophy, in which everything echoes with the discourses pronounced there in honour of the Genius of Nature; and since our professors avoid speaking about prejudices as if we had just been born, they confirm those we had already acquired by leaving us steeped in them. They inspire us with an aversion towards philosophers who disagree with them; and because they support their aversion with religion, they inspire a hatred of unfortunate unknown authors and discourage us from reading them even more effectively by the fact that they themselves have often not read the table of contents in such works because of the same scruple that they try to communicate to us.'

'Nevertheless, we treat those teachers as oracles. We say tacitly, as women do, that they appear to be clever people because they have been granted the titles and authority required to teach publicly. Thus, while our judgement is suspended, we put our memories to work by learning certain things that can be expressed only in Latin. Once we have learned this language adequately and are able to speak it, we become respected teachers, just like our own teachers before us. We gather disciples in our turn and other teachers who resemble us. In this way, our doctrine is perpetuated from year to year and from one century to another, and it spreads in the provinces. Since everyone avoids examining what they think they know by putting their trust in those who taught them, we are as convinced of this doctrine today as people were in the time of Aristotle. The same applies to all the sciences.'

'You remind me of the way that I studied in earlier days', said Timander. 'I conclude that it is not by reasoning that people usually reject some teaching, because they accept it in the first place more often by chance or custom rather than by reasoning. Since the agreement of many people about the

---

[87] Poulain compares the credulity of children's response to the stories they heard from their nurses orally (before Charles Perrault collected them in book form, in 1695), with that of the trust demanded of them when they enter school. The 'academic creed' alludes to versions of the Creed adopted by Christian churches, such as the Athanasian creed, which contained 'articles' (such as belief in the Trinity) that Christians were required to believe as a necessary condition for salvation.

same thing shows merely that it was approved rather than that it is true, we should likewise conclude from their opposition to some opinion that it was merely challenged rather than that it is erroneous, and that it had the misfortune of being the weakest opinion rather than the worst.'

'What you say is so true', said Stasimachus, 'that when some sect or opinion that seems to be novel appears, it is regarded as a monster that should be smothered at birth; people are so afraid of it spreading that they suppress it even without seeing it. If they are asked to explain this reaction, they think it is enough to reply that the opinion in question is contrary to custom and to what the ancients believed.'

'That is amusing,' said Eulalia, 'as if the ancients were wiser and less human than their descendants. But I would like to know', she added, addressing Stimachus, 'if you would reject the opinion of many people who are actually clever or reputed to be such, if they had examined some question together?'

'If they were actually clever people who got me to understand the subject matter', replied Stimachus, 'then I would readily defer to their judgement as I defer to any individual who teaches me the truth. But if they were merely reputed to be clever, and if I were actually in their company, then I would stretch civility to its limits to avoid having a row with them.'

What is the authority of an assembly of learned people?

'I agree with you', said Sophia. 'When there are so many people together, I think that one can distrust them and fear confusion. There are almost always as many interests and opinions as there are people in large assemblies. The desire to show off or the shame of conceding makes everyone hold onto their own view more stubbornly. The need to control people, the fear of not being able to defend their own opinions or of shocking those who hold a different opinion, together with the usual deference shown towards sheer numbers, cause most people to agree with the majority, so that the strongest view wins, people get their opinions from their teachers, and they usually end up agreeing with the majority view. For every person who is impartial, there are twenty who are not so. Even if they were all impartial, there would probably not be two who share the same psychological disposition. Is it not the case that everyone has their own principles and their own particular method? One person is prejudiced about one thing and another has prejudices about something else. One is ardent, quick, decisive, and zealous, while someone else is unenthusiastic, slow, and timid. Some are taught well about certain things while others are taught only poorly about them or not at all. There are some who lack focus, while others apply themselves; sometimes people pay too much attention to words, while at other times they neglect them too much; and this heterogeneous combination never produces anything worthwhile. I also know', she added, 'that the old rabbis who are steeped in prejudices defend them tooth and nail and that they force the young people to yield because they are often supported by custom and public authority, not to mention various intrigues and cabals.'

'You describe so clearly what happens in most of the learned societies', said Stasimachus, 'that if they had admitted women as a matter of course I believe you would have learned the secrets of the most important among them.'

'That results from the fact that I have read a few histories', replied Sophia, 'and partly because I am visited now and then by certain intelligent people who tell me about what they observed in the meetings they attended there. I remember', she added, 'that one of my friends who is very well informed about people, both in former times and today, was telling me one day about how bizarre were some of their opinions and customs. He made me realize that the more well-intentioned among them were forced a thousand times by considerations of state security and public order to tolerate obvious errors and the least reasonable practices.'

The Spirit of the People 'You should not be surprised at that', said Timander. 'Since people idolize their own opinions and customs, it is sometimes a sound policy to maintain them as they are. For you know that they regard them as a heritage or a vine that was bequeathed to them by their fathers. They are always ready to rise up and to take up arms, to set fire to everything and to destroy themselves in order to protect their chimerical beliefs. Wise politicians are not unreasonable to think of a people as being similar to a spirited horse that holds the reins very lightly between its teeth if it is not carefully restrained, that one has to pat it and use one's voice to calm it and prevent it from rearing up and to control it when it prances. In short, it has always been said of the people that they wish to be mistaken and to be left in their errors, and that it is dangerous to assume the challenge of correcting them.'

'This obstinacy is not limited to people who are ignorant and unsophisticated', replied Stasimachus. 'The learned are also like that, and their members are subject to convulsions and mutinies even more frequently and for longer periods than the people you were talking about.'

'Whereas a relevant doubt, a sympathetic word, or a well-turned speech can make the lower classes give up a fight that had been triggered by some other doubt; whereas a popular uprising dissipates of its own accord when it loses it leader and there is no one else to foment it; in contrast, once the flame of division has been lit among professional scholars, it causes a conflagration among them that is much more fatal because it affects the mind. Everyone assumes the role of a faction-leader, and as soon as one is defeated another appears; once they have embarked on a campaign, they are like stimulated flies that are almost impossible to contain.'

'Since they also believe they are more rational than ordinary people, it is more difficult to get them to back down. That it why is was necessary in the schools to prohibit people from speaking publicly about certain questions that were too controversial, and they were allowed to speak only favourably about other matters that reflected popular opinion, even if they did not condemn those who privately held the opposite view. Indeed, when the learned engaged in controversy they reverted to the mentality of a children's school, and the cane was the only thing that could calm them. In every century it was necessary to have recourse to the civil authorities who knew how to deploy naked power and royal authority to bring an end to riots caused by conflicting opinions.'

'It is only the least capable scholars who fall into such convulsions', said Sophia. 'I know others who have a completely different attitude, who hate quarrels and disputes so much that they even avoid places where they anticipate they might arise. But, what I most admire in them, among other things, is their love of truth. They are so impartial that even if they hold the most distinguished titles, such as those that bring most credit to scholars, they never use them in polite society, and they would never want anyone to defer to their opinions simply because they were teachers, for they do not believe that their office makes them more credible.'

'They are right', said Stasimachus. 'That status is merely a sign that those who possess it have been honoured because they were found capable of defending the opinions of the country or association where they passed the relevant examinations. If that were a proof that they knew the truth, we would have to conclude that English, Turkish, and Chinese teachers also know the truth. However, not everyone would accept that conclusion.'

'I do not wish to provide a guarantee', said Timander, 'for everyone who holds the title of a teacher. We do not have to believe that they are all orthodox, for we observe that they do not always agree and that they occasionally dispute among themselves.'

'So what is the point of those permissions to publish that I see at the back of most books?' asked Eulalia.[88]

'To provide the testimony that they offer', replied Stasimachus. 'If you had taken the trouble to read one of them, you could have noticed that they provide a guarantee that the books to which they are appended contain nothing that is contrary to religion, or to certain popular opinions of the country in question that people are not allowed to challenge. You realize that it is not good to speak publicly about truths of every kind, and since censors hold public offices, they should not allow someone to publish in a book truths that will cause controversy, even if they themselves are convinced of them.'

'Thus the approval of a book', said Eulalia, 'is not an infallible sign of its truth.'

'Not at all', replied Stasimachus, 'for apart from the fact that we approve in this century what was condemned in others and that things that are accepted in Spain are rejected in France, many philosophical and indifferent opinions slip into books, including books about religion, that one may adopt or not at one's discretion.'

Sophia turned to Eulalia, and said to her: 'Since these gentlemen have been speaking primarily for your sake, it is now up to you to draw the conclusions that result from their discussion.'

'I see clearly', replied Eulalia, 'that one should not accept public opinion as the criterion of truth in matters that we are capable of knowing by ourselves, and that the same rule applies to opinions as to fashions, namely: we do not always adopt the best or the most appropriate ones, but the first ones that we encounter.'

'You are right', said Timander. 'Customs are like great rivers that begin with a trickle of water and, so to speak, are lucky enough not to disappear near their source but to increase in size by the addition of all the streams they encounter as they flow along.'

[88] In 1623 France instituted a system that required prior royal approval (*privilège*) before a book could be published; this was printed at the end of the book. Religious authorities introduced a parallel system of condemning books, after publication, if they were judged unorthodox by a given church. Both systems of censorship evolved over time, so that some churches required their own members to obtain prior approval to publish books that included religious or theological content.

'It seems to me', he added, 'that one may conclude from this conversation that if the agreement of a whole kingdom and of many centuries were a sign of truth, then the most inconsistent opinions would be equally true or false, because there is hardly a single opinion today of which the opposite was not the prevailing view in former days or was not supported not only by those who are thought to be clever but even by whole nations.'

'These reflections', said Stasimachus to Eulalia, 'clarify the first question that I asked you, about the state of your soul and the kinds of knowledge that you possess. I am pleased that you are convinced that you know nothing with certainty, except that you have a firm and unwavering desire to know things in the best way possible. That is what you seek, namely, a reliable rule which, by providing you with discernment and precision about everything, teaches you to distinguish by their characteristic features truth and falsehood, vice and virtue, good and evil. What you are looking for is an effective remedy that will cure you of prejudice and error, will restore you to perfect health, and will protect you from the evils and relapses that you may fear. You wish for a light which dissipates the shadows that confuse and disturb your mind, which restores it to clarity and calm and re-establishes the right order that should obtain among your thoughts. Finally, by wishing to become wise you wish for a natural condition in which, once it is achieved, you would be able to see yourself and everything in your environment from the perspective of the relationships and dependencies in which nature placed you.'

Further Reading

A two-volume critical edition of Marie de Gournay's works is available for readers who wish to study the development of her ideas through various editions of her publications: *Oeuvres complètes*, ed. Jean-Claude Arnould *et al.* (Paris: Champion, 2002). There is no similar modern edition of the complete works of Anna Maria van Schurman, and most translations are based on seventeenth-century collections, such as *Opuscula Hebraea, Graeca, Latina, Gallica; Prosaica & Metrica* (Leiden: Elsevier, 1648), and on her autobiography, *Eukleria seu Melioris Partis Electio; Tractatus Brevem Vitae ejus Delineationem exhibens* (Altona: C. van der Meulen, 1673). Finally, there is a modern edition of Poulain de la Barre's three feminist tracts, *De l'égalité des deux sexes, De l'éducation des dames, De l'excellence des hommes*, ed. Marie-Frédérique Pellegrin (Paris, Vrin, 2011). *De l'égalité des deux sexes* was also published in the series *Corpus des Oeuvres de Philosophie en Langue Française* (Paris: Fayard, 1984), but this was not a facsimile edition and it contains a number of textual mistakes and omissions.

The University of Chicago Press series, 'The Other Voice in Early Modern Europe', includes separate volumes of texts in translation dedicated to each of these three authors: Marie le Jars de Gournay, *Apology for the Woman Writing*, trans. Richard Hillman and Colette Quesnel (University of Chicago Press, 2002); Anna Maria van Schurman, *Whether a Christian Woman Should be Educated and Other Writings from her Intellectual Circle*, trans. Joyce L. Irwin (University of Chicago Press, 1998), and François Poullain de la Barre, *Three Cartesian Feminist Treatises*, trans. Vivien Bosley, with an Introduction by M. M. Welch (University of Chicago Press, 2002). Many other primary texts that are mentioned by these authors or that subsequently borrowed from them are also included in this series, including Juan Luis Vives, Henricus Cornelius Agrippa, Christine de Pizan, Lucrezia Marinella, Madeleine de Scudéry, and Gabrielle Suchon. There are also anthologies of feminist writings, such as Katherina M. Wilson and Frank J. Warke, eds. *Women Writers of the Seventeenth Century* (Athens, GA: University of Georgia Press, 1989), and Frances Teague, ed., *The Early Modern Englishwoman: A Facsimile Library of Essential Works, Series II. Printed Writings, 1641–1700, Part I* (Aldershot: Ashgate, 2001). Mary Ellen Waithe has edited a four-volume selection of philosophical writings by women, *A History of Women Philosophers* (Dordrecht, 1987–95).

The intellectual context in which the seventeenth-century feminist tracts originally appeared has been studied extensively in the recent past, and there are so many excellent and relevant publications that it would be impossible to list even a representative sample of them. They include Carolyn C. Lougee, *Le Paradis des femmes: Women, Salons and Social Stratification in Seventeenth-Century France* (Princeton, NJ: Princeton University Press, 1976); Ian Maclean, *Women Triumphant: Feminism in French Literature 1610–1652* (Oxford: Clarendon Press, 1977); M. Albistur and D. Armogathe, *Histoire du féminisme français du moyen âge à nos jours* (Paris: Éditions des femmes, 1979); Joan Kelly, *Women, History and Theory* (Chicago and London: University of Chicago Press, 1984); T. Akkerman and S. Stuurman, eds. *Perspectives on Feminist Political Thought in European History: from the Middle Ages to the Present* (London and New York: Routledge, 1998). Jacqueline Broad's *Women Philosophers of the Seventeenth Century* (Cambridge: Cambridge University Press, 2002), summarizes the contributions of various women to philosophical discussions in the seventeenth century. There are comprehensive summaries of educational practices and policies that were in force in France in the relevant years in L. W. D. Brockliss, *French Higher Education in the Seventeenth and Eighteenth Centuries* (Oxford: Clarendon Press, 1987), and Henry Phillips, *Church and Culture in Seventeenth-Century France* (Cambridge: Cambridge University Press, 1997). Since Calvin's theology was so significant for Van Schurman and Poulain, readers may wish to consult one of the later editions of Calvin's *Institutes*. This text evolved over time from the first Latin edition, 1536 (which was very short), to the very much expanded Latin edition of 1559, each of which in turn was translated into French. There is a recent and accessible English translation of the 1541 French edition by Elsie Anne McKee, *Institutes of the Christian Religion: 1541 French Edition* (Grand Rapids, MI: William B. Eerdmans, 2009).

For readers seeking biographical information about the three authors, the most comprehensive life of Gournay is still Marjorie H. Ilsley, *A Daughter of the Renaissance: Marie le Jars de Gournay: Her Life and Works* (The Hague: Mouton, 1963). There are some biographical essays about van Schurman in Mirjam de Baar et al., eds., *Choosing the Better Part: Anna Maria van Schurman (1607–1678)* (Dordrecht: Kluwer, 1996), and very helpful information about her conversion to Labadism in Trevor J.

Saxby, *The Quest for a New Jerusalem: Jean de Labadie and the Labadists, 1610–1744* (Dordrecht: Nijhoff, 1987). Biographical studies of the almost undocumented life of Poulain include Marie Louise Stock, *Poulain de la Barre: A Seventeenth-Century Feminist* (PhD Dissertation, Columbia University, 1961); Madeleine Alcover, *Poullain de la Barre: une aventure philosophique* (Paris, Seattle, Tuebingen: Biblio 17, 1981); and, most comprehensively, Siep Stuurman, *François Poulain de la Barre and the Invention of Modern Equality* (Cambridge, MA: Harvard University Press, 2004).

Descartes' significance for seventeenth-century discussions of the woman question is examined in Susan Bordo, ed., *Feminist Interpretations of René Descartes* (University Park, PA: Pennsylvania State University Press, 1999) and Erica Harth, *Cartesian Women: Versions and Subversions of Rational Discourse in the Old Regime* (Ithaca and London: Cornell University Press, 1992). Eileen O'Neill reviews the extensive literature and summarizes recent debates in 'The Equality of Men and Women,' in D. M. Clarke and C. Wilson, eds., *The Oxford Handbook of Philosophy in Early Modern Europe* (Oxford: Oxford University Press, 2011), 445–74. *Women in Western Political Thought*, ed. Susan Moller Okin (Princeton, NJ: Princeton University Press, 1979/1992), examines the discussion of women by classical political theorists, while Jacqueline Broad and Karen Green, eds. *A History of Women's Political Thought in Europe, 1400–1700* (Cambridge: Cambridge University Press, 2009), summarizes the contributions of women to political theory over three centuries. The significance of women writers in Italy is examined in two books edited by Letizia Panizza, *A History of Women's Writing in Italy* (Cambridge: Cambridge University Press, 2000), and *Women in Italian Renaissance Culture and Society* (Oxford: Legenda, 2000).

The significance of Gournay, van Schurman and Poulain for subsequent feminist writers and for the eventual political recognition of the equality of women and men is the subject of ongoing research. Among those who borrowed their ideas—as they had borrowed liberally, often without acknowledgement, from earlier writers—were Marguerite Buffet, *Nouvelles observations sur la langue françoise avec Les Eloges des Illustres sçavantes, tant anciennes que modernes* (Paris: Jean Cusson, 1668), and Gabrielle Suchon, *Du Célibat volontaire ou la vie sans engagement*, ed. Séverine Auffret (Paris: Indigo, 1994; 1st edn. 1700). Simone de Beauvoir used one of Poulain's pithy arguments as an epigraph in *Le Deuxième Sexe* (Paris: Gallimard, 1949); *The Second Sex*, trans. H. M. Parshley (London: Jonathan Cape, 1953).

The translation into English of Poulain's *Discours Physique et Moral de l'Égalité des Deux Sexes*, as *The Woman as Good as the Man: or, The Equallity of Both Sexes* (London, 1677), provided the inspiration for many subsequent defences of women's rights in England. Its main theses were plagiarized in the anonymous pamphlet by 'Sophia': *Woman Not Inferior to Man; or, A Short and Modest Vindication of the Natural Right of the FAIR-SEX to a Perfect Equality of Power, Dignity, and Esteem, with the Men* (London, 1739), which was reissued as *Beauty's Triumph or, The Superiority of the Fair Sex invincibly proved* (London, 1751). Poulain's work subsequently appeared in a pirated English translation (which omitted paragraphs that were specific to France and might have caused suspicions about its author) as *Female Rights Vindicated; or The Equality of the Sexes Morally and Physically Proved. By a Lady* (London, 1758) This was republished as *Female Restoration, by a Physical and Moral Vindication of Female Talents; in opposition to all dogmatical assertions relative to Disparity in the Sexes* (London, 1780) and, with the addition of chapter divisions, it was reissued in northern England as *Female Rights Vindicated; or, the Equality of the Sexes Proved* (South Shields: James Jollie, 1833). The influence of Poulain's work on eighteenth- and nineteenth-century discussions of women's rights in England has been extensively investigated by Guyonne Leduc, in *Réécritures anglaises au XVIIIe siècle de l'ÉGALITÉ DES DEUX SEXES (1673) de François Poulain de la Barre* (Paris: l'Harmattan, 2010).

Mary Wollstonecraft seems to have borrowed at least her title from the pirated translation of Poulain, in *A Vindication of the Rights of Woman* (London, 1792); there is a modern edition of the latter, edited by Janet Todd in *A Vindication of the Rights of Men; A Vindication of the Rights of Woman; A Historical and Moral View of the French Revolution* (Oxford University Press, 1994/2008). William Thompson's *Appeal of One-Half of the Human Race, Women, Against the Pretensions of the Other Half, Men, To Retain them in Political and Thence in Civil and Domestic Slavery* (London, 1825) has also been reissued, edited by Dolores Dooley (Cork University Press, 1997), and the more familiar treatise by John Stuart Mill, *The Subjection of Women* (London, 1869) has been republished in various modern editions; see *On Liberty, with The Subjection of Women*, ed. Stefan Collini (Cambridge University Press, 1989).

There are extensive summaries and frequently updated bibliographies for many issues in contemporary feminism in *The Stanford Encyclopedia of Philosophy*, at <http://plato.stanford.edu>.

Index

academies 130, 178
Aeneid 64, 67, 71
Agrippa, C. 3, 61
amazons 67, 149, 184
Amyraut, M. 37
ancients, authority of 126, 151, 196,
 205–7
Anna (biblical prophetess) 66, 72
Anonymous (a lady), 12–13
Anonymous (Sophia), 9, 12, 35, 43–4
Antisthenes 78
appearances 39–40, 122, 192
Appia, St 68
appointments, purchase of 132
Arete 57
Aristotle 10, 15, 34, 50, 61, 83, 88, 99,
 109, 115, 197–8, 205, 206
arts 82, 86, 96, 101, 115
Aspasia 58
astrology 140
astronomy 161
Augustine, St 21, 26, 27, 109, 112, 118
authority
 critique of 10, 36, 147
 of Scripture 1, 24, 36, 55
Axiothea 59

baptism 69
Basil, St 17, 30, 65–6, 70, 78, 87, 96
beard, defining masculinity 66, 75, 76
beauty 131, 178, 186
Bible
 Colossians 48
 I Corinthians 19, 48, 93
 Ecclesiastes 113
 Ephesians 73
 Genesis 17, 18, 19, 26, 50, 65, 66, 73
 Mark 1
 Matthew 10, 12
 I Peter 26, 105
 Romans 118
 I Timothy 26, 32, 48, 103–4
 Titus 85
biblical interpretation 11, 20, 21, 24, 26,
 36, 105, 117

biblical languages 27, 29, 81, 101, 105,
 106, 110, 116
blood circulation 136, 159
Boccaccio, G. 3, 61
body 42, 158, 184, 186
Brahe, T. 57
brain 42, 44, 50, 158, 180

Calvin, J. 7, 33
Camilla (queen of Volscians) 67
canon law 167
Carneades 74
cartesianism 10
Castiglione, B. 62n
Catherine of Siena, St 69
Cato 116, 199
censorship 210
chatter 192–3
children 133, 143, 145
Christ 17, 65, 72
Cicero 56, 97, 205
Clement of Alexandria, St 30, 87
common sense 135, 157
commonwealth 149, 164
convents 144, 189
conversion, religious 8, 11
Cordemoy, G. de 43, 46
Corina 62
Cornelia 56
councils (church)
 Lateran V 15, 16, 41
 Trent 20, 29
crafts 156–7, 184
creation 78, 83
custom 29, 91, 108, 125–6

Damo 56
Deborah 66
Democritus 199
dependence 152–3
Descartes, R. 10, 39–40, 41–2, 45, 46–7
Diogenes 198
Diotema 58
distaff 54, 104
Drake, J. 13

dualism 42–4, 154, 158
Du Soucy, F. 3
Du Tillet, J. 63

education
    of men 46, 133–4, 137
    of women 21–3, 30–5, 45–7, 59–60,
        79–93 *passim*, 98, 108, 120, 141–2,
        144–5, 160, 178, 187–90, 196,
        201–11 *passim*
Elizabeth, Princess of Bohemia 108–9
eloquence 138–9, 148
Epicharis 67
Equality
    and difference, 49–51
    defence of 13–14
    natural 202
    of opportunity 51–2
Erasmus, D. 2, 61, 83, 89
Erinna 63
esteem 149–50
Eustochium 70
explanation, *see* hypothetical

faith 26–7
fallacy, *see* incapacity
Fathers of the Church 17, 20, 21, 55
Feckenham, J. 101
Fénelon, F. 46
form (substantial) 15, 31, 41–2, 65, 82
Francis de Sales, St 68
Fulgose (Battista Fregosa) 63

Galilei, G. 20, 26, 27–8, 36, 122
gender 43, 52
Génébrard, G. 68
Gilbert, G. 3
God 20, 86, 129, 135, 136, 159, 192
    knowledge of 35
Gourney, Marie le Jars de, 4–6,
        110–11
    Equality of Men and Women 5, 15, 23,
        54–73, 78, 97, 105, 107
    The Ladies' Complaint 5, 14, 51, 74–8
    Promenade of Monsieur de Montaigne 5
Gracchi, mother of 56–7
Gregory of Nazianzus, St 70, 84
Gregory of Nyssa, St 17
Grey, J. 101–2
Guevara, A. de 64
Guillaume, J. 3

happiness 98, 168–9
head 158–9, 178–9
heresy 29–30, 86
historians 150–2
historical conjecture 127–31
Homer 63
Hortensia 57
Hôtel-Dieu 143
Hotman, F. 63
Huldah 66
Hume, D. 43–4
Hypatia 56
hypothetical explanations 40–1, 45,
        127–31

ideas 40, 155–6, 202
idleness 84, 96
ignorance 5, 30, 88–9, 90, 100, 115
illiteracy 31
incapacity fallacy 38, 125
incarnation 19–20, 72

Jerome, St 69–70, 71, 78, 110
Joan of Arc, St 71
John, St 70
Judith 70–1
justice 52
Juvenal 148

Kepler, J. 26
knowledge
    and belief 210–11 *passim*
    natural desire for 34, 82–3, 99
    required for virtue 100, 169–71

Labadie, J. de, 7–8, 25, 28, 29
ladies 55n, 141
Laelia 57
Laertius, D. 63
La Forge, L. de 43, 46
Lastheneia 59
Latin 46, 56, 57, 110, 137, 139, 166, 206
law, divine and human 33, 97, 164
lawyers 44, 152–3
Leaena 67
liquidity 155
Livy 165
Locke, J. 26–7, 28

Maccabees, mother of 67
Machon, L. 3

Malebranche, N. 44, 50
Marinella, L. 23, 107
marriage 19, 153
Mary Magdalene 68, 71
Mary (Miriam, sister of Moses) 66
Matthieu, P. 63
Maximus of Tyre 58
medicine 140
metaphysics 159
method 46, 161
Michelangelo Florio 101
mind (human) 15, 42, 50, 157–8, 179
Molière, J.-B., P. de 45, 148
Montaigne, M. de, 4–5, 14, 17, 45, 60–61,
     76, 77
moral diversity 165
More, T. 98
Moyne, P. le, 3

natural philosophy 155–6, 159
nature 18, 19, 31, 41, 44, 60, 66
needlework 156, 184, 189
nobility 182

orators 147

passions 160
Paterculus, V. 68
Paul, St 19, 21, 26, 28, 48, 68, 70
Pausanius 63
Pentheselia 67
perfection (concept of) 180–1, 183
Peter, St 70
Petronilla, St 68
Pharamond 63
Philo of Alexandria 198
philosophers 153
Piéron, H. 12
Plato 2, 10, 56, 58, 59, 61, 78, 89,
     197
Plutarch 50–1, 60, 63, 78, 92
poets 147
Politian (Angelo Ambrogini) 61
Pomponazzi, P. 15, 16
popular opinion 147, 201–2
Porcia (Portia) 67
Port Royal Logic 46
Poulain de la Barre, F. 9–13
     A Physical and Moral Discourse 11,
        36–48, 119–200
     Doctrine of Protestants 36–7

The Education of Ladies 11, 37, 48,
     201–11
The Excellence of Men 11
predestination 8, 30
prejudice 38–9, 89, 119–20, 122–3, 151,
     154–5, 207–8
prescription 167–8, 173, 205
princes 129, 150
propriety (idea of) 182
pyrrhonism 17
Pythagoras 56

Queen of Sheba 58
querelle des femmes 2
Quintillian 57
Quintus Curtius 165

Ravier, M. 11
reason 36–7, 204
regencies 103, 130
religion 129–30
rhetoric 47, 148, 163
Rivet, A. 22, 23, 25–6, 28, 32, 34–5,
     94–108 passim, 114, 115
Rohault, J. 39, 43, 46
Rolet, [L.S.R.] 3
Ronsard, P. de 67

sacraments 33, 69
Salic law 63, 64
salons 99, 133, 178
Sappho 59, 62
Sarasin, J.-F. 148
scholars 134, 137, 154, 205, 208–9
scholasticism 9, 16, 31, 38, 41, 109, 136,
     154
schools 32, 91, 105
Schurman, A. M. van, 6–9, 57
     correspondence 94–111
     Dissertation 6–9, 18, 22–35, 79–93
     Eukleria 112–18
Schurman, J. G. van, 7
science (definition of) xii–xiii, 155
     types of 84, 161–2
Scripture, see Bible
Scudéry, Madeleine de, 3
self-interest 38–9, 123–4, 151,
     152
Seneca 60, 67, 78, 85, 96, 104
sexual difference 65
Socrates 56, 59, 78

soul 15, 16, 41, 44, 65, 99, 136
spindle 97, 104
strength 40, 42, 51, 65, 185
study, objectives of 32, 34–5, 86, 89–90,
      92, 103–4, 172–3, 178
substance 42
Suidas (encyclopedia) 63

Tabarin (A. Girard) 199
Tacitus 62, 64, 65
Tasso, T. 61
taste 160
temperament 83, 183–4, 185–7
Tertullian 21
Theano 56
Thecla, St 68
Themistoclea 56
Theodoret of Cyrrhus 17–18, 58
theology 80, 98, 114, 116
Thesbe (Phoebe) 68
Thomas à Kempis 24, 25
Thomas Aquinas, St 139
Toland, J. 37
transubstantiation 37
Trousset, A. (alias J. Olivier) 1, 2, 24
truth, criterion of 120, 147, 210–11

Ulpian 96
Utrecht 6, 7, 113

Verboquet 199
Vigoureux, M. 1

virtue 5, 34, 60, 66, 74, 85, 88–9, 107,
      142, 169–70, 187
Vives, J. L. 46, 105, 108
vocation 92–3, 103
Voetius, G. 6, 7, 8, 29, 113

wisdom 95
witches 12
Wollstonecraft, M. 13
women
   alleged faults of 124–5, 171, 188, 190–6
   and various disciplines 81, 142, 159,
         160–8
   army generals 176
   charitable 143–4
   excluded from employments 33, 103,
         124–5, 128–9, 174
   excluded from sciences 130, 168–9, 208
   inferiority of 2–3, 148–9
   in marriage 145, 153
   images of God 19, 73
   judges 177
   lawyers 139, 166
   learned 141, 175, 177
   pastors/ministers of religion 47, 68,
         129–30, 175
   queens 176
   superiority of 3, 233, 106–7, 186

Xenophon 59

Zwinger, T. 64